You, Your Child, and "Special" Education

You, Your Child, and "Special" Education

A Guide to Dealing with the System

REVISED EDITION

by

Barbara Coyne Cutler, Ed.D.
Autism National Committee

with

Sue Pratt, M.A.
Consultant

·P·A·U·L·H·
BROOKES
PUBLISHING Cᵒ ®

Baltimore • London • Sydney

Paul H. Brookes Publishing Co.
Post Office Box 10624
Baltimore, Maryland 21285-0624
USA

www.brookespublishing.com

Typeset by Broad Books, Baltimore, Maryland.
Manufactured in the United States of America by
Versa Press, Inc., East Peoria, Illinois.

The individuals described in this book are composites or real people whose situations are masked and are based on the authors' experiences. In all instances, names and identifying details have been changed to protect confidentiality.

Library of Congress Cataloging-in-Publication Data

Cutler, Barbara Coyne.
    You, your child, and "special" education : a guide to dealing with the system / By Barbara Coyne Cutler with Sue Pratt. — Rev. ed.
        p.   cm.
    Includes index.
    ISBN-13: 978-1-59857-123-3 (pbk.)
    ISBN-10: 1-59857-123-0 (pbk.)
1. Special education—Parent participation—United States   2. Special education—Law and legislation—United States.   I. Pratt, Sue.   II. Title.
    LC4031.C89 2010
    371.90973—dc22   2010029074

British Library Cataloguing in Publication data are available from the British Library.

2014   2013   2012   2011   2010

10   9   8   7   6   5   4   3   2   1

Contents

About the Authors

Barbara Coyne Cutler, Ed.D., got her advocacy training the hard way. Divorced and with two small children to raise, she began to search out services for her son with autism. It took her almost 10 years to realize that being a patient, no-trouble-at-all parent was not the way to get attention or services. She learned painfully through her personal experience that a parent has to become vocal, visible, knowledgeable, and relentless in order to become an effective advocate. As a parent of a now middle-age son in continuing need of services, Dr. Cutler has been through the system in the dark days when her small son seemed to have no rights at all through the early days of the educational rights movement and later into the adult service system. From a once quiet and compliant parent she has become a leading advocate for people with disabilities and their families. Aware of deficiencies in systems serving people with disabilities, Dr. Cutler worked on her own professional development, acquiring bachelor's and master's degrees from Harvard (where she was also a Merrill Fellow of the Radcliffe Institute) and a doctorate in special education from Boston University.

Dr. Cutler has directed educational, supported works and community resource programs, including the Autism National Committee (http://www.autcom.org), which she serves on now; facilitated the development of a model respite care program; trained parents and professionals in positive behavior support programs; and provided individual consultation in various states to public schools dealing with the needs of students with autism and developmental disabilities.

In her more than 30 years of service, she has continued to advocate as a member of boards of service, state, and advocacy organizations including her local Commission on Disability and Regional Developmental Disabilities Council. She has presented throughout the United States, Puerto Rico, and Canada. She has published chapters in various disability-related books and newsletters.

Looking back, she realizes that because of her son's disability, her career was chosen for her. "I've made my personal and career decisions by dealing with the crises that parents of children with disabilities learn to expect as part of their daily routine. It's a life that's sometimes harrowing, sometimes rewarding—but never, never dull. I have never regretted my decisions. Without strong parent advocates, our sons and daughters could be overlooked and poorly served."

Dr. Cutler lives next door to her son, George, and his wife, Sherrie, and across the street from her son, Robert. The family is often together on weekends and is always available to support each other.

Sue Pratt, M.A., has advocated for students with special needs for more than 35 years. She claims she keeps trying to quit, but people like her friend Dr. Cutler and parents in need keep her "keeping on." Ms. Pratt received her bachelor of science degree in elementary education from St. John College in Cleveland, Ohio, and her master of arts in education from Western Michigan in Kalamazoo. She has taught for 11 years and worked for or directed the parent center in Michigan (Citizens Alliance to Uphold Special Education [CAUSE]) for 25 years. Among her accomplishments, she lobbied with great zeal to change the wording in The Individuals with Disabilities Education Act (IDEA) from *behavior management* to *positive behavior support* for the 1997 reauthorization. She also worked with the Office of Civil Rights and CAUSE staff to produce the first guide for professionals and parents to obtain services under Section 504 of the Rehabilitation Act for students with disabilities not in special education.

Foreword to the Revised Edition

I am delighted to write a foreword for this excellent book. The year 2010 marks the 35th anniversary of the Education for All Handicapped Children Act of 1975 (PL 94–142), the landmark and revolutionary law for children with disabilities, which changed its name in 1990 to the Individuals with Disabilities Education Act (IDEA) and has been amended several times. IDEA has changed the lives of millions of children with disabilities, and parents have played a pivotal role as advocates for their children. Yet, parents need to continue to know their rights and responsibilities and forge new directions to ensure that the laws for people with disabilities stay strong, are implemented, and reach new frontiers.

As Eleanor Roosevelt said, "The future belongs to those who believe in the beauty of their dreams." Parents have dreams for their children with disabilities and as the most effective advocates their children will ever have, parents can help those dreams become a reality. When parents combine their commitment to their children with high expectations and effective advocacy skills, their children can become as independent and productive as possible.

This book is written by two mothers who have seen dreams become reality for their sons with disabilities and who continue to have dreams for their sons. Barbara Coyne Cutler and Sue Pratt have not only been strong and effective advocates for their own children but also for countless of families in this nation. Both of these women have experienced special education from its inception. They both came from the professional world of education prior to having sons with disabilities. They have gained insight and wisdom from more than 35 years of experience in advocating for students with disabilities and their families.

Barbara and Sue have spent a major portion of their lives working to support students with disabilities and their families so that students can reach their maximum potential and become contributing members of society. Both women have been successful in ensuring that their sons participate and live in their communities. Often Barbara and Sue have had to struggle against the odds and be strong advocates because some professionals did not understand their dreams for their sons. Their success and their guidance through the maze that faces parents should be a beacon to families, showing them that their children can surprise the world with their abilities.

It is my hope that Barbara and Sue's efforts will contribute to the dreams, high expectations, and success for families advocating for their children across this nation. I know it is with this goal in mind that the authors have labored to share their acquired wisdom with all parents who seek advice and guidance.

Paula F. Goldberg
Executive Director and Founder
PACER Center
Minneapolis, Minnesota

Foreword to the 1993 Edition

More than 4 decades ago, parents of children with disabilities throughout the United States and in quite a few other countries in the industrialized world revolted against the neglect and often total exclusion of their children by the educational system. Very significant victories have been gained in the ensuing years, but much is yet to be achieved in the parents' campaign, which has been increasingly joined by activists in the education profession.

On the national level, this campaign's success is anchored in a long line of federal legislation, beginning with some modest enactments in the late 1950s and culminating in the Education of the Handicapped Act (EHA) of 1970 (PL 91-230) and the Education for All Handicapped Children Act of 1975 (PL 91-142). The EHA was amended several times throughout the 1980s until the name of the legislation was changed to the Individuals with Disabilities Education Act (IDEA) of 1990 (PL 101-476).

However, far too often, parents realize that the goal and philosophy of fully integrated education as expressed in IDEA are in stark contrast to the neglect that they and their children face in their local school systems. In fact, IDEA's goals and everyday reality are often so far apart that parents see no way to achieve those goals for their children.

Dr. Cutler's aim in this book is to reassure parents that there are not only ways to negotiate with school people on behalf of their children but that they, as parents, are needed and included in IDEA as active participants in the development of their children's individualized education programs (IEPs). Dr. Cutler provides a clear blueprint as, step by step, she walks through the process outlined in IDEA. While she points to pitfalls in that process and to possible conflicts among parents and school people, her book is written positively and reflects her basic belief that the law provides a sound basis for effective collaboration between parents and professionals.

Over the past 2 decades, a wealth of literature has been available on the new developments in the philosophy and practice of special education. The value of Barbara Cutler's contribution lies in her direct approach to parents' concerns regarding the school needs of their children and what they, as parents, can do about these needs. Dr. Cutler does not just exhort parents to be "in communication" with the school, but painstakingly provides guidance for writing letters or arranging visits to the school that may seem nonresponsive. The vignettes throughout the book exemplify specific problems and are more helpful to the average parent than the well-formulated broad pronouncements on legal, regulatory, and procedural issues that are found in textbooks. And above all, this book encourages parents to value their own good judgment and what they themselves hear and experience with their children and to share this with school people as they participate in developing IEPs.

Rosemary Dybwad, Ph.D.
Gunnar Dybwad, Ph.D.
Heller School
Brandeis University
Waltham, Massachusetts

Preface

This book was written to help parents understand and protect their child's educational rights provided by the Individuals with Disabilities Education Improvement Act (IDEA) of 2004 so that they can be effective in getting at least some or all of the services their children need and to which they are entitled.

It is more than 30 years since Congress defined and mandated educational rights for students with disabilities. Earlier attempts to include children with disabilities were perceived as not binding for school systems, which occasionally provided services but did not feel required to provide for most children with disabilities. In 1975 Congress sent a clear message to *all* public school systems that *all* children have a right to a *free appropriate public education.*

Since then the law has been amended and reauthorized to include an expanded age range (3–21), a stronger emphasis on inclusion (*least restrictive environment*), early intervention programs for infants and toddlers, assistive technology services, and transition planning for adulthood. With these additions have come some challenges.

The burden of proof for poor education is now borne more by parents than school systems, and schools increasingly use discipline codes to exclude or suspend students with disabilities for behaviors that are caused by or related to their disabilities.

Still, with these improvements and additions to IDEA in place and in spite of these challenges, surely you can expect the school systems to provide the services your child needs! Unfortunately, you cannot—and especially not without your active participation. Although there are schools that will work with you to comply with the law, some schools may seem indifferent to your child's unique needs and to your efforts to get more appropriate education. You may feel bewildered, angry, and sometimes defeated. For a very few parents, there are some schools that may actively resist both their efforts and setting up appropriate programs. These are the schools for which you may need professional advocates to help you, the parent advocate, to get the appropriate individualized education program for your child.

However your school system treats you, your child depends on you, and so you will persevere with this book and other resources, especially the Parent Information Centers listed along with other resources in the appendixes, to guide and support you. With new information and skills you can not only get a better education for your child but also you may even help your school system change to better serve all of its children.

For parents who may now be frustrated, confused, or uninformed about their children's educational rights, you should know that parents have told us that the information in this book has helped to strengthen them for those meetings that will get the services their children need and to which they are entitled.

For those of you with children who will require services beyond their school years, the information you gain from this book will provide you with the skills you will need to deal with adult service systems. Although there are likely to be fewer entitlements for adult services, you will be prepared and strengthened for the long haul (as the author can personally attest).

Although this book is written primarily for you, the parent, it can be useful to caring professionals. It can help them to understand the experiences of families and to see the value of parents as essential partners in developing appropriate education with its necessary supports and services. When informed professionals collaborate with parents, good things do happen.

Acknowledgments

It was Marty Kozloff who first insisted I had something to say that parents and school people needed to know. He had the vision and he gave me the time and space to write this book. Without his caring, support, and encouragement, this book would not have been written.

Gunnar Dybwad, my mentor, colleague, friend, and critic, adopted the book as one of his favorites and supported the book and my advocacy efforts for the rest of his life. I could not have remained so committed without his support.

And to Frank Garfunkel, who gave me the highest praise when he complained of the first book: "I couldn't find any fault with it." Many thanks.

Other professionals to whom I am grateful include Doug Biklen who—consistent with his commitment to individuals and families in disability—was an early promoter of the book, sending me to Iowa for my first forum in informing and strengthening parents; Barry Prizant, who listened and trusted parents when it was not popular to do so; Barbara Bruno Golden, who went with me to my first IEP and showed me the importance of having your personal advocate with you at the IEP meeting; Bill Condon and Herb Lovett, models for us all, who recognized competence in and gave respect to individuals with disabilities long before the self-advocacy movement was established; and to Jeff Strully, who keeps pushing us forward.

Worthy of thanks are the teachers who showed me how insightful and supportive a good and caring teacher can be even in, and maybe especially in, some of the remote places I have traveled to. Students in my consultations, many of whom not only charmed me but also taught me about their needs and how they could be met, are worthy of praise for their daily efforts and struggles within the education system.

This book only happened because of parents who drove the government to recognize the injustice in education and to correct it, however. There are parents such as Martha Ziegler and Paula F. Goldberg, who organized Parent Information Centers to inform and train parents in using the law; others, such as Barbara Domingue, who served and supported parents; still others who inspire for the long haul, such as Marlene Ross and Poly Cobb; my personal resources, such as Susan Goodman and Sue Pratt (who made sure this book matched the sometimes changing law); and my first partner in advocacy, the Northeast Regional Conference on Autism, which took on the education of parents and professionals when there were few local and regional conferences to go to.

All of these people have contributed to the shaping of the ideas and experiences that have gone into the writing of this book and its revisions. Some will recognize their stories and their contributions, others will agree with the substance, and a few may wonder how I managed to come to "that conclusion." The applications and interpretations are my own, but I am grateful to all of the people who said, "You go, girl!" "The book is needed. Just do it!" and "Do it again!"

Paul H. Brookes Publishing Co. has been especially kind in picking up this book and publishing it twice. I am grateful to all of the Brookes staff who have supported me in the last 20 years: Melissa Behm, Steve Plocher, Leslie Eckard, Roslyn Udris, and most of all, the ever-patient Rebecca Lazo, who waited while I dithered for 9 years on whether to revise the book again. I had become uncomfortable with some changes in IDEA, but it was a parent, Jeanne Wu, whose challenges with her son's services pushed me to decide to move forward because it was clear that parents needed this book.

Parents are always a very special and continuous resource, always open and generous with their ideas and experiences, even when those experiences are painful and demeaning. They struggle for services for their children, and if they fail, hope the sharing of their failures will help other parents and students toward success. That great sharing from parents paid off. New and younger parents have told me that reading this book, even on the eve of their child's IEP meeting, has strengthened them. Yet one thing parents know is that our experiences make us all "family." To the many families who made this book possible, much is owed. Thanks for sharing the pain, the success, and the hope.

To my own family, Rob, George, and Sherrie, thank you for your support, understanding, commitment, love, and encouragement. Family is all.

To
Tom Gilhool
who started it all
and
to our children,
who are both inspiration and support,
Rob, George, and Sherrie (BCC)
and
David Jr., Daniel Pratt James, and grandson David T. (SP)

1

It's About Rights

*rights and responsibilities • special strengths •
the law • becoming an advocate • the six
characteristics of a strong advocate • rights are
not favors • using this book • chapter by chapter*

If you are just getting started as an active parent advocate for your
child because he or she has been diagnosed with a disability or is suspected of having a disability, you may be feeling suddenly overwhelmed. How will you—a mere parent—be able to work or deal with
professionals in the education systems?

You will do what other parents have done before you.

You will begin by knowing that your child has a right to a free appropriate public education (commonly referred to as *FAPE*), without
expense to you.

You will begin by understanding that the law gives you certain rights
and responsibilities to ensure that your child's rights to education
are recognized and protected.

You will begin because your child depends on you. You accept your
role as a parent advocate whether it's for only a few years or for your
child's entire school career, or, if your child has disabilities severe
enough to require some form of lifelong support, you are there for
the long haul.

The purpose of this book is to equip you for dealing with the school
system and to help you to not feel overwhelmed in working with
school systems. A big job? Yes. But if you understand that you have

some special strengths that only a parent can have, you will be your child's best ally and advocate.

If you have some experience, you may be thinking, "It's not so bad," and many times, the meetings and plans for your child may not present problems. Right! (Or you may be thinking, "It was tough.") But if or when challenges present themselves, it is important that you believe in yourself and your child and have some skills to support your beliefs and your efforts.

Let's begin by understanding your child's basic rights to a free appropriate public education. As a parent, you should know that education rights for children with disabilities were not always honored. Prior to 1975, there were no clear rights to education. The programs that existed were likely in church basements and rarely in public schools (and when they were, they were usually conducted in the basements); some children stayed home, and some went into state institutions. It wasn't fair, and the situation did in fact violate children's constitutional rights to an education. Parents at that time did not know their children had any rights to education or appropriate education.

Eventually, it was parents, with the help of lawyers, who became the aggressive advocates, leading the struggle to realize their children's right to education. Sadly, it was not educators who led the fight. In fact, there was resistance from many education professionals.

Always keep in mind: Parents were the advocates, and they worked hard for all children with disabilities. Many conditions have improved because of parent action:

- Students with disabilities once attended separate schools (or separate wings of the school building, with classrooms perhaps located next to the boiler room) or attended class in church basements. Today, students with disabilities are educated in classrooms located on the main floors in community schools.

- Students with disabilities who were once isolated from contact with "mainstream" students are now educated with typical students for an array of subjects.

- Teenagers who in earlier years would have been encouraged to leave school for sheltered workshops when they turned 16 are now staying in high school.

- Students with physical disabilities are being included in schools made accessible by the Individuals with Disabilities Education Act

(IDEA) of 1990 (PL 101-476) and also by the Americans with Disabilities Act (ADA) of 1990 (PL 101-336).

- Students who need special assistance are getting the services of therapists and specialists in general education schools and often within general education classrooms.

- Students who once would have been denied any form of education are now receiving extended-year (12-month) and even extended-day programs.

- Many students are learning to read, write, talk (or communicate by signing, picture systems, or computers), participate in recreation and extracurricular activities, demonstrate skills once considered beyond their reach, and participate in school life with their typical, age-appropriate peers.

Since the law once known as the Education for All Handicapped Children Act of 1975 (PL 94-142) and now called the Individuals with Disabilities Education Improvement Act (IDEA) of 2004 (PL 108-446) was first passed by Congress and signed into law by the president, changes have been made. Some changes—such as early intervention and preschool programs—are good, and some serve to weaken children's rights and parents' ability to advocate. Because the law is regularly reauthorized and there are frequent court cases that can affect interpretations of it, it will continue to change. In addition to this book, you will need to have access to resources for up-to-date information. You will find some of these in the appendixes in the back of this book.

As you go through this book, you will read about some changes and additions, such as inclusion, functional behavioral assessment (FBA), transition plans, and other components of an individualized education program (IEP). We will alert you to some common problems and even some extreme situations. Stories about services and problems will illustrate what some parents have gone through. Right now you need to know that your child is entitled to a free appropriate public education and that those services are provided at public expense, not your expense, through an IEP developed by the team, which includes you. You are an active participant working with school personnel. The IEP is written to meet your individual child's needs; that is what *appropriate* means. It is not written for a group of children, nor is the plan based on available space, funding, or school personnel's convenience. Special education is not a place; it is a service or program of services designed to meet the needs of one child.

The law is a guarantee of these services. However, the full or best implementation of those FAPE services depends on you. It can be a little frightening at first and a lot of work, but without your active participation, your child's education may be limited and/or inappropriate. You make the difference.

Of course you are thinking, "I want to help my child get the education he or she needs and is entitled to, but don't you have to have professional skills and special knowledge to be an advocate? Don't you have to be some kind of recognized expert to do the job? How can I, a mere parent, become an effective advocate? After all, I've often heard lawyers referred to as advocates, and they are the experts in interpreting the law."

It may help you to know that lawyers have in fact looked to skillful and knowledgeable parent advocates for advice in dealing with school systems and for information about the law. These parent advocates were not lawyers or educators; they were just good advocates who learned through hard work and practice how to do the job well. Any parent can become a good advocate. Some parents with training will become exceptional advocates and work for other parents. It will also help you to know from the start that you can take someone with you who can support you through all meetings dealing with your child's IEP. In fact, you should always take your personal advocate with you. (We'll talk more about your personal advocate later.)

If you know your rights and use this book to learn skills and strategies, your child will be represented by a strong and capable advocate—you. Remember that IDEA ensures that you, as a parent, have a central and powerful role to play. Through its insistence that schools make every effort to involve parents, the law invites parents to become advocates for their children. It clearly gives parents the power and freedom to act on behalf of their children and the responsibility to take action and to do it well. You can do it!

HOW DO YOU BECOME A GOOD ADVOCATE?

Let's list and discuss the basic characteristics of a good advocate. The following list presents the most essential traits and skills.

Characteristics of an Effective Advocate

1. *Greatest concern for the child's best interests* rather than for the concerns or interests of the school system

2. *Long-term commitment to the child's welfare* and to being the child's advocate

3. *Knowledge of the present needs of the child,* the ability to recognize those needs, and the complete history of the child

4. *Assertiveness* in persistently pointing out the child's needs to the people responsible for meeting those needs

5. *Ability to work with others* (e.g., professionals, paraprofessionals, other parents, advocates) to develop appropriate and beneficial educational goals and plans for the child

6. *Ability to find and use information, allies, and resources* to put the needed educational plans to work

This list may seem overwhelming at first, but you can see that there is no requirement that you have to be a lawyer, an educator, or a doctor. It includes only personal characteristics that you may already have, can strengthen and adapt, or can acquire with some self-instruction and practice. Measure yourself against the definitions that follow.

Greatest Concern

Who cares more than you about what is happening to your child and what the future will hold for him or her? Yes, there are and will be some professionals and others who care about your child and who are on your side, but they probably have tens or hundreds of other students or clients to be concerned about. As a parent, your love and concern is deeper, stronger, and more enduring. No one cares more than you.

Long-Term Commitment

Who has been and will be around your child longer than you? Professionals come and go, sometimes yearly, and they may leave when you feel you need them most. That teacher who was so kind and interested just moved to another part of the country, or that sympathetic psychologist has opened a practice a hundred miles away. You, however, will be there with your child no matter what throughout his or her entire educational career and beyond, if needed.

Knowledge of Your Child

Who knows more about your child's growth, personality, special needs, and special skills than you? You know how hard he or she tries to do certain things, how well he or she gets along with the neighbor-hood children, or how lonely he or she feels sometimes watching life go on around and without him or her. You are the best source of infor-mation about your child: You are the expert in residence. As useful as medical and school records are, they explain only part of your child's experiences. You may not know everything, but you know more than anyone else. You are the best available expert with the broadest overview of your child, always open to learning more information about you child's strengths and needs.

Stop here for a moment to recognize that on these three points—caring, constancy, and knowledge—you lead the field of potential advocates for your child. You come by these qualifications naturally because you are the parent. Parents are the natural advo-cates for their children—they are the first and last resource. Others can help you do the job (and you will want their help), but there is no one as qualified as you in these three basic requirements for being an effective advocate.

Now, for the last three qualifications, you probably need some help in dealing with the system. Most people do, including profession-als. You can give yourself the help you need through reading, getting online, contacting agencies for up-to-date information, signing up for parent workshops, preparing for meetings, having your friend or per-sonal advocate beside you, and so forth.

Assertiveness

Being assertive simply means speaking up and hanging in there. Some of us are better (and bolder) at this than others. But even if you are shy or lack confidence, you can learn to be more assertive. You may already be feeling a little surge of confidence from realizing that, as the natural advocate, you have some powerful qualifications that no one else can match. With the guidance of the later chapters in this book, you will work on developing more confidence and on learning to state your child's case more assertively. You won't become mean or aggressive, just firm and persistent.

Working with Others

Working with others is something you have done before, but you may have yet to work as equals with school staff. Luckily, school people react in the same way as anybody else to courtesy, praise, diplomacy, or persuasion. Your ways of dealing with pleasant and unpleasant neighbors or coworkers will help you work with school staff of both sorts. After you have rid yourself of some ideas you may have about "mere" parents and about experts who have "all" of the answers, you will become more comfortable in working with professionals. You will draw on your everyday experience and skills to learn how to cooperate with, disagree with, and, occasionally, even manipulate school personnel. And you will be doing this for your child.

Finding Information and Allies

You may feel sure that you are weak in obtaining information and discovering allies and resources, but you have some skills in this area, even if you haven't applied them to getting educational services for your child. For example, you have probably used a computer to sift through information. You read the directions and the guarantee for the toaster; if you couldn't understand the information or directions, you probably asked the right friend to explain them to you—and if your friend suggested that you write to the company or the Better Business Bureau, chances are you followed up on the suggestion. (Some of these friends may later become your personal advocates in helping you through the IEP process.) Or you went back to the computer or library to obtain information, maybe checking several sources. These are everyday skills you may already be using. They are the basis for developing special advocacy skills for finding and using information, allies, and resources you will need and use for the IEP meeting. Give yourself credit.

Sure, it will take some time, effort, practice, experience, and more practice for you to become skilled or more skilled in these last three items, and for some parents, it will take more than a little courage. But you will be doing what other parents have already done. In a short time, you will be able to say, as one parent has said:

> "I surprised myself at the school meeting! I sounded so calm. I told them what I wanted for Tiffany and why she needed it. I thought I was losing, but I stuck to my guns. By the time they agreed to give her the extra time with the therapist, I was exhausted. But when I left the meeting, did I feel good! It was worth it. Next time we meet I won't be so scared and it will be a little easier for me."

As you use the skills that you will be learning or improving, you will keep getting better at using them. You will become more relaxed about or at least less frightened of your meetings with the professionals. It will never be really easy, and you can never become casual about any meetings that will affect your child's education. You may not get everything you ask for, but you will feel great satisfaction from your personal successes as an effective advocate and even greater satisfaction from the better education and improved services your child will receive as a result of your advocacy.

YOU'RE ENTITLED

The first thing you need to understand about legal rights is that rights are not favors. They are not gifts of administrators or teachers, they are not windfalls that have come because there's a little extra money left over in the school budget, and they are not special privileges given to the children of parents who are pleasantly accommodating and who don't make any "trouble" for school staff.

Having rights under the law means that your child is entitled to certain services and that you are entitled to participate in the process of determining the amounts and types of services he or she receives. You need never argue with anyone about whether your child should have a public education. People who withhold services and interventions from your child or who deny you the opportunity to get involved in shaping his or her program are themselves breaking the law. School systems are obliged to take the rights of children with disabilities very seriously.

In fact, school systems should have been serious about the education of students with disabilities long before the enactment of IDEA because children have had the right to a public education all along. Public education, by definition, is a service that the community provides to its citizens—all of them, without discrimination. Think about other public services that your town provides, such as police protection. If someone broke into your house, you would expect the police to come, not to tell you, "We only investigate incidents on the east side of town. It's too bad you live on the west side." If you got a response like that, you would probably complain to some higher authority. If that higher authority told you that there was not enough money in the budget to serve residents from the west side, you would carry your complaint to a still higher authority. You would not passively accept this treatment, because you know that as a resident of your community, you have an equal right to protection.

Unfortunately, parents of children with disabilities have too often allowed public administrators to approach their children as special cases, which often meant with discrimination. Some school administrators can make parents who ask for services for their sons and daughters feel that they are somehow depriving so-called "typical" students of the services they need. Not only is this unfair and untrue but also the whole notion of students with disabilities draining resources from students without disabilities is just one more burdensome myth that parents have to deal with. Do not be taken in. Parents of children with disabilities have been paying taxes to support public services that have been provided to other children while their own children may have been denied some or even all services. A reminder that you, too, are a taxpayer is in order when someone tries to justify withholding services to your child by telling you that "the taxpayers won't stand for any increase in school costs." This argument for parents of children with disabilities is both unjust and illegal.

If you are beginning to feel a little nervous or even a bit overwhelmed about becoming an advocate, you are on the right track. In advocacy, the stakes are high, the work is hard, and the outcome is crucial, so you need special assistance to achieve better services for your child. Knowing about IDEA is a major step in the right direction, but it is not enough to create a successful advocate. You must also know how school systems operate and what you as a parent and a nonprofessional, concerned spokesperson for your child can do to bring about changes that will benefit him or her. In short, you need to know how to deal with the system. This book is designed to help you to understand how the school system operates and how to get it to provide the services your child needs.

WHAT YOU NEED TO KNOW

Chapter 2 provides information about the most important changes and additions in the law since it was first passed. Most amendments to the law have been positive, although some have been troublesome or just confusing. We briefly describe to you the elements of FAPE. On the positive side, the amendments have expanded the original age eligibility for students from 6 to 18 in 1975 to birth to 21 in 1990. More children and adolescents are now required to be served in the least restrictive environment (commonly referred to as *LRE*), and more services such as assistive technology, the individualized family service plan (IFSP) for preschoolers, integration, and inclusion must be provided. PL 94-142 and its amendments are most recently known as the

Individuals with Disabilities Education Improvement Act (IDEA) of 2004 (more commonly known as IDEA 2004).

Chapter 3 explains how school systems try to control parents through the perpetuation of myths that keep parents at a distance and in awe of the professionals and that have sometimes been effective in keeping students with disabilities in inadequate programs or even out of programs.

Chapter 4 examines the power structure of school systems, explores how school politics can limit the performance of even the most competent and caring teachers and administrators, and helps you learn how to recognize the educators who can and want to help you and how to deal with those school personnel who might stand between your child and a better educational program. You will learn how to separate fact from fiction and what you must do to counter the effects of myths and snow jobs.

In **Chapter 5,** just when you are beginning to feel that the politics and pressures of the school system are assuming unmanageable proportions, we help you to discover *your* hidden talents—your daily living skills and your potential allies and resources. This chapter shows you how to turn everyday skills into effective advocacy tools and yourself into a confident and competent advocate.

In **Chapter 6,** you will learn how to use and test your personal skills and common sense when you visit your child's classroom. You will be guided step by step through the program evaluation, from your very first request to visit to the time you sit down to discuss your questions, concerns, and careful observations with your child's teacher. Your developing skills and sound judgment will not equip you to take over the classroom (that is not your intention!), but you may find for the first time in your life that you are actually taking part in a discussion with a teacher, if not as a potential partner, then at least as an equal participant who knows that he or she has valuable information to share.

At this point, you will have in your repertoire enough information, experience, practice, and preparation to sit down with the school people in the IEP process. The IEP is the very heart of IDEA. It is the blueprint for your child's daily school program. If it's not written in the IEP, it doesn't exist. Promises are meaningless and likely to be forgotten.

Without an IEP, your child has no guaranteed educational services; without a good IEP, your child may be cheated out of some of the services he or she needs. Your job is to get that good IEP.

Chapter 7 walks you through the whole IEP process, from the first notice you receive (perhaps at your request), through the hammering out of the specifics of the educational program, to the final resolution, which should result in a good IEP for your child.

"Hold on," you may think to yourself. "What's this 'should' business? Doesn't all this work I'm about to do promise me a good program for my child? Why should I do all this work for nothing?" Although active participation as a parent advocate will bring about a good IEP with more and improved services for the child in the majority of cases, a small number of parents will not reach agreement with school staff, and those parents will feel forced to reject the IEP. They might wonder what more they can then do to help their child. Their work has not been in vain.

Chapter 8 addresses the problem of the rejected IEP. Parents who have rejected the IEP still have options—such as mediation, resolution, and appeals. All of the work they have done and all of the information they have collected will be used to their advantage when they have to confront the school system. Confrontation is a difficult experience for parents (as it is for many school professionals) and is not to be entered into casually. But when there are serious deficiencies in the IEP and irresolvable differences between parents and school people, then the parents must be determined to go all of the way. Chapter 8 tells you how to use confrontation to your child's advantage, what kind of help you need and where and how to find it, how to file a complaint, and how to survive the difficulties of confrontation.

When you achieve your goal—an appropriate IEP designed to meet your child's educational needs—and are looking forward to a well-deserved rest, **Chapter 9,** the final chapter, prepares you for monitoring the implementation of your child's IEP. The hardest and most time-consuming work will be behind you, but your long-term commitment and concern and vigilance for your child will require you to continue as the advocate and participate in the educational process. You will want to ensure that the IEP is not merely a paper product, but is rather a daily working plan for the teachers and specialists who are educating your child—that your child is in fact receiving all of the services written and agreed upon in the IEP. This chapter tells you how to watch over the program, what to look for in your monitoring of it, and what to do when you find your school is noncompliant— that is, not delivering the agreed-upon IEP.

As you use this book, you will read about the experiences of other parents who decided to take on the system and learned how to deal with it. Some parents learned how to become effective advocates on their own through trial and error, success and failure; others, thwarted by their lack of confidence and information, gave up after some valiant, but brief, attempts. You will have the benefit of their experience as you prepare to deal with the school system and make it work for your child.

This book won't promise you that your child will have an ideal IEP, be given a private school education, or have unlimited access to the services of a dozen different specialists. It can promise that your child will at the very least have a better IEP and school program because you took advantage of your legal right as a parent to advocate for your child's educational needs.

Let's begin by looking at those special provisions and critical services that Congress has put in place over the past 3 decades.

2

Keeping Up with IDEA

changes in the law and additions • early intervention • preschool • inclusion • assistive technology • accommodations • functional behavioral assessment • behavioral intervention plan • No Child Left Behind • individual transition plan • mediation

In this chapter, we introduce you to some significant changes in educational rights that have taken place over the years. It's not that schools couldn't provide certain services since IDEA was first authorized by Congress; some states did. For example, since 1975, some states authorized services for preschool children with disabilities. From the beginning, Michigan provided educational services up to age 26. No other state has provided such extensive services. States and schools have often chosen what they will provide, sometimes even in violation of the law. IDEA sets minimum requirements for each state. A state can do more than the federal law requires, but it can't do less.

Some of you may be told, "Oh! We can't do that!" when you ask, "Can't Anna go to the Sunshine Nursery School instead of that regional segregated program you run 30 miles out of town?" The answer is "Of course she can!"—and this might even be required if the Sunshine Nursery School is the most appropriately inclusive or the least restrictive environment. If you are the parent of a young child or a child who has recently been diagnosed, some of this language may seem strange to you. *Least restrictive environment* simply means that a student who has a disability should have the opportunity to be educated with typical peers to the greatest extent possible.

Here is an example of why you need to know what the law provides so you will understand your options, know what you want to ask for, and know which services your child is entitled to receive.

Anna's mother was moved to tears when her little 3-year-old got off the big school bus and rushed to her mother's arms, worried and shaken, and whispered softly, "I came home," after a day of not understanding why she was taken so far from her home and family or if she would return. Her mother wanted Anna to attend the nursery school in town, but the special education director said that wasn't possible. Anna's mother didn't know enough about IDEA to question the appropriateness of sending a toddler so far away to preschool.

If you are the parent of a young or newly diagnosed child with a disability (or a child suspected of having a disability), just the thought of all of this—learning about the law and seeking and asking for services while you cope with understanding and coming to terms with your child's diagnosis or difficulty—is probably overwhelming. You want desperately to trust the professionals to give your child the right and needed services; after all, they are the professionals. And often, many children are provided with the free appropriate public education Congress promises. But childhood is short, and you need to take full advantage of the educational system and not waste time in being manipulated by school personnel who may be more concerned about the school budget or administrative convenience than the rights of your child.

You can't do everything, but you can do something. In fact, you already have—you are reading this book. Let's take a brief look at components that have been added to the original law. These will appear throughout the book. You may not need all of them, but for now you should just know what they are. You can come back to this chapter when you need to. For now, you should know the following terms and services: *early intervention, preschool, least restrictive environment (LRE), assistive technology, accommodations, functional behavioral assessment (FBA), behavioral intervention plan, individualized transition plan (ITP), mediation,* and *due process.* This chapter also familiarizes you with other important laws, including the Americans with Disabilities Act (ADA) of 1990, Section 504, and the No Child Left Behind Act of 2001 (NCLB; PL 107-110).

EARLY INTERVENTION

If your child is under 3 years of age and has been diagnosed with a disability or is considered at risk, IDEA directs states to develop and implement programs to meet the needs of infants and toddlers up to age 3 and their families through the individualized family service plan (IFSP). Note that this plan makes clear that the family is getting services, too. As part of this process, parents are members of a multidisciplinary team that usually includes a nurse, a speech-language therapist, an occupational or physical therapist, and a behavior specialist. Many parents will tell you that they never felt they had as much support and understanding as with those professionals who served their children in early intervention (EI).

Evaluations by these various EI specialists are a key part of the program. Those evaluations are important now, but you may find they are still important as your child grows older. Difficulties with movement and sensory issues and diagnoses such as attention-deficit/hyperactivity disorder may be forgotten by school personnel over the school years and be relabeled "behavior problems." Instead of therapy; support; and/or accommodations for neurological, sensory, or other difficulties, the focus is on getting students to "behave." In future meetings with schools, you may need to remind or inform them of these early findings as you seek support and/or accommodations and point out from your comprehensive home files that these behaviors are the result of unmet needs. This shows you the importance of saving all of your child's school records and evaluations, as well as any communications you may have received from staff or other professionals.

In the IFSP, in addition to the child's specific needs for supports and services, the strengths and concerns of the family as a whole are incorporated into the supports the child receives. This is the only time the family concerns are considered, and support and services are to be family-directed.

A number of different elements should be considered when developing an IFSP for your child, such as your strengths, your needs, the needs of your other children, the time you have available, your priorities in terms of EI services (in addition to how much, where, when, and how it will affect your family), and what supports will be provided to aid your entire family in assisting the child with the disability.

The transition from EI to preschool can be particularly difficult for families, who often feel less included in the planning process once their child leaves EI programs. No longer are the needs of the family considered as they were in the IFSP. Parents may feel a loss of partnership, and if their child has only been considered a child at risk and has no diagnostic label, their child will lose services. If an assessment to determine a diagnosis is necessary in the transition to preschool, then time will be lost while waiting for the assessment to take place. You should ask for assessments early.

PRESCHOOL

The plan for transitioning to preschool (also called *early childhood programs*) should begin at least 3 months before a child turns 3 years of age. Better yet, start the process when your child is 2 years and 6 months by asking the EI professionals to help and advise you.

Remember, the school system must have your written permission for evaluations to take place. Your child's IEP must be completed—including assessments—and ready to go by your child's 3rd birthday; otherwise your child may stay at home waiting for services.

———◆———

Mrs. Perreira tried to set up an early meeting but was told to wait until her daughter turned 3 years old in September and that she should just "trust the team." However, the placement the team offered in September did not fit her daughter's needs. Had the team done the transition planning early enough, they would have realized that their recommended placement based solely on the diagnostic label did not really meet Maria's needs. As a result, Maria waited while the school scurried to find a more appropriate program.

———◆———

The assessments conducted to determine necessary services are an important part of the transition to preschool. When assessments have been completed, the IEP team will meet to review the data from the assessments and plan an appropriate educational program for your child. By law, you are an essential member of the IEP team. You bring the most important voice to this meeting, and you have the most knowledge of your child. Yes, the responsibility is heavy, so you should always try to take someone you can trust with you to the meeting.

Although the receiving school personnel may feel that they can do the planning by themselves, the EI specialists who worked with your child are supposed to be part of the transition meeting and planning process, and you will probably want and need them there. Again, the IEP must be ready to be implemented on your child's 3rd birthday, or your child will have to wait for services.

———◆———

Harry Anderson used his business skills and style to prepare for his son's transition. He visited a number of early childhood special education programs and prepared a presentation complete with slides for his son's first IEP, much to the astonishment of the other members of the team. Harry wanted to establish a collaborative relationship with the people in the system—but wanted them to know that he knew what his son needed. In addition, he had the involvement of educational advocates to assist him with the interpretation of the law.

———◆———

Your child's transition can be a very emotional and vulnerable process. Parents handle this differently—some are intimidated and allow the school system to take control, others line up their facts and information. Be as prepared as you can be (computer presentations are optional), and seek support where and when you need to. Mr. Anderson, with his degree of preparation, established himself as a person to be reckoned with from the start. He did not want to burn his bridges, but he was trying to establish a mutually respectful, positive working relationship in which he shared his knowledge of his son with the schools.

INCLUSION

From the start, the federal law has been clear that students with disabilities must be educated to the extent possible in the LRE. Thinking about how to use LRE to provide a more inclusive education has been ongoing since IDEA was first written and passed by Congress as the Education for All Handicapped Children Act of 1975 (PL 94-142). There are many ways in which a student can be included, fully or partially. Possible models of inclusion from least to most inclusive are reverse mainstreaming, partial inclusion, social inclusion, academic inclusion, and full inclusion. However, just being in class with students without disabilities does not mean a student is included. Without preparation and accommodation, it means he or she is merely *placed*.

Some still question whether students with disabilities should be included. Are they ready to be included? Will this take away from the other students in the classroom? Couldn't and shouldn't special education serve these students better somewhere else?

A wide range of comfort levels with inclusive education remains, but regardless of differences of opinion, the basic premise—giving students with disabilities the opportunity to learn alongside their typical peers—is the focus of IDEA.

It used to be that students were required to have the same knowledge, skills, and performance ability as their peers in a given area of study before they could enter a class with same-age peers. They would have to be "prepared." This practice of "getting ready" for inclusion excluded many students whom the schools decided did not have the proper prerequisite skills to be in a typical age-appropriate classroom. In the meantime, students needing special education services received their education in a separate setting. *Reverse mainstreaming* is a minimalist way for students with and without disabilities to be in class together: Students from regular or general education classrooms come for short periods to "special classes" as "helpers" or visitors.

Julio often put his hands over his ears when the speech therapist visited the special class. The speech therapist unfortunately had a rather shrill voice. Nine-year-old class visitor, Tony, on seeing Julio raise his hands to his ears, immediately commanded, "Hands down!" Julio not only ignored Tony but also moved away from him. This experience provided little social or educational opportunity here for either Julio or Tony.

Today, many, but not all, educators believe that students should be able to participate in general education classes to the best of their abilities. Our students have the right to be educated and socialize with other students their age. "Readiness" is not an excuse for exclusion; accommodations can and must be made. Most students can be included in general education classes, except for the occasional pull-out for certain interventions or services. Making those inclusion opportunities meaningful is the challenge.

———————•———————

Maria was fortunate because her small town was committed to inclusion. In her school's efforts to include her, they realized that she knew more than they had previously thought and that her challenges came from motor difficulties. Once understood, Mr. Grace, her classroom teacher, began to scan the class tests into the computer and modified them by selecting the most critical questions from the tests. He set Maria up to use the computer because writing and printing was so labor-intensive for her that even with fewer questions, she would not be able to finish in time with her class. Mr. Grace was pleased to be able to accommodate Maria with just a little extra effort, and Maria was happy to be truly a part of her class and not just "present."

———————•———————

Sometimes it can be helpful for students coming into an inclusive class/school to provide information in advance, especially if challenging behaviors may be exhibited, and to help other students understand that accommodations and supports are not special privileges. Maria's classmates understood that she worked as hard and as long on her shortened tests as they did with their full-length tests. No favoritism was seen there. If information is to be provided in advance, it must be done respectfully and begin with the students' strengths and not merely focus on their differences.

———————•———————

Ms. Washington knew Alysha was a good reader, but sometimes the classroom noise level became stressful for her. The teacher created a comfortable reading corner where Alysha could go when the noise level got too high. She told her other students that if they wanted to quietly read after their work was done, they could go to the reading corner too. Alysha had her safe space, and some other students who liked the reading corner became better readers than Ms. Washington had expected.

———————•———————

Students with disabilities may be included in many meaningful and respectful ways—ways in which typical students can be both understanding and accepting.

There are also many ways to do inclusion wrong. Just placing a student in a general education class without understanding, supports, and accommodations is not enough and can actually be harmful. Such arrangements tend to highlight differences and isolate the student in the mainstream mix, even possibly resulting in more stigmatization. It is also dangerous to focus on a student's differences in the guise of supporting the student.

———◆———

Lamar was included in the general education fifth grade, and at first glance everything looked good. One day, all of the students including Lamar were working on their papers as the teacher was writing the next part of the lesson on the board. Lamar was humming softly. No one seemed to be paying attention to Lamar's humming except Lamar's behavior specialist and inclusion specialist, who were monitoring him. As soon as they realized he was humming they swooped down on him and yanked him out of the classroom. No one in the classroom had been aware of or bothered by Lamar's humming, but everyone had a chance to see the specialists dragging him from the classroom. Later, when the teacher gave a homework assignment in which the students were asked to write about their "absolutely favorite thing," poor Lamar, who loved horses, was told by the specialists that his assignment would be to write about how to enter a classroom quietly.

———◆———

Inclusion specialists are a relatively new position in schools. They can be helpful in transitioning and including students with disabilities in classes with their same-age peers without disabilities. It is important that they understand the individual student's disabilities and differences, or these inclusion specialists they should have access to a professional who understands the disability so they can consider any accommodations that might be needed. In Lamar's case, the specialists made him stand out. Although decreasing humming was a reasonable goal, their approach to controlling behavior was more disruptive than anything Lamar was doing. The denial of Lamar's opportunity to write about his favorite topic as the rest of the class would do seemed unfair and in effect denied his fellow students the opportunity to know Lamar better.

Sometimes the behaviors we demand of students with disabilities are more than we expect of typical students, and we should make sure that our responses are not unreasonable.

———◆———

> *Stavros was in a special (segregated) class at the high school, where he*
> *had few opportunities to be included. On the day the class was to attend*
> *a movie with the entire student body, Stavros was forced to sit at a table*
> *just outside the auditorium where he would be seen by everyone. His*
> *teacher had decided Stavros should not see the movie with the others*
> *because he had not finished his paperwork. Stavros's mother had a hard*
> *time believing that Stavros was the only student among the 1,000 high*
> *school students watching the movie who had not finished his work, and*
> *she was furious and saddened by the humiliation of her son before the*
> *entire school.*

———◆———

Demanding the same or extra work in an apparent effort to be fair (e.g., same task, same format, same length of time to complete, same instruments) may actually deny the student's right to respond in ways that show his or her abilities. Unreasonably high expectations and practices merely highlight differences and disabilities and effectively deny the student his or her right to an appropriate education.

ASSISTIVE TECHNOLOGY

Over time, Congress realized that for a significant number of students to be successfully included in education, other assists and accommodations were needed for students with hearing, vision, motor, and communication difficulties, and it authorized the inclusion of assistive technology services and devices in the Individuals with Disabilities Education Act Amendments of 1991 (PL 102-119). There are many technological devices that are available to help students to participate more fully and fairly in the classroom; in other words, to get an appropriate and adequate education.

The basics—computers and scanners—are available in just about all schools. Many devices can be used with computers. Various keyboards are available—standard, foldable, larger letters, larger keys, voice-activated, eye-gaze–activated, and even "indestructible." Computer mouses also come in many styles and options: standard, trackball, joystick, big button, foot mouse, head mouse, and various switches. In addition, an array of specialized voice devices and software exists, such as talking dictionaries, voice synthesizer software, voice output readers, voice memo, talking timers and calculators, talking clocks and watches, and vibrating alarm clocks; and without a doubt still more are in development.

You get the idea: There is something to assist just about everyone with a special need. Think of your child and his or her needs. If dyslexia, intellectual disability, or speech is the issue, wouldn't a talking software program on the computer help? Such programs are essential for students who are blind, but they can also help students with reading or language needs. For children with visual impairment, large print and better lighting can help. Those with physical difficulties have a variety of "switches" (e.g., big ball, eye- or voice-activated). So many educational devices are available, and the information is out there for you.

School staff, when faced with an extensive list of hardware and software, might groan, "Good Lord! The school budget!" Assistive technology can be expensive, but it doesn't always have to be.

———◆———

Tyler's advocate, Mrs. Vartinian, approached the IEP team with a request for a laptop to accompany him to every class so that he could fully partici-pate during the school day. After a few protesting gasps from some mem-bers of the team, Mrs. V. suggested they might consider an AlphaSmart, a keyboard device with a small screen that can be downloaded onto a regu-lar computer and printed out at any time during the day. "It costs less than $200," she told them. "What do you think? There may be other models available at the office stores for the same price or a bit more." The principal, recovering from the imagined $1,000-plus figure, responded, "We can check that out and find something to help Tyler."

Tyler's special need was communication, and this technological support provided another opportunity. He was able to "talk" to his classmates and teachers, offering him social as well as strictly educational benefits in his inclusive classroom.

———◆———

Emily, another student in an inclusive class, benefits from her teacher's use of computer hardware, scanner, software, and skills in meeting needs addressed in her IEP.

Mr. Moody regularly scans classroom work into the computer and modifies the papers for Emily so that she can do and complete the work along with her classmates. Emily has difficulties processing visual information, so asking her to do the same amount of closely printed paperwork as the other students would put an unfair burden on her. Mr. Moody knows he can test her work adequately by carefully selecting fewer questions. Larger print and extra spacing between the questions allow Emily enough space to process visual information more easily. Emily is then able to participate in class discussions about the work along with the rest of the class. Such simple use of technology provides Emily with both social and academic opportunities.

———◆———

At times a student's equipment needs may cost big sums, but if that is necessary to provide the student with an appropriate education, IDEA requires that the school provide what is needed. As a parent, you will want to seek out disability organizations and public agencies to get advice and see what is available. New products are being developed all of the time, and your child will benefit from your up-to-date knowledge. This research is extra work for the parent and teacher too, but the payoff is satisfying.

ACCOMMODATIONS

We have been focusing on technological assistance and accommodations, but there are other simpler accommodations we need to consider. You, the parent, need to be aware of these accommodations, which will help the school to include and educate your child.

Because of ADA, passed by Congress in 1990 and amended in 2008, public buildings and services to the public must be made accessible to all, including people with all kinds of disabilities. Buildings and services have been made accessible through an array of supports, ranging from braille signs to auditory enhancement systems to elevators and chair lifts.

Section 504 of the Rehabilitation Act of 1973 (PL 93-112) was passed before ADA and even before IDEA in its earliest forms. This law required, since the early 1970s, that all public entities, state and federal, using federal funds were to be made accessible to people with disabilities. Many schools have been made accessible through these federal funding sources and requirements, and federal law requires that these schools have a Section 504 coordinator to deal with access issues.

The ADA is better known than Section 504 because of aggressive advocacy by groups of people with any kind of disability who fought for its passage by Congress in 1990. It covers all services available to the public, such as handrails in restrooms, curb cuts, and doorways wide enough to accommodate wheelchairs. However, when there is a problem with old schools (and mindsets), your best help for the protection of your child's civil rights to equal access is Section 504.

———◆———

Sanjay uses a wheelchair. He was able to get into the first floor of his school, where he was being educated in the third grade with his age-appropriate classmates. As his IEP was being planned for the next year, his mother expected Sanjay would move with his class to the fourth grade. Because of the structure of the building, she expected that the fourth grade would be moved to the first floor. Instead, she was told that Sanjay needed another year in the third grade. This would result in separation from the students he had been with for 4 years and possible loss of friendships. She protested that Sanjay seemed to be keeping up with the class work. The principal shook her head, saying simply, "In our professional opinion…." Sadly, Sanjay's mother gave in. "What can a poor parent do?" But Sanjay's mother will be haunted by questions about his ability to move on with this class to the fourth grade. Whatever the school's reasoning, Sanjay was excluded from his peers and friends.

———◆———

Ramps, elevators, and chair lifts are obvious accommodations. But many other accommodations, often simpler and costing little, can and should be provided for individual students.

———◆———

Sasha had difficulty coping in physical education class. It was hard to say whether it was the open space, the noise, or the constantly changing activities. It was painful to watch her discomfort and awkwardness. At the IEP meeting, Mrs. Rostov addressed the team: "We have tried gym for years, and it is just not working. Isn't there some way to set up an individualized program of activities that would satisfy the state regulations and give Sasha the physical activity she needs?" The occupational therapist who had been working with Sasha for the past 2 years offered a tailor-made program for Sasha. Sasha liked walking and she loved to swim. The principal approved this substitute plan, and Mrs. Rostov was pleased because these were activities Sasha could carry forward through the rest of her life.

———◆———

Simple classroom accommodations are numerous, such as giving preferential seating for the easily distractible student near the front of the classroom or sparing an acutely auditorily defensive student unnecessary discomfort by warning him or her that a fire drill is scheduled later in the morning. Other accommodations may not be so easily determined, such as those that might help students whose seizures may be brought on by the flickering of florescent lights. It is important for teachers in those classrooms with florescent lights to suspect that what looks like a student's inattention may be partial or absence seizures. Incandescent lights or alternative florescent lights that flicker at a different frequency are accommodations that can be installed.

Any accommodations that are needed should be written into the IEP by the whole team. It may occasionally be costly and sometimes inconvenient, but in many cases school staff and parents working as a team can develop reasonable accommodations at low cost.

It can be helpful to consider the needs for assistive technology and other accommodations before the FBA (described next), and certainly as part of the FBA, because it helps everyone to really take a good look at the student and provide a stronger assessment.

FUNCTIONAL BEHAVIORAL ASSESSMENT

FBA is a systematic process for collecting information. It is a way to analyze a student's needs to try to determine better ways to meet those needs. The information (data) the team collects will be used to help determine why "problem behaviors" occur and help identify ways to address behaviors that interfere with learning. FBAs must be done by a team of people who have contact with the student daily or at least weekly. Out of this should come a positive behavior program. Parents and professionals need to become good observers, seeing the student with a wide lens and not just using a simple behavior checklist. A functional assessment does not always end with a behavioral support plan; it might end with some environmental or program changes or even some simple changes in teaching methods.

Although the added behavioral language in IDEA '97 may seem to promote one method of instruction, parents who want a less restrictive and more responsive approach need not be concerned that every student must now submit to a strict behavior program. Within the behavioristic language of the law, there is room for a more individually responsive assessment, planning, and supports. For example, an FBA, if conducted properly, might lead to a new or improved communication system (maybe even a laptop) for a student with little or no spoken language, or students with sensorimotor needs may at last have both environmental and academic accommodations made. However, there are many parents who believe in strictly behavioral programs for teaching their children self-control, and this will be an option they want to explore.

The new language of FBAs uses the term *problems* in describing behavior when *needs* might be a better way of thinking. Many children have "behavior problems" that are part of their disability. Without the needed accommodations, these behaviors may make it difficult to learn, cause harm to the child or others, or isolate a child from other students. Some children, such as those with Tourette syndrome, have behaviors that are hard to control, or sensorimotor issues, that may make extended sitting in the classroom difficult.

———————◆———————

Jason was lucky that Mr. DuBois understood that sometimes the classroom noise and activity overwhelmed him. The teacher remembered the occupational therapist at the IEP meeting talking about how helpful it would be if Jason could sometimes walk off his anxiety. Mr. DuBois spoke to the principal in advance about sending Jason with notes to the head office just to give Jason a chance to relax before returning to the classroom ready to learn. He also occasionally and randomly did the same for other students so as not to single Jason out too obviously. Mr. Dubois shared this information as part of the FBA, and it became part of Jason's plan. Over time Jason became more relaxed, as these walks kept him from becoming overloaded, and soon fewer walks were needed. A careful assessment of the environment can be critical.

———————◆———————

A few students simply have not learned positive ways to have their needs met. Here, direct instruction and coaching with or without a behavior program may be helpful. If behaviors interfere with the students' ability to learn the skills that they need to be successful, they must be assessed comprehensively, and that must include what goes on in the classroom, the physical environment, materials, time of day, and so forth. If we look more widely, there may be some surprises.

———◆———

Will sat restlessly with his peers at the edge of the circle as the teacher reviewed the alphabet. Ms. Campbell held up a card—"This is K. What is this?"—and the circle would answer "K." But Will, who had a language disability, would look up and away every time, seemingly noncompliant. The visiting inclusion specialist started to look in the direction Will was looking, and after several alphabet cards, realized that whatever card was held up, Will was turning to look at the matching letter of the alphabet posted up on the wall. Rather than being noncompliant, Will was actually doing more work than the other students.

———◆———

Assessment should be comprehensive, and *comprehensive* means looking at everything, and listening, too.

Still, there are children who, through lack of opportunity, need to learn better or improve their social skills. Sometimes, for students with language disabilities, the behavior is a way of saying no. We can target and teach better ways that are more productive for students. Teachers have little control over some situations (e.g., a fire drill), but a good teacher can be sympathetic while moving a child along or, if a student has extremely sensitive hearing, warn that individual student of the fire drill that is to come to lessen the impact of an unexpected and noxious noise.

To conduct the most accurate FBA, we need to understand the student's disability. Too frequently, what were seen as disabilities in EI and preschool (e.g., motor, sensory, or communication issues) somehow in elementary and middle school become "problems" and noncompliance issues. It is up to you, as the parent, to make sure the IEP team remembers or has access to this early information about your child's special needs. Team members need to understand the disability and the basic needs associated with it. When the student's difficulties are ignored, "problem behaviors" can result.

Through the process of FBA, we can learn about when, where, and why behaviors are likely to happen. The team's responsibility is to gather information in the different school environments and activities to help understand why a student has problem behaviors. The result of collecting information and data across the school day should lead to a hypothesis about why the behaviors occur. A *hypothesis* is merely an educated best guess based on the information the team has gathered. The results of the assessment are then used to develop a behavioral intervention plan.

BEHAVIORAL INTERVENTION PLAN

From the FBA, the team should have a clear idea of the student's needs that trigger problem behaviors. The team can now begin to plan positive strategies to respond to needs and teach new behaviors and to provide materials or equipment to meet those needs. Interventions can include improved communication methods, supports for various physical and sensory difficulties, sensory diet, assistive technology, and so forth—in other words, those supports indicated as a result of the FBA to meet the individual student needs. Changes may be made in classrooms and other environments to support desired behaviors and to reduce or eliminate any difficulties that tend to result in so-called problem behaviors.

These strategies targeted to meet the student's needs are usually called *positive behavior support*. The goal of teachers and parents is to use the information from the FBA to help a child learn new skills and provide new opportunities for learning. This is not a discipline or punishment plan. It is a plan to help meet the educational needs of the student.

If at any time you feel your child's behavioral intervention (methods, equipment, supports) plan is not meeting his or her needs, you can ask for another FBA to be done.

NO CHILD LEFT BEHIND

At first glance, NCLB may not seem to offer much to students in need of special education services. Yet NCLB can benefit students with disabilities by requiring that teachers be highly qualified. This means, in the language of the law, that a teacher has full state certification or qualifies under a plan known as "high, objective, uniform State standards of evaluation." This rule does not allow the placement of any unassigned teacher where there is an opening. Now a teacher who teaches math must be certified as highly qualified. The same rule applies to special education teachers.

At one time, "special classes" in some schools were where less able teachers finished out their careers until retirement. (And in some cities, special education classes were moved from district to district to balance district racial composition.) Now with high teacher requirements, special education can no longer be used to maintain unqualified teachers.

If your child's teacher is not certified and you feel that this lack of qualification weakens the implementation of your child's IEP, you are entitled to file a complaint with your state department of education.

NCLB also has clear student testing requirements in reading, math, and science. Some people are concerned that the requirements for schools to have acceptable test scores might push students with disabilities out of general education classes and back into segregated special education classes or force them to repeat the year in typical classes. Here, NCLB may unfavorably affect some students receiving special educations services who will not be able to test well because of their disabilities. Assistive technology and other accommodations may help some but not all students. In addition, the option of alternate assessment for students with a range of disabilities is meant to allow as many students as possible to participate in state and national testing. The challenges of testing may move school personnel to better recognize the needs determined by the disabilities and improve the ways (e.g., equipment, more time) they test their students with disabilities so that the results are more fair and accurate. This could be a benefit to your child. You will certainly be discussing these standardized tests when the team writes the IEP.

INDIVIDUALIZED TRANSITION PLAN

As your child goes through his or her education from EI until he or she graduates, or finishes on his or her 22nd birthday, you will know that you have gone through many transitions—people, services, methods, schools, and even a crisis now and again. An individualized transition plan (ITP), however, is a formal plan of transition required of the school by IDEA when your child becomes a teenager. Any type of transition always includes present and future staff and takes place with sufficient time to visit any new setting and meet new staff.

The goal of an ITP is to prepare the student for the transition to adult life. It focuses on finding the right amounts of academics and work skills and training for community and independent living skills. By law, an ITP must be prepared when the student turns 16 (some states start at 14 or even sooner), and his or her presence and participation in the ITP process is required for all meetings. It starts with a vision, which includes the interests and preferences of the student, and continues to be refined over the next 6 years (or fewer if the student graduates earlier). If your student is expected to need continued services into adulthood, a representative of a public agency or agencies such as public health, developmental, or rehabilitation services will attend the later planning meetings.

The planning may start at age 14, but it's good to remember that many typical students don't or can't make life choices at 14. Be flexible and carefully consider choices before tracking your child who may need lifelong supports into programs that may remove him or her from participating in school life with the typical students. Those early friendships and connections can also be useful social supports for adult life in the community.

MEDIATION/DUE PROCESS

An important part of IDEA is *due process,* which means that you, the parent, have the right to reject the IEP, including the behavioral intervention plan or any other portion you think would be wrong for your child. Due process comes into play when you and the school disagree on what's in the plan or what's not in the plan. Perhaps some vital service you want put into the IEP, often speech or physical therapy, is not there, or not in the amounts you think are necessary for your child. If the school disagrees with your rejection, then your first efforts should go to resolve the problem through mediation.

The mediator is often appointed by the state for these mediation hearings and is expected to be impartial and work with you and the school to resolve your differences. If you are dissatisfied with the mediation process, you are always entitled to go to court. But because most of you won't even go to mediation, we will save that information for later in this book (see Chapter 8).

Mediation is a confidential process in which you and the school staff sit down with a mediator to come to some agreement. You are not required to go to mediation; it is voluntary for you, but mediation is always preferable to more formal hearings. It can help you find a way to continue to work with school staff for your child's benefit. Your state department of education is required to have this process and provide the qualified and impartial mediators. In some states the local school sets up the process and mediators; this seems a conflict of interest to some advocates. Still, it is valuable to go through the process to find any agreements you can and to identify the most serious disagreements.

―――――◆―――――

Tiffany Jones was about to enter middle school—new building, new teacher, new aide, and even some new students. Tiffany did not do well with changes. Her mom wanted the school to ease her in by having her visit the teacher and aide in the new school a few times in the week before school opened. The principal rejected this request. "She has already visited the building in the spring with all of the other students. We can't do special favors for everyone." But Mrs. Jones made her case that Tiffany came home from the visit agitated and fearful of her future. Tiffany's neighbor shared what she knew about Tiffany. Mrs. Jones asked for mediation to resolve the problem.

The mediator had a few questions: "Are the teachers in the building that week?" "Yes." "Will it cost any more to have Tiffany visit?" "No." "I recommend you do it. It would be hard to defend your not doing it." So Tiffany visited the empty school building, sat in her classroom, met her teacher and aide for 1 or 2 hours for 3 days, and started the new school year with relative ease.

―――――◆―――――

In mediation, it is best to take your personal advocate with you. For this meeting, it can be a neighbor like Tiffany's or a friend. Later you will read more about your personal advocate, but for now, know that you always take someone with you who is on your side.

Mediation is likely to work more easily when your requests are not big-budget items or are easy to implement. The mediator can bring both sides together. If you and the school agree, then an agreement that is legally binding is drawn up and signed by both sides. If you cannot agree, you can then move to the next level. If you choose to go to hearing, a more formal process, the law now requires that you first go to a resolution session.

You may never need to use due process. However, if you do, you will find more information on this topic in Chapter 8.

REAL STORIES TO HELP YOU ON YOUR WAY

Some of you may be wondering about the stories in this book. Yes, they are real. The names, of course, have been changed, the genders some of the time, and the details only as necessary to preserve confidentiality. You will learn from their experiences and with hope from their successes.

Now you want to prepare yourself, the most promising advocate for your child, by learning to challenge the myths that persist in some schools and by acquiring new skills and determination to do the job.

3

The Myths Stop Here
Substituting Fact for Fiction

the myths in action • "troublesome" parents • practicing your advocacy • self-statements help • it isn't easy • the fantasies unwind • the persistent parent advocate • still in the learning mode

"It's hard for parents to be objective."

"Let's just leave the teaching to the teachers."

"A full school day is just too much for your child."

"We can't place your daughter in a 'regular' class. It would be unfair to disrupt the regular students. Besides, she'd be lost."

"The principal is a very busy person with many responsibilities. He will get back to you when he has more time."

"The methodology of this teaching program is quite complex and would be hard for you to understand. Trust the professionals to do the job right. Just sign here, please."

Many parents have heard statements such as these when they have tried to obtain services, gain admittance to their children's classrooms, offer suggestions for change, or simply get information from school staff. These statements all have one thing in common. They are all based on myths—that is, they are half-truths that are accepted by many people and are used by a minority of people to control the behavior of individuals who would question the workings of the system.

When parents question the school system, insecure school professionals who feel threatened by them use just these kinds of statements to keep parents from "meddling" in "school business." Many parents accept such statements without any attempt to defend themselves and their special value as participants in their children's education. Some are so intimidated that they find themselves nodding in agreement to end a difficult situation. Others are uncomfortable or even resent these remarks, but because they do not have the necessary facts or skills to correct or counter the statements, they may retreat in silence. In this way, parents allow themselves to become victims of myths that have been used by school systems for too many years, in spite of parents having the expert knowledge about their children.

Fortunately, IDEA clearly states and protects the rights of parents to participate (or "meddle") in the educational process. But in order to fully contribute to the process, parents must discover some of the hidden meanings in the myths and acquire the skills to dispel myths that can undermine their effectiveness or even prevent them from helping to shape their children's educational future. Parents must understand why the myths have survived in order to be able to deal with them now.

THE PERSISTENCE OF MYTHS

Why do these myths persist if they tend to prevent or limit the involvement of concerned parents and if they do little to improve the education of children with disabilities? They persist because there is an element of truth in every myth; however, that truth is only partial. Of course, the educator is a specially trained expert, but parents know their children best and have seen what they can do outside of the school setting. Yes, parents are not always objective, but experts aren't 100% objective either; no one is. And a child may indeed have trouble with a full school day, but it may be the content of the school day that is the problem and not the length of the time spent in school.

Myths also persist because they seem to work. They are effective in keeping a smokescreen around the human and everyday limitations and imperfections of the people who work for school systems, and, to the extent that they silence or confuse parents, they provide security to "threatened" school personnel. However, these myths do not really benefit anyone—children, parents, or even school personnel.

HOW TO DEAL WITH MYTHS

Dealing with myths is a little like cleaning house: You have to keep doing it. Unlike housecleaning, however, each time you confront, counter, and dispel myths, you will find yourself doing less and less. In this chapter, we identify and discuss the types of myths about parents, teachers and other professional educators, and students with disabilities. We will examine a number of specific myths drawn from the experience of many parents, focus on the behaviors of both parents and school personnel that support the myths, offer some explanations of why the myths are wrong or counterproductive, and then develop some ideas about things parents can do to overcome the harm done by the myths. You will learn to recognize and understand the myths in operation, make statements to yourself that will strengthen your resolution to counter these fictions with facts, and make statements to school staff that will demonstrate to them that the myths are in error.

THE MYTHS ABOUT "MERE PARENTS"

The "mere parents" myths have their foundation in a collection of beliefs held by some school people that parents always know less and are less capable than professionals (because to them, a lack of professional training means a lack of objectivity and good judgment) and that parents will waste hours of the professionals' valuable time if they are allowed to participate in their children's education. This kind of thinking puts you on the receiving end of professional expertise and in a defensive posture when you try to deal with the school people. Thus you may feel that you must argue for your ideas and requests while the professionals simply pass judgment. Measured against the professionals (and by the professionals), you, the parent, are always found wanting. Time is wasted if staff expect to understand your child's needs without acknowledging that you, the parent, carry the most comprehensive knowledge of your child's learning history.

All parents and educators are affected by the "mere parents" myths, and to some degree, all believe them (this includes assertive parents and well-intentioned educators). It is important to keep in mind that both parents and educators are victims of these beliefs—parents because they are prevented from fully stating the case for their children and educators because they deprive themselves of a necessary source of information about their students. (Keep in mind that you have a great deal of factual information about your child and that the school people need your information now and throughout your child's school years.) Here are the primary "mere parents" myths that have too often kept parents "in their place":

- Parents are naive laypersons who can't and shouldn't teach.
- Parents are too emotionally involved to evaluate their children.
- Some parents aren't really interested.
- Parents are still obedient school pupils who should be seen and not heard.

Parents Are Naive Laypersons Who Can't and Shouldn't Teach

The thinking behind this myth goes like this:

> *"Parents don't know anything about teaching. They have not had professional training. Yet some parents are always trying to give the professionals advice on how to work with their children and even how to run the classroom, in spite of the fact that they are totally ignorant of the sophisticated instructional and evaluative methods that modern teachers and specialists employ. Usually a reminder that the teacher has had special training, years of experience, or an advanced degree will put an end to their questions and demands. Parents may mean well, but they just don't know enough about teaching."*

Some teachers and other professionals feel very strongly about this myth. Their training is very important to them. For some professionals, this is because they have unquestioningly followed the dictates of methods that may now be considered outmoded or at least in need of some thoughtful revision; for others, it's because they have a personal need for a social and professional status that puts them at least a notch above the "average guy."

The open and competent teacher, however, welcomes questions from all quarters to help in his or her ongoing search for new educational methods and directions and, although proud to be a school professional, is more concerned with doing the job well than with personal prestige. Although very few parents are also trained educators, the secure teacher recognizes that parents are the students' first "teachers," and that they continue to teach their children throughout their growing years and have useful information for the teachers and/or specialists.

Let's look at the myth in action. In her parent–teacher conference, Beverly Jackson brings up the subject of reading with some excitement. She tells the teacher that her son, Darren, who has been diagnosed with an intellectual disability, is able to select his favorite soup, Chicken Zucchini, from the many soup cans on the kitchen shelf.

Mrs. Jackson: *I know he can't read, but he always picks out the right can, even though all the soup cans look alike. He must be recognizing some of the letters. Do you think he could begin to learn to read?*

Teacher: *Mrs. Jackson, Darren is now 15. If he hasn't learned to read by now, it's highly unlikely that he will ever learn. I can show you in his folder that when he was 12, his former teacher tried him on a new reading readiness program, which he couldn't do at all. We have used the most up-to-date methods. Reading is simply beyond Darren's ability.*

Mrs. Jackson: *But how do you explain the fact that he can pick out the right can every time?*

Teacher: *Well-meaning parents often give cues to their children without even being aware that they are doing it. You probably smile at him when he touches the right can. We have tested Darren and we know that reading is beyond his ability. You really should leave the teaching to the teachers and not torment yourself with unreasonable hopes. In a few minutes, I have another meeting. I would like to use this time to discuss Darren's inattentive behavior in class.*

Mrs. Jackson (sighs): *What's wrong with Darren's behavior in school?*

This parent has presented vital information to the teacher, but because the teacher hasn't seen it himself or herself, it is discredited. The open and responsive teacher would ask for more information and plan to check it out in school on the chance that Darren is a potential reader, even if only of a small list of words.

Roy Armijo is another example. He is explaining to the IEP team that he thinks his son, Simon, is ready for a full day of school.

Mr. Armijo: *And my wife tells me that when Simon comes home, he's after her to take him to the store or to let him go to the playground. But we can't let him go to the school playground because school is still in session. It seems to me that he has plenty of energy for a full day of school.*

Teacher: *Energy is not the issue, Mr. Armijo. Simon is not yet ready to handle the strain of a full school day. He becomes increasingly frustrated after 2 hours in school. Three hours is the maximum amount of time he can manage in school without being disruptive.*

Mr. Armijo: *I know he can get restless, because I've been helping him at home with his homework. He's only good for 15 minutes at a time. So we alternate. Fifteen minutes on his school work, then we may go outside and shoot a few baskets. We'll come back in and work for another 15 minutes. I don't know why it works but it sure seems to help. Is there something like that on-and-off stuff you could do in school?*

Teacher: *What would you suggest, Mr. Armijo?*

Mr. Armijo: *I don't know. I thought you might have some ideas.*

Psychologist: *These emotionally disturbed children, Mr. Armijo, have to learn to accept limits. Simon is just now slowly learning to manage the classroom according to its rules. If we make special rules for him, he will become confused, and we could have a lot of testing behavior in school, which would be detrimental. [Smiles.] After all, he can hardly play basketball in the classroom, can he? Maybe next year he will be ready for a full day. His progress is slow but steady. You don't want to disrupt that, do you?*

> **Mr. Armijo:** It seems awfully slow to me, and I worry that he's missing so much school.
>
> **Principal:** I understand your impatience, but rules are important.
>
> **Mr. Armijo:** Nothing more you can do now?
>
> **Principal:** All in good time, Mr. Armijo, all in good time. We'll let you know when we feel he's ready for more.

This parent also has some important information for the school. He doesn't have all of the answers, and he is looking to the professionals to find a way to use this information he has provided to help his son. If the team had been receptive, Roy Armijo might have heard this response:

> *"It sounds like you are having some success in working with Simon at home. Of course, we don't have the same freedom and flexibility you have at home, but we might adapt your approach. If we could schedule some gym activities for late morning, he might be able to stay into the afternoon. We want to be cautious, but we need to be thinking about ways we could expand Simon's day."*

Instead of responding to Mr. Armijo's urgent request to try some supports or changes that can later be evaluated, Simon's present team believes they have all the answers. Their frequent references to the rules may reflect the concern that this parent is breaking one of their unspoken rules: Parents shouldn't interfere by trying to teach or making recommendations for teaching. In their efforts to control this parent, the team members discard information that could help them do a better job.

When parents present the kind of valuable information as illustrated in these examples, the team members should look beyond behaviors and try to make use of the information to improve the school program. Darren Jackson may be ready to read at least some key words, even if he is 15. And Roy Armijo seems to be working well with Simon. In fact, the parents may be having more success at home than the teachers are having in school. Open and responsive teachers would be asking the parents for more information, rather than cutting the parents off (or down!), and would be planning ways to test and use the information. For example, Darren's teacher might try some meaningful (to Darren) sight words on cards or even collect soup labels for a start—perhaps the earlier reading readiness program held little meaning for Darren or focused on his weakest learning modes. Likewise, Simon's teacher could be thinking about alternating desk work with physical activity, such as having Simon erase the blackboard, get milk, or carry notes to the office, to see if this pattern of activity could help.

When parents' information is simply ignored or discredited, they feel bewildered and frustrated. They may respond by assuming that the knowledgeable professional is right and that their information is unimportant. This "mere parents" myth survives because it is based on the true statement that parents have not been trained as professionals. But parents aren't asking to run the classroom; they only want the professionals to know their children and to pay some attention to what they have seen, heard, and experienced with their children. Yet some school professionals interpret parents' lack of professional training as evidence that parents know nothing about teaching their children and can't or shouldn't teach at home or offer suggestions to teachers.

What educators forget when they engage in this kind of thinking is that parents were the children's first teachers. They taught their children language (e.g., "doggie," "car"); concepts (e.g., "Go bye-bye," "Stove hot"); manual skills (e.g., using a spoon, a fork, and a knife, in that order); social skills (e.g., "Thank you," "I need help"); and even some academics, such as colors, counting, and table games. Depending on their children's difficulties, parents may have varied in their rates of success, but they did teach. When their children reached school age, the parents expected the schools to provide education, but they did not forget how to observe and how to help.

In many cases, parents of students with disabilities usually do more teaching at home than parents of children without disabilities. They do this out of necessity to help their children overcome some of the obstacles presented by disability and the denial of educational services. Most of these parents do a remarkable job, but their extraordinary achievements may go unrecognized by school people. Parents of students with disabilities may even be seen as less able or "defective" because they have produced a "defective" child. Of course, this kind of thinking and treatment is nonsense and grossly unfair to both parents and children, but it exists. Parents can deal with these attitudes by asserting their children's rights and by reminding themselves of their past achievements with their children.

If you are treated in any of the ways discussed, you may begin to doubt your own reason, ears, and eyes. When you find yourself asking, "Who am I, a mere parent, to question the statements of experts?"

or if you find yourself retreating, think about the good things you have helped your child achieve. Make some self-statements to strengthen your determination to keep everybody on the right track: dealing with the educational issues you have raised. To yourself, you might say things such as these:

"It is my right to be here actively participating in my child's education."

"I don't have to be a professional to know what I have seen my child do."

"My information about my child is valuable and useful."

"It doesn't take a mechanic to tell someone he or she has a flat tire."

"My requests are reasonable."

"If they need more information, I am willing to give it."

These statements are the basic ideas to keep in your head. Whenever you have any reason to expect difficulty, you might practice saying these things to yourself (using your own words) before the meeting, and maybe even write them down to refer to for support and encouragement during the meeting. You can also review in Chapter 1 the reasons why you are and can be the best advocate for your child.

For example, to the professionals, Beverly Jackson might say the following:

> *"I honestly believe that Darren is ready to read; I have seen him choose his favorite soup from cans with identical labels. If it would be helpful, I am willing to observe him more carefully in the next weeks. My husband and other children will help me check my observations. In the meantime, I would like you to look for ways you can further help Darren in school through other methods or materials you know. Then let's meet again to see if there's something more that can be done to help him learn to read."*

When you make these kinds of statements to the professionals, you are doing several things:

- Demonstrating your ability to work cooperatively and in a businesslike way with the professionals

- Involving them actively by referring to what they can do (they can seek methods and materials that will build on your successful efforts or meet your child's needs)

- Demonstrating your objectivity by seeking more information through your own efforts and by asking the professionals to check out the information you have presented

- Letting the professionals know that you intend to stay with the problem or issue until it is resolved

Note that you do not allow the professionals to dismiss or belittle your requests. Giving in would only confirm their belief in their own "absolute" expertise. However, in spite of your feelings of frustration, never argue and insist they do it your way. Arguing gives them a reason to label you an "emotional" parent and ignore your requests. The myth of emotional parents who do not see their children objectively is another powerful prejudice you may need to overcome.

Parents Are Too Emotionally Involved to Evaluate Their Children

The thinking behind the myth goes something like this:

> *"Parents can't be objective because they are so emotionally involved with their children. They can't get enough distance from their children to gain a realistic perspective and evaluate the real problem. Only someone who is outside the family and professionally trained can be truly objective about the problem and about what needs to be done. Teachers and specialists know more about the child's actual educational needs than do parents."*

Let's look at two examples.

At her conference with the teacher, Alma Jones asked if her daughter, Briana, who has cerebral palsy, could leave the classroom 5 minutes before lunchtime in order to get down the stairs before the lunch bell rings. Briana had told her mother that it has been difficult for her to get through the milling students to the cafeteria, that she always arrives last, and that she only has enough time to eat half her lunch. The teacher smiles and says, "Now, Mrs. Jones, we shouldn't baby Briana. I know mothers do like to protect their children, but Briana shouldn't get special treatment. Don't you want her to be treated like the other students? If she is going to learn to be self-sufficient, then let her take her knocks with the other children instead of asking for special favors. Briana is just trying to get your sympathy."

Mrs. Jones is confused. She tries to let Briana do as much for herself as possible, but is she still being overprotective? She drops the subject.

At the IEP meeting, Roger and Joan Backman asked whether their son, Ray, who has a mild intellectual disability, can be accepted on one of the intramural basketball teams. The guidance counselor responds:

"Ray would have a difficult time keeping up with all the other players who are not disabled and are so much faster and smarter than he is. He seems to be doing well in school, and the other children are just beginning to accept him. I know that you would like him to be as able as your other children, but he is disabled, after all. You shouldn't be pushing him too hard."

Mr. Backman answers: "But you should see him play with the other kids in the neighborhood. He's as good as any of them, at least in the basketball game."

There are some knowing smiles around the table as the guidance counselor says, "Perhaps his friends make allowances for him. I think we should stick to Ray's educational plan so that his teachers will have time at this meeting to talk about his work in math, which is quite poor."

Mr. Backman looks angry, turns to his wife, shrugs his shoulders, and is silent.

In these two examples, the parents are seen by the school people as being too emotionally involved with their children to be able to make valid judgments or recommendations. For example, Alma Jones wants to "baby" her daughter and hold her back. Roger and Joan Backman want to "push" their son into situations for which he is not ready. Sometimes the perspective of the school people shifts, depending on parents' current requests: Last year's pushy parent may become this year's overprotective parent. No wonder some parents are confused about their ability to be objective; they try, but for one reason or another, they never quite seem to make the grade.

Often, professionals patronize parents by making assumptions about parents' motives. When asked to explain or support their assumptions, they will sometimes dredge up the worse possible example of parent behavior they can remember, such as the parent who insisted on driving his able-bodied 10-year-old child two blocks to school any time it threatened to rain. Of course, there are a few parents who are pushy or protective and who are determined to do things their way without considering the effect of their actions on their child's growth and welfare, but they are in the extreme and should not be cited as examples of average parents. Most parents are primarily concerned about their children's welfare and give long and serious thought to how much protection ("babying") their children need and how much challenge ("pushing") their children can successfully manage.

In both examples, the parents have allowed the myths to go unquestioned. Instead of pursuing the discussion with the teachers, Alma Jones begins to question herself. Although Roger Backman is angry and frustrated by the patronizing way the group treats his request to have his son take part in school sports, he feels people aren't really listening to him anyway and so he withdraws in silence. His wife goes along by saying nothing. The myth remains effective in keeping parents in their place.

How might parents respond to the "emotionally involved" parents myth in a positive, practical, and productive way? First, they must examine the myth to discover the element of truth on which the myth is based. Then they must question the conclusions that have been drawn from that element of truth. The truth here is that parents are emotionally involved with their children. Of course they are. Imagine what it would be like raising children if you were not emotionally involved! Your emotional involvement is your antenna that tells you when something good or bad is happening to your child. Your love for your child keeps you interested in the many small steps of your child's growth and development (making you the rich source of information that you are) when others, less involved, would lose interest or forget. Sure, sometimes you may have hesitated or been too eager for your child, but you probably weren't too far off the mark, and when you discussed it with someone who was interested and treated you as a competent person, did you decide to ease up or be a little more cautious? Your emotional involvement is not only a good thing for you and your child, but it is also essential for your child's development.

Unfortunately, professionals sometimes assume that parental emotional involvement is a drawback, a set of blinders parents wear, and a hindrance to professionals in their efforts to help parents see their children more objectively. They may discount the value of the information presented by a parent without at least checking it out because of one past experience with a truly "emotional" or biased parent. Roger Backman has seen his son play basketball; Briana has told her mother that lunchtime is difficult for her. Yet what these parents have seen and heard is being ignored. They are understandably frustrated, angry, or depressed.

When parents hear professionals devalue or ignore the information or request they are making, they should react in the following ways:

- Recognize the value of emotional involvement.

- Learn to make statements to themselves such as, "Of course I care. Where would my child be if I didn't care?"

- Keep the professionals on task by not allowing them to close the discussion (e.g., "Yes, we don't want to give her more help than she needs, but we still have to figure out how to get her to the lunchroom in time to eat her lunch. What can we do?").

- Continue the discussion by asking what more information is needed by school personnel to make the request acceptable for them to begin to consider possible solutions to the request the parent is presenting.

Let's go back to Alma Jones. Here is a possible scenario:

Teacher:	*. . .instead of asking for special favors. Briana is just trying to get your sympathy.*
Mrs. Jones:	*Yes, I do appreciate the effort Briana puts into keeping up with her classmates. But I am concerned that we may be asking too much of her in this case. Is it possible for her to leave class 5 minutes early for lunch?*
Teacher:	*Well, yes. I suppose it is. But it would make the other students even more aware of her differences.*
Mrs. Jones:	*Can you think of any ways to minimize these differences or perhaps other solutions that might be better?*
Teacher:	*Give me some time to think about it.*
Mrs. Jones:	*Would you call me in a day or two to let me know what you have done? I'm especially concerned because Briana isn't finishing her lunch and she is a little underweight. Could you let me know how much of her meal she is actually missing?*
Teacher:	*But, Mrs. Jones, I'm not in the lunchroom. We have aides for that.*

Mrs. Jones: *I didn't know that. (Stifles a groan and takes a deep breath.) I know teachers need their breaks. But you know Briana better than the lunchroom aide. I'm sure with your experience, if you monitored the situation for only a day or two, you would find the right solution to the problem. (Mrs. Jones then arranges to talk with the teacher by phone toward the end of the week.)*

Notice that the "new" Alma Jones acknowledges her emotional involvement ("I appreciate Briana's effort"), ignores the teachers' assumptions (the parent is babying Briana), and keeps the discussion going by asking questions that involve the teacher in monitoring the situation and solving the problem. Instead of being put off by the teacher's remarks about babying Briana, Alma Jones perseveres, politely and firmly, and arranges for further consultation. By presenting herself as a rational, on-task, and caring parent, the new Alma Jones refuses to play along with this "mere parent" myth. If Roger Backman can stay on task by asking the IEP team to have the gym teacher check out his son's basketball playing skills before allowing the discussion to be closed, then maybe he too can become an effective advocate for his son.

Even if it sounds easy, it isn't. It may get better over time, but it will always be a challenge. If you have any reason to expect the "overly emotionally involved parent" treatment, then you must practice dealing with the myth before you go to the school. Practice with two sets of statements: those you may need to make to yourself ("I am a good, caring, and concerned parent. I know my child. I am here to find solutions") and those you make to teachers and others ("I am asking you to meet a real need my child has. What information do you need? How can you find out? What solutions can you find or can we find together? How can I help?"). If necessary, write statements down in your own words and refer to them at the meeting. With practice and experience, you will become more confident about your own contributions and eventually encounter fewer people who will attempt to use this myth to put down your efforts. When they do try, your calm and firm manner will help you to keep going as your child's best advocate.

For those of you who have successfully maneuvered in situations involving this myth, or for those who have been fortunate in dealing with educators who feel that parents are reasonably objective and therefore useful as sources of information, there is another myth waiting in the wings for you to face and manage.

For any of you confronted by this myth, you should know that there are parents with advanced degrees in education, psychology, and other specialties who have been put down by this kind of thinking. You should know that Evelyn, a competent physical therapist who consulted regularly to Middletown School System and participated in many IEPs as a member of the team, also faced difficulties in the IEP process after she adopted 5-year-old Eric, a child with physical motor challenges. She reports the following:

> *"I couldn't believe it. I worked with these people for years in developing IEPs for other children. Now they hardly paid any attention to my recommendations for Eric. I told them, 'I'm the same person I have always been. My observations should count.' But they just smiled and suggested that my observations were colored by my emotional involvement. I was an adoptive parent for 5 months and I was being patronized."*

Evelyn, because of her expertise and past and even ongoing professional relationships with the school staff, was shocked by their response. Only 5 months an adoptive parent, the team solidly viewed her as too emotionally involved to be objective.

Some Parents Are Just Not that Interested

Some parents are put down by schools for lack of interest, sometimes through no fault of their own; some parents have babysitting problems or lack transportation or have become burned out by earlier experience in trying to get the right services for their child. Other parents might have difficulty getting time off from work to meet with school staff during the school day, and some parents may receive notices they don't understand because of their legalistic style, or they may not even receive adequate notice at all.

Ellie Pierce showed up at Parent–Teacher Night concerned that she had no contact with the school. She was greeted with "Why, Mrs. Pierce, we did not expect you to come tonight!"

Mrs. Pierce:	*Why would you think that?*
Principal:	*We called you and were never able to reach you so we assumed you weren't interested. We tried several times.*
Mrs. Pierce:	*I never received any calls. I did not know you were trying to reach me.*
Principal:	*You were never home.*
Mrs. Pierce:	*I was working. Did it ever occur to you to call at night or weekends when you could reach me?*
Principal:	*Well, school closes and we are out of the building by 3 p.m.*

The school may have made minimal effort, but the parent is blamed for lack of interest. IDEA tells us that meetings should be set up at the convenience of all IEP team members, which means parents, too. Too often meetings are set up at the convenience of the schools ("teacher contracts"). Rarely are meetings held after school and almost never are they held in the parents' home. As a parent, you have the right to insist that you be given adequate notice and that the school make at least some effort to accommodate your work and family needs.

Parents Are Still Obedient School Pupils Who Should Be Seen and Not Heard

Most parents stand at least a little in awe of school people and systems because schools represent our childhood images of authority and mystifying expertise. We are all products of school systems and we still retain a number of childlike school behaviors based on the old rules: "Stand in line," "No gum chewing," and "No talking out of turn."

The school building can bring out these old feelings and behaviors in practically everyone who doesn't work in a school. Those school people who feel most secure in authoritarian roles tend to exploit this habitual response to shore up their status with almost everyone who is not a regular part of the system. They may use a commanding tone of voice, keep people waiting in the outer office or halls, require silence as you walk the corridors, and generally treat parents as children and intruders. They make it clear that everyone in the building has a particular place, and the parent's place is that of the child.

Parents who are in the school building advocating for perhaps the first time may feel threatened and see themselves as disruptive. Old habits, like school behaviors, do die hard. Years of training as school pupils develop a knee-jerk kind of response in parents when they find themselves in the setting that trained those behaviors. Whether it's 10, 20, or more than 20 years since you were in school, those old habits stand ready to resurface. But your days of being an elementary school student are gone forever. You can't be sent to the office or to detention. The school's former power over you is gone. School staff do, however, have a new power—the power to decide your child's future. When concern for your child makes you nervous, you may find your old school habits emerge to make you feel even more nervous. Fortunately, you can learn to recognize these behaviors and feelings as old and excess baggage, dismiss them as silly, and get on with the grown-up business of advocacy.

When you find yourself becoming uncomfortable in the school setting, you must learn to examine your discomfort:

- Am I sitting here quietly waiting in the principal's office because I am a courteous adult who will allow a reasonable delay before my appointment, or because I am the old school pupil who dares not speak up?

- Do I hesitate to visit my child's classroom because I want to carefully review the educational program first or because I am fearful of being in a place where I don't "belong"?

When you examine your feelings, you will learn how your behaviors support this myth and how school people can use your discomfort to keep you from becoming involved in your child's education. Put the burden of being an old school pupil behind you by saying some of the following things to yourself:

"As a concerned parent, I have the right to be here for this visit."

"My presence here is not disruptive. I am here for important reasons."

"I expect to act and be treated as an adult."

Statements like these will weaken the old, unnecessary behaviors that make your job of advocacy more difficult. When you understand the effects of the myth, you will become more assured and effective when you present yourself at the school as a concerned adult acting on behalf of your child. It will take practice and experience to strengthen your ability to advocate, but other parents have done it, and you can, too.

You may find yourself facing any one or even all four of the "mere parents" myths at any given meeting. It will help if you know what you are up against so that you can adapt and strengthen your own positive behaviors. Asking yourself these questions can help you determine which myths are operating in the situation:

- Am I being treated like a naive person or like one whose information is meaningless or even worthless?

- Am I being treated like a sentimental, overindulgent, unreasonable, or disinterested parent?

- Am I being treated or feeling like an old school pupil?

When you identify the myths that are creating problems at meetings with educators, search your memory for helpful self-statements you can use. If you are especially nervous or expect things to be difficult for you, prepare yourself by writing down in a notebook those bolstering self-statements you may think you need, and then refer to them when you feel uncomfortable or pressured. In this way, you can carry your supportive slogans with you. Each time you think them or read them, you will be a little more reassured about your ability and right to advocate.

This reassurance will help you to present yourself as a calm, rational, and strong person who is determined to be the best advocate for your child's education. Your attitude will help to shatter the myths held by educators. Nevertheless, the first time you deal with a teacher or group of professionals, you may feel you botched it (e.g., "I gave in too easily," "I forgot to mention some important things," "I let myself get upset"). Even if you are new at being an advocate, you did some things right: By meeting with the school people, you shared your concern about your child's program and you presented important information. If you prepared yourself with self-statements, you probably found you were doing well for at least some of the time. Next time you will do better because you are becoming aware of how the myths operate and learning how to defend yourself against them. You are also learning how to present yourself. But you will need to be aware of other myths in addition to the parent myths that may influence the behavior of school people in their dealings with you.

THE MYTHS ABOUT EDUCATORS

In addition to parent myths, there are persistent educator myths that can limit the effectiveness of teachers, specialists, and others involved in the education of students with disabilities. The ones that most frequently undermine the establishment of a parent–educator partnership that could benefit the children are the following:

- Educators are super experts in their field.
- Educators are totally objective.
- Educators are free agents.

If these myths sound familiar, it is because they are the other side of the parent myths. As parents are expected to behave in emotional, naive, and dependent ways, educators carry the burdens of the opposite expectations—total knowledge of the field, complete objectivity, and full freedom to act. This is a heavy burden because it is simply not possible for any one person to have all of these qualities. Educators may feel threatened when unrealistic demands (on the part of society, parents, or the professional community) are made on them, and they may feel they need to insist more strongly that these myths are true.

Educators Are Super Experts in Their Field

Education is not unique in maintaining the myth that the professional has all of the answers and that laypersons are not only lacking in knowledge of the profession but are also incapable of understanding explanations given by the professionals. Unfortunately, many professions perpetuate such mystiques. Members of the medical profession often support a super expert myth. Many parents have presented questions or information to their children's doctors only to be told that they are just anxious parents, perhaps delaying a diagnosis that may be essential to early intervention services. In a number of cases, the doctors may announce the following year their "discovery" of a serious condition to the parents, who were concerned all along. Like educators, physicians should pay attention to the information that parents have about their children. The most famous historical example of doctors and parents working together led to the development of phenylketonuria testing and early treatment, which followed a doctor's interest in mothers' reports about symptoms (such as unusual urine odor in their seemingly normal infants).

Although it is true that educators have special skills and understanding that have been acquired through years of training, the field of education is so broad that no individual educator (or even several educators working together) can know every method or technique. Because they work with various numbers of students, educators' time for observations may be limited, and therefore, those observations of students' needs may also be limited. It may be impossible for educators to know every facet of every student—strengths, weaknesses, and most effective teaching methods for each individual. Parents can add their observations to those of educators, thus enlarging the amount of information available about the individual needs of students with disabilities. If, in an effort to appear expert and competent to lay people, an educator ignores information that the parents offer, everyone loses, including the educator. To be a competent educator requires not only a foundation of special skills, but also an active involvement in seeking educational solutions by using personal observations and information from parents, who are also experts with regard to their own children.

Professionals caught in the super expert myth try to maintain the appearance of knowing all out of fear that parents or colleagues will question their competence otherwise. Furthermore, the need to appear super competent may become more imperative if school budgets are tightened and more people vie for fewer school positions. School personnel may feel financially and professionally threatened if they confess that they do not have all of the educational answers at their fingertips. They may sometimes overstep the limits of their own field of expertise in an effort to appear knowledgeable, as in the following example:

———◆———

Janet McDonald is concerned because she thinks her young son with an intellectual disability has problems with his vision. At the school meeting, she asks the professionals about Andy's performance in school and whether they think he is having any problem with his vision.

They answer, "No," and go on to develop Andy's educational plan for the next year without suggesting that Mrs. McDonald consult a medical expert.

Janet McDonald fortunately continues to observe on her own. Two months later, she takes Andy to the eye doctor, who tells her that her son has a serious vision problem and will probably need to wear strong glasses for the rest of his life.

When Andy starts wearing the glasses, he becomes less clumsy and can do things more successfully.

———◆———

An alternative scenario, in which the educators are interested in the parents' information, might be as follows:

Mrs. McDonald:	*Do you think Andy has any vision problems?*
Special Education Director:	*Why do you ask? Have you noticed anything different in his behavior?*
Mrs. McDonald:	*He seems to be getting clumsier, and he squints funny at his fork when he's eating.*
Teacher:	*I haven't noticed anything, but I'll watch more carefully now that you've raised the issue.*
Special Education Director *(to teacher and parent):*	*I hope you two will keep in close communication. If either of you feels there is a question about Andy's vision, I think he should be tested by an ophthalmologist. The IEP can be delayed if you want to wait for the medical report, or we can proceed and revise it later.*

In the first scenario, the school people played "expert" beyond their limits and crossed over the line of educational expertise when they "diagnosed" Andy as having no visual problems. Their expertise should have helped them recognize, on the basis of Andy's performance in school, that he was facing some new difficulty. Instead, they assumed that Andy's problems of clumsiness, odd gestures, and poor performance were all part of his intellectual disability. Fortunately for Andy, his mother was concerned and wise enough to follow through on her own observations and eventually to seek out the right expert for the job—in this case, the eye doctor.

What could this mother have done at the IEP meeting instead of accepting the school people's opinion? She could have given a fuller explanation of what she had seen at home. If that did not arouse the suspicion and interest of the educators, she could then have insisted that Andy be tested before his IEP could be developed. To support herself in this undertaking, she might have made self-statements such as, "I don't have to be a pro to know what I have seen my child do" or, "If I'm going to help Andy, I have to be persistent."

The burden of being an all-knowing expert is as unfair to the educator as it is to the parent. Sooner or later, the expert will be found out and will then appear to the parent to be untrustworthy or incompetent. Many parents are more comfortable and more trusting with the professional who can occasionally say, "I don't know." It has been the authors' experience in working with parents in training programs that the "I don't know" answer can help to establish a cooperative and trusting relationship between parents and professionals. Too many parents have been given absolute or definitive answers in the past that have been proven wrong over time (e.g., Darren did learn to read, with the help of new teachers, Ray now plays on a regular basketball team in the community center).

When parents suspect that they are dealing with educators whose behavior seems to be controlled by this myth, it is important that they do not insult the training, experience, or intelligence of the educators. Because parents have to work with these same educators to develop a good IEP, they must stick to the facts about what they have seen and heard their children do and make it clear to the professionals that they, the parents, are not trying to assume a professional role. Rather, they are caring parents who are acting as responsible advocates for their children by keeping important facts before the professional as services are being planned, developed, and reviewed.

Parents must be ready to support the educators who can say, "I don't know the answer" by appreciating their honesty and by cooperating with them to find the answers. Real experts know their resources and look to parents as a powerful and special resource for information about their students. But educators who present themselves as all-knowing experts may be convinced that they are more qualified than parents because they have a need to believe that they are completely objective. This is another myth.

Educators Are Totally Objective

Many educators and other professionals believe that parents' statements about their children are to be taken with a large grain of salt because parents are emotionally involved and lack the special training that develops the objective judgment that professionals have. The parents see the tree, but the professionals see the forest.

Of course, it is true that most parents are more emotionally involved with their children than teachers are and that occasionally their emotional concern can cloud their judgment, but educators are not as free of emotional involvement as they would like to believe. Their objectivity can be distorted by their personal need to support and justify their years of specialized training and work with students.

If a parent questions a teacher on the use and effectiveness of a particular method with his or her child, then that teacher may be faced with a dilemma: "If this isn't the best method, then maybe I have not effectively taught a number of students or have even failed to teach some students because of my reliance on this method." It may be easier for a weak teacher to believe that the parent is wrong and that the method, which has been used for so many years, is still the right one.

A strong teacher, however, would be able to accept parents' suggestions of information or even criticism of a given method because he or she knows the effective methods will stand the test of parents' questions and because he or she expects to be learning more every year about new methods, theories, techniques, and ideas that will help meet individual students' needs. The strong teacher accepts the responsibility for searching out new methods and answers in order to teach more effectively, unlike the weak teacher, who tries to defend past performance and protect the present position by emphasizing the years of training and denying the value of parental input. Let's look at an example:

Mrs. Costa: *I know Manny has had a hard time with math. He sometimes gets very upset doing his homework, even though it is only a few problems. I try to help him. Yesterday I had him using his fingers to count and it really helped him.*

Teacher: *I do not allow him to count on his fingers in class, and I would prefer that he not do this at home. He must learn to do the sums in his head.*

Mrs. Costa: *But he can't get the right answers that way, and he's so upset when he makes mistakes.*

Teacher: *He can't go through life counting on his fingers. He will have to learn like others with his kind of disability—through practice, practice, practice. You know, I have worked with children like Manny for many years, and I know what they need. They learn by rote; they must do things over and over until they learn to do it right.*

The poor parent is in a bind. If she helps Manny by letting him use his fingers, Manny will be in trouble at school. Yet without that extra help, Manny is condemned to practice failure over and over until he learns to hate arithmetic.

The secure teacher might have said something like this:

> *"I know Manny is having a hard time with math, and I appreciate getting this information from you. If using his fingers helps him get the right answers, maybe I should be trying it in class. Let me check it out. Also, there may be other materials in my files that might help me give Manny the extra help he seems to need. We'll stay in touch regarding how he progresses in math."*

Or, the teacher might have said something like this:

> *"You know, there was a time when we discouraged children from using their fingers to do math, but now we feel differently. In school Manny has used blocks to do his work, and right now he's using lines drawn with numbers to help him do his sums. I'm impressed that you noticed he needed something to count and let him use his fingers. He needs the success of doing it right. And I'm pleased you spend time with him on his homework. Don't worry that he'll use his fingers forever. As he makes progress, he'll rely less and less on learning aids like fingers and number lines."*

In this case, the information is well received by the teacher, who is willing to either try another approach as suggested by the parent or acknowledge the value of the parent's observations and efforts.

There are other times when educators' objectivity is on the line. The teacher or specialist may see a need for more individualized instruction or some special supports, but he or she is in no position to ask for more services or help from the system, which claims to be short on money and staff. The educator experiences a conflict between his or her professional judgment and the resources available to him or her. Because it is hard for anyone to live with this kind of conflict day after day, soon the educator may begin to believe that perhaps the need is not so great after all and eventually may come to dismiss the student's need for additional services. In this way, the educator can escape from the uncomfortable realization that the student has serious needs that he or she is powerless to meet and can maintain the feeling that he or she is providing a good program or service. Consider the following example:

> **Mr. Harrison:** *But last spring you said Sara needed more speech therapy.*
>
> **Teacher:** *Well, I have given it much more thought. You know, there are a lot of pressures on children like Sara, and she is a very sensitive child. If we stress her speech problems, she may become more socially withdrawn.*
>
> **Mr. Harrison:** *I think her poor speech interferes with her social development. Because other children have difficulty understanding her, she is often left alone or, at best, is the last one to be included.*
>
> **Teacher:** *Let's give her time to develop at her own pace and see what she can do naturally and without pressure.*

This type of switch is not made to meet the child's education needs, but to sustain the teacher's own feelings of self-esteem and self-worth: He or she needs to believe that his or her job is worthwhile and efforts are not wasted. Everyone, including parents, uses this kind of mental gymnastics or adaptation. For example, one family may make financial sacrifices for a child's braces because they feel that orthodontia is essential for his or her physical and social well-being; another family may be so poor that they have nothing to sacrifice and come to believe that their child doesn't really need braces. Yet both children may have the same need. And sometimes parent advocates, in efforts to get the right services for their children, may find themselves beginning to believe that the professionals are doing a good job, because believing that is easier than continuing the frustration of the struggle to get services.

It is important for parents to understand that educators may also unintentionally make these kinds of mental adjustments to preserve their sense of professional worth, and parents should recognize that educators are not always free to act solely on the basis of their professional judgment to pursue and develop the programs they once realized were needed.

Educators Are Free Agents

Many parents ask why, if the school personnel know a program is needed, they don't just set it up. Because it is the school's job to educate all children, parents expect that school staff will do what is necessary.

What parents need to know is that people who work for school systems are not free to pick their resources—people, time, space, or materials. The school system sets limits on what is available to any employee and on what means school personnel can use to request or pressure for more resources. Parents don't realize that they may have more freedom to act than school people often do. When parents understand that educators are limited by the rules and structure of the system and that parents can more freely speak out, act, or even badger for services, then parents will realize that their advocacy efforts can help competent and concerned educators get needed services. Chapter 4 takes a close look at how the system operates and what kinds of experiences parents may have when they try to deal with the school system.

All of these myths about educators persist because many parents and professionals would like to believe that educators are all-knowing experts, clear-sighted and clear-headed, free of bias, and free to act on the children's needs as they see them. These myths place enormous burdens on educators who, like everyone, have both skills and shortcomings. They also need and want the resources necessary to do their jobs well, and they may need parents as allies to get the needed resources from a resistant school system.

THE MYTHS ABOUT STUDENTS WITH DISABILITIES

Parents can also help educators, themselves, and their children by learning to recognize and dispel some common myths about students with disabilities. Here are some important myths that you may have come across:

- These children's disabilities are the source of all problems.
- These children can only learn by rote.
- These children can't handle a full day.
- Children can be so cruel.

These Children's Disabilities Are the Source of All Problems

This myth is used to explain anything that goes wrong in school or with the child. It's as if the child is no longer a person but has become the disability. There is no need to search for new understanding or teaching methods because the child has a label of, for example, intellectual disability, learning disability, cerebral palsy, or autism. Whatever the child does, the educators can point knowingly to the label. For example, Andy, the boy with an undiagnosed visual problem discussed earlier in this chapter, does not warrant attention from the educators as he becomes more clumsy because he is labeled with an intellectual disability: The assumption is that his intellectual disability is the cause of his clumsiness (until his mother takes him to the ophthalmologist). If Andy were a typical student, his behavior might have prompted concern and action from the educators, who would be asking the parents about his vision and the need for testing. But, like Andy, students with other disabilities may have problems simply blamed on their labels. For example:

Danny, who is labeled with emotional disturbances and learning disabilities, has had his new baseball cap stolen at school. He bought the cap with money earned for doing chores at home. The teacher, who makes little effort to get it back for him, dismisses his loss. Every day for a week Danny asks the teacher, "Where is my hat?" and is told not to talk about it. The following Monday he asks again, but now the teacher forbids him to mention the hat again or he will have to leave the classroom. Danny swears at the teacher and is sent home. Danny now has no hat, no understanding, no justice, and, for a few days or more, no education. The teacher explains that Danny is distressed because he is "emotionally disturbed"; she does not see that his distress is an appropriate response to the loss of something he valued and worked hard to obtain.

Jenny, who is nonverbal and labeled autistic, is working on her usual morning puzzle, which she has already done twice and is expected to do three times. The teacher prods her to keep working and tells her to finish if she wants her gold star. Jenny, making noises, looks away and claps her hands rapidly. The teacher takes the puzzle away, says, "No star, Jenny," turns to the aide and says, "These kids with autism can't do their work for very long. Now she's going to keep up this weird clapping behavior." Jenny smiles a little and begins to clap again. Jenny's behavior is considered "weird." But her refusal to do the puzzle still one more time might make sense to the teacher if she were asking the right questions: "Is Jenny's behavior telling me she doesn't want to do the puzzle?" "Are puzzles still a useful activity for Jenny?" Instead, the teacher makes the assumption that

Jenny's "weird" behaviors stem from her autism and not from her boredom, which is a normal, human response to a lack of stimulation.

———◆———

Whatever problems these children encounter in the classroom are explained away by the educators on the basis of the children's primary labels: Andy is clumsy because he has an intellectual disability, Danny is upset because he has emotional disturbance, and Jenny won't work because she has autism. Instead of searching for more or new information to engage their students and solve the problems, the educators locate all problems squarely in the child. In this way, they can absolve themselves of the responsibility to do more careful observation, seek new approaches, and develop new solutions.

Of course, these children have disabilities (that is the kernel of truth behind this myth), but, like all children, they have human needs for recognition, understanding, support, stimulation, and novelty, and these needs are often overlooked or minimized by educators. Because many school systems are now serving a range of children with special needs, providing the right supports and programs may not be easy; educators must search out new methods, information, and insights to do the job. They must avoid assumptions that go with labels. Parents must continue to observe their children, looking for strengths, weaknesses, and supports that work. They must share (and even insist on sharing) information about their children with the educators, keeping the educators aware that their children have basic human needs that require attention in addition to their special, disability-related needs.

These Children Can Learn Only by Rote

Unfortunately, some educators believe that students with disabilities must be subjected to endless drill and practice to achieve any gains in their educational programs. They believe that rote learning is the answer; thus the more severe the student's disability, the more likely that student is to have learning drummed into him or her.

Although it may be true that the more difficult a task is, the more practice may be needed for mastery, it is also true that any child, no matter how serious his or her disability, can become bored or frustrated through repetition of meaningless tasks. Every child needs to not only be supported but also to be stimulated. For example, after months, maybe even years, of doing puzzles, Jenny is possibly just bored. This task may have once been interesting when she was gaining mastery in a visual-motor (e.g., coordination of eye–hand) skill, but seemingly endless repetition may have reduced her motivation and even tolerance. On some occasions, Jenny is compliant; on others, she may be expressing her reluctance through "inappropriate" behavior. Perhaps it's time to introduce some new visual-motor activities to get her working again.

Manny's failures in math when he is not allowed to count on his fingers should be signaling his teacher that simple rote learning is not effective; his parents have already recognized the importance of successful attempts based on counting aids. The answers he is trying to learn by rote are probably meaningless to him since he is so often wrong. Unlike Jenny, he continues to try, but for how long? A child's behaviors—failure, frustration, or boredom—are messages that the materials and/or methods are not working, and that the teacher should try for other ways to help. There are other tasks Manny could do to support and stimulate his math learning, such as counting out food cans or setting the table at home, building structures and counting the number of floors or pieces to make a new floor, or playing math games using dice and counting moves (at home or in school). The possibilities are endless: counting and sorting balloons of different colors for a party; sorting socks (basic two table for addition or multiplication); and even using regular playing cards for counting, sorting, matching, and playing games. And don't forget the computer programs for all ages and levels. This technology should be at least as available for students with disabilities as it is for other students. These activities can be fun, at least some of the time, and should seem important to the student because he or she is actively engaged in his or her own education.

Too often, both teachers and parents feel so overwhelmed by the burden of a child's disability that, in efforts to overcome or limit its effects, they fall back on drill and routine practice (forgetting that writing or doing something one hundred times can be used as a form of punishment). They try to drum learning into children's heads, as if battering would do the job, when children need stimulation and normal activities that they can enjoy, that they feel are important (even grown-up), and that make sense. Parents or teachers may fail to take advantage of the normal opportunities that can aid in the development of early academic skills.

What can you, as a parent, do? Do not be afraid to test your child's developing skills around the home. In this way, you can learn about your child's strengths, weaknesses, and the kind of help or modifications needed to promote active learning. You should, at the same time, keep a simple record of your observations that you can share with the educators. Your information can stimulate them to question their assumptions about how various students with disabilities learn. It will require effort on your part and perhaps a little repetition to get the educators to take a careful look at your child's performance or needs; however, once they realize you are really concerned and serious about your child's program and that your observations are accurate, they may begin to investigate new materials and methods.

These Children Can't Handle a Full Day

Many people equate disability with fragility or a lack of stamina. They expect that children with cognitive and/or physical disabilities will require less activity and considerably more resting periods than children without disabilities. They tend to become protective in ways that can limit the learning of students with disabilities; for example, planning rest periods or even shorter days for adolescents with intellectual disabilities who might benefit more from the regularly scheduled gym periods provided to typical students.

Because of this myth, parents and teachers may see weakness where none may exist. They may see evidence of weakness in children's boredom, frustration, or disruptive behavior, all of which may result more from the programs' inability to meet the students' needs than from any lack of stamina in the students. When students are bored, frustrated, or disruptive, it is harder for the teacher to work with them. Sometimes, it is really the stamina of the teacher that is called into question: He or she may be the one who needs a shorter day with the more challenging students.

Of course there are some students who, because of certain conditions, such as heart and respiratory problems, are less able to maintain a constant level of activity or to engage in strenuous activity. The energies of these students should be conserved in school. For example, an educator may tell a parent, "I just feel so badly for poor little Lisa when she starts getting cranky. I know the school day is just too much for her." Lisa's father shares the educator's concern about his child's heart condition and the fatigue he sees in her at the end of the school day. But he also notes that her classroom is on the third floor and the lunchroom and recess area are on the ground floor. He raises the possibility that his daughter is exhausted from climbing the stairs. He plans to ask if the school can accommodate Lisa's needs by relocating the classroom on the first floor to spare her the unnecessary physical effort of mounting so many flights of stairs.

If you are in doubt about a full day of school for your child, think about your child's performance at home. Is he or she raring to go out and play as soon as school is over? Is he or she still awake for the 11 p.m. news or up at the crack of dawn when everyone else is still sleeping? If you don't see evidence of fatigue at home on school days or weekends, the problem at school may be something other than lack of stamina.

If you still have questions about your child's ability to withstand a full day of school, you should consult your child's physician. Like the educators, the doctor also needs the facts that only a parent can provide. Because every child is different and you know more about your child than anyone else, share with the doctor your observations about your child. If the fully informed doctor says that your child requires more rest for medical reasons, you should explore with the educators the options for your child to have rest periods at school so that he or she may miss as little schooling as possible. If the educators feel the school program is too mentally or physically taxing for some students, they can gear the classroom to the learning and activity/rest needs of the students by using the appropriate materials, methods, and activities and by adjusting the pace to fit the students.

When you are told your child is not strong enough to be in school all day and you know his or her physical health and energy levels are good, you may rightly suspect that it's the teacher who can't handle a full day. He or she may not be skilled enough or may have too many students with not enough help in the classroom. Ask for an aide for the teacher. Or, perhaps the program isn't the right one for your child, and therefore your child reacts out of frustration. You have the right to ask to change the program—totally or in part.

This myth of "weakness" has in the past deprived a number of children with disabilities of full educational opportunity. Your information, questions, and insights can help the educators develop new ways of thinking that can lead to a better program for your child (and possibly for other children with disabilities as well).

Children Can Be So Cruel

This is a myth you may hear when you are asking for your child to be included. It is an excuse. Schools control many aspects of students' behavior: Students are expected to get to school on time, sit in their chairs, raise their hands when they want to answer, answer when they are called on, not chew gum or use cell phones, get permission to use the bathroom, adhere to any dress code the school enforces, and so forth. Given the current national interest in controlling bullying, students are also told not to injure, harass, or insult their fellow students. This applies equally to students with disabilities, and schools expect all of their students to behave accordingly.

Schools can also be proactive about supporting good relationships among students of all abilities. Some schools have what they call a "lunch bunch," where a group of students, including one or two students with disabilities, get preferential treatment by meeting for lunch in the conference room with a counselor or teacher, maybe with an occasional pizza. School cafeterias are places where teachers can see the relationships or absence of relationships among students of all abilities. A teacher is apt to know her students better than a lunchroom aide and may be able to foster relationships in that most social part of the day—lunch. Unfortunately, most teachers are in the teachers' room and miss this important opportunity to support their students. Segregating all students with disabilities at one table does nothing but magnify any differences among students, even if a typical student can be convinced to occasionally visit.

Assigning a typical high school student to a student with a disability as a way to earn points for community service does little to develop any real friendship between the students. This arrangement tends to make the student with a disability more an object of pity than a peer or friend.

There is no reason that schools can't help to develop some good supports for inclusion and some good relationships among students of all abilities, and they should be held accountable for their support of students with disabilities.

THE SHATTERING OF MYTHS

We have discussed some common myths about parents, educators, and children with disabilities. The myths persist because people believe them. Shattering myths is tough work and can only be done by consistently giving the lie to the myths through your busi-nesslike presentation of yourself as a concerned parent, your state-ments of observations you have collected about your child, and your determination to see that the important issues you raise are not ignored or forgotten.

If reading about these myths has not yet struck a familiar chord in your experience, when you begin to deal with the school system, you will see how pervasive they can be. You may not experience all of them, but as a parent advocate, you will not let a myth slide by in silence; your silence could be interpreted as acceptance of the myth. However, you need not argue; you dispel the myths by demonstrating that you are a reliable, informed parent who deals in facts and that your child (one of "these children") can in fact benefit from a full edu-cational program designed to meet his or her needs.

When you find yourself in a situation in which several myths appear to be operating, try to deal with one at a time.

————◆————

When the educators at the IEP meeting tell Peg Olson that children like Bert have very short attention spans and she is probably exaggerating his skill, she pulls out her notes from watching Bert at home and says, "I appreciate your skills and experience, but I have seen Bert perform at home. His atten-tion span is longer than the 2 minutes he seems to have in school."

She looks at her notes and describes Bert's behavior. (Her opening statement deals with the myth of educators as super experts. Her careful notes and statements about Bert's behavior deny the myth of emotional parents who can't be objective.) Mrs. Olson continued, "I don't know every-thing about children like Bert, but I do know my son. This is the way we help him at home so he can do the work. When he is having difficulty with his homework, his father or I stay close by to offer him help when he asks for it. But after he understands the problem, he will work on his own as long as 15 minutes."

Once again, she acknowledged the expertise of the educator without denying what she knew about her son and the help she has given him. She also refused to play the game of "these children" by telling the educators that whatever they know about children like Bert, at least he can work independently for 15 minutes when he is supported and understands what is expected of him.

After a while, the educators stopped talking about "these children" and stuck to Bert. At this point, they may start listening to Mrs. Olson's information because it is factual. She can then continue to participate in the planning process as an effective parent advocate. Her son may need more of this and less of that, but he doesn't need any myths to interfere with planning his program.

———————

Obviously, this is hard work. Chances are, in your first meeting, you may not be successful in dealing with any myths that arise or even in recognizing them because you, too, are learning to disbelieve them through understanding and practice (using supportive self-statements). As you improve, however, the myths will appear like red flags to call you to action. Your careful and thoughtful responses will begin to educate the educators to the erroneous assumptions that the myths embody.

We have presented some examples of myths in operation and of the kinds of things you can say to yourself and to educators to advance the development of your child's education. You now are beginning to understand some of the things that may have gone wrong in the past when you dealt with the school system. Perhaps you are thinking about making that first telephone contact, but don't rush out yet. There is still more you need to know about dealing with the system before you become the cool, controlled, and effective advocate.

4

Services and Snow Jobs
Understanding Your School System

the hierarchy and pecking order • a map for the system • "good" guys and "bad" guys • polite, assertive, and relentless • recognizing and protecting the good guys • working with the system, for better or worse • "reasons" for exclusion • bringing down the barriers

---

Elsie Chen is always ready to help at the school Christmas fair, go on field trips when teachers need an extra parent, and volunteer in the school library. The principal has told her she is a caring and concerned parent, a real asset to the school, and that he has been working hard for 3 years to get extra speech-language therapy for her son, but the budget is getting tighter all of the time. Mrs. Chen waits patiently.

Donald Kowalski got fed up with waiting for the school to provide a full day for his daughter. He went to the Parent–Teacher Association (PTA) meeting to corner the principal, who had not returned any of his calls. In the school halls, he loudly threatened that he would pull his daughter out of school if she did not get better service. Afterwards he felt worse because his daughter loves to go to school and he never intended to keep her home.

These parents may understand their children's needs and the meaning of IDEA, but they do not understand how to work with school personnel. Let's take a closer look at the day-to-day operation of the school system, the behavior of the individuals working in it, and your own behavior when you approach and try to deal with that system to get services for your child. If you intend to be an effective advocate, you will need to know how to ask for services in ways that get the system moving, how to tell the "good" guys from the "bad" guys, and how to modify your own behavior and acquire new skills so that you get what you ask for (or at least most of it).

A LOOK AT SCHOOL SYSTEMS

School systems, like other bureaucracies, tend to be conservative. Most are not quick to change, nor are they noted for their flexibility. Their mottoes could be "We've always done things this way" or "Business as usual." The business of schools has generally been to provide a standard service (education) to a standard group of people (average children) at a standard cost. The quality and cost of education may vary from community to community, but within each community, the school system tries to educate children in the same way. If a child fits the mold, fine—he or she gets an education. Children who don't fit that average mold, however, tend to get pushed out of school, or if they are well-behaved and don't look too different from that "average" mold, they may get pushed to the back of the classroom.

Of course, you may have met individual school people who have cared about the children who don't fit the mold and who have really tried to help, but who found there was only so much they could do. You may even have known teachers who weren't offered a new contract or who chose to move on after a year because they asked too many times for more support services or for new ways of doing things, or for trying to move their students toward the least restrictive environment and were denied. They didn't fit into the system either.

When you asked why these people were no longer with the system, the system response (if you persisted) may have been that they were not good team members. Translated, this means they could have been good teachers and good administrators, but they asked for change—new methods, new services, or more supports and inclusion. Change is not a typical goal of school systems; they want to deliver the same service with maximum efficiency and a minimum of fuss.

Systems tend to resist change: Otherwise, IDEA would be fully implemented because it has been the law of the land for years, every student with a disability would be in a program that meets his or her needs, and this book on how to get services would be unnecessary. Although systems don't like change, they can be changed by pressure from the community, by strong advocates who assert their rights and their children's rights under the law, and by the threat or initiation of legal action. Making waves works.

The Hierarchy/Pecking Order

In order to make waves with success, you need to know who to approach in the system and when. Like all bureaucracies, the school system has a hierarchical structure: Everyone working in it is working directly under someone else. The teacher answers to the special education director or principal or both and so do the inclusion specialists, and the special education director answers to the pupil personnel director (like the principal), who in turn answers to the superintendent, who answers to the school board, which must account to the elected officials or directly to the voters. Every person has a certain status with particular responsibilities, powers, and limitations.

The *teacher* can choose classroom activities, but he or she must arrange with other teachers and specialists for when and how much the children are to be included; receive support services; and have access to facilities such as the gym, arts and crafts room, or cooking room. He or she may have to get approval through the principal's office, just as he or she does for classroom materials and equipment. However, special education teachers often have a lower status than general education teachers and may have less access to facilities, which is why segregated special education classes may have physical education only twice a week, when general education classes have it three or more times per week. Status and stigma, rather than the students' needs, often determine the availability of services and facilities. Therefore, the committed parent advocate can become a trusted ally of the teacher, whose power in the classroom evaporates in the school halls and front office because of such discriminatory attitudes.

Inclusions specialists and school psychologists may answer to the special education director, the principal, the director of pupil personnel, or all of the above. Their power in moving the system forward is little better than the teachers'.

The *principal*, who is responsible for all of the children in the school, has the power to make decisions about how to use personnel and space in his or her domain within certain limits, and those limits are primarily financial. The general rule is to stay within the budget and not ask for more money. But at times, you will also see personal relationships determining the use of staff and space; for example, a teacher favored by the principal may get a nicer classroom.

Not every school principal believes in or supports IDEA's requirement of placing the student in the least restrictive environment (e.g., "I have 300 kids to be concerned about. I can't spend half my time worrying about 10"). You may encounter problems for special education students (e.g., poor support for teachers, isolated space, a separate wing, a poorly located classroom, a resistance to inclusive programs) and unavailability of facilities at suitable times with principals who feel they have had special education thrust upon them. A fair principal will try to provide at least equal access and time to students with disabilities; a caring principal will supply what it takes to meet every student's special needs.

The *special education director* works with personnel who provide special education in the school. He may supervise the special education teachers, the inclusion specialist, and support staff; set up a method and format for developing IEPs; share in the hiring and firing of special education staff with principals; develop budgets that must go to the director of pupil personnel (or pupil services) for approval; and generally plan for and coordinate special education and inclusive services with other administrators who probably have more power. The special education director is knowledgeable about the education of students with disabilities, but because the number of children he or she serves may be fewer than those served by a principal, he or she may have less authority or impact on decisions than other administrators. Sometimes there can be tension between the special education director and an individual principal if the principal resists having special classes in "his or her" building. Although the special education director is the administrator with whom you may deal most often, you should recognize that his or her power is limited. On the totem pole of administrators, he or she may be at the very bottom.

The *director of pupil personnel* may be responsible for all hiring and firing of teachers and specialists and for preparation of school personnel budgets. In spite of direct access to the superintendent of schools, covering several or more schools may spread him or her thin.

Large school systems may also include *assistant superintendents* for elementary and secondary education who present budgets, based on all of the program plans developed, to the *superintendent,* who then brings everything to the *school board* for approval, cuts, or disapproval.

The Map of the Power Structure

The map of the power structure or hierarchy, shown below, illustrates how the administration interacts with the personnel and students in a school system. Note that most of the power to make decisions is located at the top and that the students and services are at the bottom. The unbroken lines denote active, working relationships between school people. The broken lines show you the people who may or may not work together. For example, in one school, the

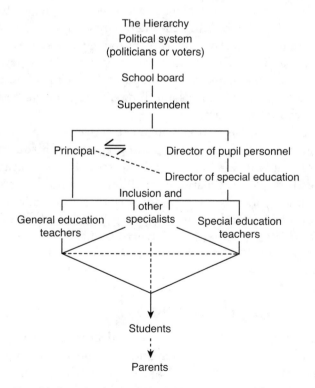

Map of the hierarchy of a typical school system.

principal rules with an iron hand and has only a nodding acquaintance with the special education director, whereas in another school, both general education and special education teachers meet together with the inclusion specialist and plan regularly for the students who are their joint responsibility.

Your school system may differ a little from this basic diagram. It may be smaller (two or three principals and a superintendent) and therefore easier to maneuver. You may even know the administrators and school board members personally. Or it may be even larger, and you will need to add a few more rungs and titles to the ladder. But this diagram of a hierarchy can serve as your basic map of how to get from the bottom of the system to the top when you need to. Most of the time you may be working with your child's teacher and the special education director. However, at times your child may not be getting the services he or she needs, and you will want to reach someone with more clout. Know who's who in the hierarchy.

This discussion must seem like a long way from your child's classroom and your request for some extra speech-language therapy or gym time. But understanding the hierarchy of a school system can help you be a more effective advocate by giving you a sense of the lines of authority and the checkpoints for information and power. That way, the next time a request disappears between administrators' offices or is transformed into something different in the budget, you will know whom to contact.

This does not mean that you must concern yourself with the school budget in order to get an appropriate service for your child. But sometimes you will want to remind the school administrators that special needs of your child and other children are not being met, and at other times you will want to support concerned administrators when they need your help in defending part or all of the school budget. Your familiarity with the structure of the hierarchy will help you to recognize who wields the power of the purse over services, supports, and schedules.

The "Good Guys" and the "Bad Guys"

Besides a map of the system, you may need a script and maybe even a scorecard to understand the action and know how to tell the so-called "good guys" from the "bad guys." As you work with people inside the school system, you will discover very few, if any, real villains—people who genuinely dislike you or your child, put in their time only to collect their paychecks, or enjoy having the power to make decisions that can make the lives of other people (e.g., parents, children, or school personnel) miserable. Most people are well-intentioned. But people who work in a system are usually not free to act on their good intentions: They must play certain roles, say certain things, and perform certain actions. Within the limits of these system requirements, some school personnel will be effective resources in getting good services for your child. Because your goal is an educational program that benefits your child, you can define these people as the "good guys." People who interfere with or prevent you from getting good services for your child are, by definition, the "bad guys." Some school staff will shift back and forth from being resources ("good guys") one time to being obstacles ("bad guys") another time. In order to decide who will be your best resources, you need to understand a little about the experiences and motives of schools' staff and how their experiences may have weakened their good intentions.

Most people, especially those who go into special education, begin their educational careers with good intentions and lofty ideals, such as the following:

- Every child is unique.

- All students (no matter how severe the disability) are learners.

- Schools should help students to acquire the skills they will need to function as adults in society.

- Schools can help students develop good self-images and feelings of competence.

- Learning can be an exciting and rewarding experience.

Somewhere between "go" and the time when you encounter them, school people may have lost some of their idealism, energy, commitment, and feelings of effectiveness. But what happened to them and to the ideals with which they started off? Their experience may have worn them down.

If they are teachers, they may have been responsible for too large a class, found too few support services (speech and physical therapists may not have been available or perhaps were available for so little time that it didn't make much difference), or worked under a principal who viewed educating students with disabilities as his or her special cross to bear. These teachers may have asked many times for more services and space only to be refused, ignored, or intimidated through subtle messages that their contracts might not be renewed if they continued to bother people. When they compared notes with friends, they found other school systems were not really different. They grew tired of asking and getting nothing in return for their efforts.

If the disillusioned people are administrators, their experience may have been the same: too much work, too few resources to build effective programs, too many requests for personnel denied, and too many attempts to create new ways of doing things that were frustrated by a system insisting that "we've always done things this way."

It helps you to understand that most people start out with good intentions, but when their efforts are continually thwarted by the system, many of them learn to adjust to the system's demands. They become "well-adjusted," and this conformity—this giving in or up—can result in an education for your child that may not meet his or her needs. Some of these well-intentioned people are still hopeful or even still requesting more in spite of getting very little; they can often be revived by the appearance of a parent who means business about education and advocacy. Others will need more cordiality, convincing, and even coaxing on your part to trust you as the ally they need and may have been waiting for. But there will be some who are burnt out and will be no help to you at all. In fact, they may even stand in the way of your getting services for your child. Unfortunately, they have become the "bad guys"—you must move beyond them.

Let's look at some examples of "good" and "bad guys" talking to parents:

Mr. D'Amico *(finishing a long talk about his child's language needs):*	*. . . and I really feel Kelly needs to be evaluated by a speech-language therapist and get some regular speech-language therapy.*
Teacher:	*Well, I do see a lot of what you're talking about in the classroom.*
Mr. D'Amico:	*Don't you think she needs more help?*
Teacher:	*Oh, boy! (Hesitates) Well . . . frankly, I do. But I've asked several times, and there's only one speech-language therapist for the entire school.*

Mr. D'Amico:	*What can I do? Is there someone I can ask? I'm going to do anything I can to get help for Kelly.*
Teacher:	*Good for you! My asking won't help, but maybe I can tell you who you should be talking to and help you plan what to say. Let's start with . . .*

This teacher is a "good guy." He's been waiting for someone like this parent for too long and is ready to offer the benefit of his knowledge and experience. Together, they will go after the service: Mr. D'Amico, the assertive parent, and this teacher, his silent partner.

But look at another example:

Mrs. Wu:	*He doesn't seem to remember a lot of things you tell him, and I think he really tries.*
Teacher:	*Harry is often inattentive. He isn't motivated to do his work.*
Mrs. Wu:	*But I was reading about something called "auditory memory" problems, and the article said . . . .*
Teacher:	*I'm quite familiar with the concept, Mrs. Wu. You'll simply have to face up to the fact that your child is lazy. Have you talked to him about trying harder?*
Mrs. Wu:	*Yes, I have. Thank you for your time, but I have a dentist appointment in 10 minutes.*

This teacher is a "bad guy." Notice how the problem is shifted back to Harry and his parent. "Your child is lazy" and "you should talk to him." The learning problem (auditory memory) is not even considered.

The following is an example of one kind of principal–parent interaction:

Mr. Howard:	*And Walter really needs more attention in his physical education program. I looked in and he was just wandering around the gym.*
Principal:	*He's getting gym time twice a week. What more can you expect?*

Mr. Howard: *His IEP says three times a week, and the program is supposed to be set up and supervised by an adaptive physical education specialist.*

Principal: *We don't have an adaptive physical education specialist any more. She's on maternity leave. And given the fact that your son doesn't do much in gym, I see no point in giving him or others like him more time when all of these normal kids can benefit from more time in the gym.*

The parent could continue the discussion by arguing that if Walter had more time and teaching, he might benefit more from physical education. But this principal is bad news; she sounds like she thinks she's doing Walter a favor by letting him into the gym at all.

Another principal might be more responsive:

Principal: *Well, Mrs. Foster, our therapist is gone. And I've asked the pupil personnel director for a replacement, but she's so frantic about the budget that I've gotten nowhere.*

Mrs. Foster: *Isn't there something you can do?*

Principal: *I've tried. But you know, sometimes a parent can make more waves than a principal.*

Mrs. Foster: *Are you suggesting that I should go over your head?*

Principal: *Not at all! But I'd like to have that therapist, too.*

This principal is a "good guy" because she's admitting that she's powerless and is subtly suggesting that maybe a person outside the system can do more. She is not wasting the parent's time by pretending that the service may or may not be provided at some vague future time. Her honesty is definitely helpful in this situation.

When you meet someone who is willing to say, "I can't get the service. You may need to go to my boss," you will need to protect that person who has shown you that he or she is willing to feed you the information that you need to do your job well. When you go to the pupil personnel director or the superintendent, you will say only, "I am coming to you because my child is not getting the service that is in the IEP." Then you will explain to him or her why it is essential that your child get that service now and that you expect that service to be delivered.

Other administrators (e.g., special education directors, superintendents) and specialists (who, like teachers, give direct service) will fall into the same groups: There will be "good guys" and there will be "bad guys." You will learn to sort them out through their words and efforts, through their advice and direction, and through their up-front and behind-the-scenes actions on behalf of students with disabilities. Did you get the needed service? Yes? That's a "good guy"!

When you first begin to work as an advocate, some people will confuse you. They will warmly greet you by name when they see you, and sooner or later they call you back on the telephone. But did you get the service or are you on your way to getting the service? That is the measure. The warm smiles and handshakes you get will not educate your child.

Now and again, a "bad guy" falls into the position of a "good guy" by mistake, default, entrapment, or even change of heart. For example, you may overhear the principal at a PTA meeting telling another teacher or parent that there is a new speech-language therapist on board. You can jump in with, "I'm so glad you were able to get the therapist. Now Kimberly can get the extra help she needs. I appreciate your efforts."

You know about the therapist, the principal knows you know, and your praise is hard to ignore. Or the principal may have seen a film at a conference and returned to school convinced that inclusion is the answer to the needs of his or her students with disabilities. He or she pushes and gets the necessary supports. Your child's services improve. The principal is now your "good guy," even if he or she wasn't on your side last week.

It is important that you continually think about how effective and how helpful are the school staff with whom you are trying to work. First impressions can be misleading, individuals do have bad days, people do change their attitudes, and when there are personnel changes in the system, the power of an individual may increase or decrease. Yesterday's friends may be today's hindrances but tomorrow's supports as they respond to the pressures and priorities of the system. Sure, it would be great if school people were always friendly and consistent in their support, or even consistently difficult so that you could know what to expect. But they aren't. You will have to deal with them where they are at any given time. You can also get more insights into the system by going to a PTA or school board meeting once or twice a year.

INEFFECTIVE WAYS TO DEAL WITH THE SYSTEM

Parents deal with school systems in a variety of ways, some effective and some not. Either their work with schools is productive (they get what they want) or counterproductive (they get little or nothing, or they even lose something). Let's look at the counterproductive patterns of exchanges first.

Isolation

This exchange is no exchange at all: The parents never see or rarely talk to the school people. Some parents do this because they have complete trust. They believe that the school system has the child's best interests at heart and is doing all it can. These parents may not be aware of the pressures school boards and finance committees apply to school personnel. Or worse, they may not understand their children's right to education and may actually believe the school is doing them a favor in educating their children with disabilities.

Then there are the parents who have no confidence in what they know about their children (the "mere parents" people). They will tell you that the teachers and specialists are professionals trained to do the job. What can a mere emotional and ignorant parent do but let the professionals do their job without bothering them? They have no problem signing whatever IEP the school hands them.

Mrs. Yoon, for example, found her son Charlie's IEP document in his backpack with a note that said "Sign and return." Mrs. Yoon had no questions. She wasn't sure she understood the document, but she signed it and put it in Charlie's backpack ready for the next school day.

Other parents give up (if they ever started) because they believe that you can't fight city hall or that one person can't change the system. Such apathetic parents take what they get without gratitude and without hope. They probably know their children should have more; they certainly know they need more.

Some parents who are afraid of rocking the school system work hard at being "good," quiet parents who don't bother school staff. They take what they get out of fear that, if they complain, their children will get worse service, less service, or even no service. Unfortunately, people who expect nothing generally get nothing. When services are being cut, the children of these "good parents who don't complain" may suffer the most. These parents—the trusting, the apathetic, and the fearful—take what they get because they don't realize what their children are entitled to, what power and competence parents have or can develop, and that even the most difficult system can be changed by strong, committed advocates.

Co-opting

Some trusting and fearful parents do have contact with school staff. Because they believe that the school system can do the best professional job without any meddling from the parents, or that their speaking up might jeopardize their children's services, many of these parents tend to become servants of the system; that is, they become co-opted by the system. They accept what their children get without question, and they are grateful. They will do what is asked of them, from baking cakes for the sales and helping out in the lunchroom to signing the IEP. Their actions are based on proving their gratitude by demonstrating their respect for the professionals and their constant willingness to be helpful. Co-opted parents are also "good" parents.

Besides trusting and fearful parents, the so-called "good" parents may also be "seduced" parents, ones who may have started out as advocates and who have become co-opted through attention and friendly gestures. Their struggle for services makes them grateful for kind words and special relationships. Over time, they too become the "good" parents of the system.

The "good" parents give the system no trouble. Some schools are experts at recognizing these parents and do just enough to keep them in an ingratiating posture: a few kind words (e.g., "It's nice to have a parent who understands the problem"), a little threat (e.g., "Let's not rock the boat by making too much noise about Aaron's speech needs or they may cut back on what he has now"), or a special concession (e.g., "I'll try to get more, but you know how tight the budget is this year"). These parents are grateful for crumbs, and their children get educational crumbs instead of services.

Be wary of the teacher or administrator who tells you that you are not like other parents (because "you are so understanding and realistic"), who shares his or her problems with you, who is always in when you call, and who is unusually prompt about returning your calls. He or she may be trying to make you a "friend" for his or her own purposes: Aren't friends sympathetic and helpful? Don't they make allowances for each other, give each other more time when needed, and not criticize, at least not in front of anybody else?

In the beginning of a personal relationship with a school person, you may get a slight improvement in services and a well-massaged ego. As time passes, you, the understanding, "rational" parent, may find yourself sympathizing more and more and getting fewer services.

While this parent seduction or co-optation is going on, your child is in limbo. You have made a "friend," but is your child getting the education he or she deserves?

Co-optation is a hard pattern to change because the seduction of parents is a gradual, even insidious process during which you have many occasions to develop the habit of supporting and sympathizing with the school person. However, you can learn not to personalize your relationships with school people through some careful planning and role playing in which you rehearse with your own personal advocate how to become your child's strong advocate instead of the school's pal. You are out to influence people and gain services, not to win friends. When co-opted parents learn about their children's educational rights, they can begin to disengage themselves from personal ties with the school system and to look for methods and skills to help them become the strong and independent advocates that their children need.

Reactive Confrontation

Sometimes when parents first learn about the rights of their children with disabilities to education, they react with bewilderment, anger, and frustration. In an attempt to right the wrong that may have been done to the child, an outraged parent may go with fire in his or her eyes and heart to confront the teacher or administrator, and shout, "What are they paying you for? You ought to be out sweeping streets for all you know about these kids!" or "You never liked my kid anyway, you poor excuse for a teacher!" The reactive parent, in venting anger upon the first representative of the system that he or she is able to contact, sometimes blames an individual who may in fact be powerless to meet the parent's demands to correct the school system's failure. Parents who flare up like this think the school staff will now move because they really told those people off.

Occasionally, this may bring immediate but short-range results; most of the time, however, these parents have just given teachers or administrators a good reason for dealing with them as little as possible. The school staff, being on the receiving end of such fireworks, will often, with some justification, react with anger of their own. Although they may attempt to placate, threaten, or ignore the parent at the time of the confrontation because of the parent's "irrational" behavior, they feel they now have good cause to minimize the parent's participation in the planning of educational services for his or her child, or they conclude that with a parent such as this, no wonder the child has problems. After all, schools can't be expected to do much to help a child from an unstable home situation. If the school staff feel justified in avoiding the parents or even refusing to see them, how can parents be effective?

When school people avoid parents after such a confrontation and do not improve services for the children involved, parents become more frustrated and demoralized; they have done their worst and still the system didn't budge, so they feel that they might as well give up. Obviously, "you can't fight city hall!"

School systems, which have years of experience in dealing with all kinds of parents, know that most parents who use reactive confrontation are not likely to continue because of the emotional drain and exhaustion involved; such parents usually give only one performance and then return to isolation. School people reason, "If we can ride out the storm, these parents will eventually leave us alone."

If you are a parent who has used reactive confrontation, you probably know already that fireworks behavior is a mistake. It is a mistake, however, that you can repair. It may require an apology on your part: You can say that you are sorry for the things you said at the meeting, that you don't know what came over you but that you were really worried about Maria's progress, and, in addition, that you are having problems in your job, all of your children have been sick, Aunt Martha is in the hospital, or the pipes burst. Of course you can exaggerate and embellish your excuses in your apology. You may still believe that the person is incompetent or heartless, but you are not going to say it to his or her face ever again. Besides, you can't prove the person doesn't like your child, should be sweeping streets, or is a poor excuse for a teacher. Do not say anything you can't back up with specific information or data. However, you can, if necessary, be apologetic; it's for a good cause—your child's future.

If you can't get past the secretary, leave a message that you want to apologize for your behavior the other day and hope the teacher or administrator will get back to you. If necessary, leave a note. It's hard for school people to refuse an apology, especially when they are bent on showing how rational, cool, and objective they are in contrast to your emotional behavior. It may be hard for you to apologize. Just toughen up and file it under advocacy training.

Once contact has been reestablished, you can set about the business of advocacy through preparation and planning. If you know you have a short fuse or tend to get easily excited, your preparation should include more role playing, possibly reading a book on relaxation (and learning how to do it), and always taking someone with you who will keep you on task and under control.

EFFECTIVE WAYS TO DEAL WITH THE SYSTEM

Remember that you can change your behavior and direction at any time; in fact, to be a good advocate, you are always acquiring new behaviors, changing old ones, and increasing your advocacy skills. When parents learn skills and strategies, as well as rights, they can start to act in more productive ways with school systems. Your most important resource is likely to be your personal advocate. When the system is working for you, that advocate can be a friend or neighbor.

Productive Assertiveness

Parents who have been fearful, naive about their children's rights, trusting (but now disillusioned), and drained by emotional confrontations must start their self-training program by developing productive assertiveness. (The outraged parent was extremely assertive, but that kind of assertiveness is not productive. He or she burnt out quickly and the school system returned to business as usual.)

What does productive assertiveness involve? First, it means knowledgeable parents. You know what the law promises and what it means for your child; you know what is in your child's IEP, what evaluations have been done on your child and what they show, what specific kinds of services will benefit your child, and what sources and resources for information and support are available to you. You have done your homework. And you know your child.

Then, because you are well-informed, you prepare yourself to present your case to the school staff. You examine your strengths and weaknesses, including some assumptions like "I'm only a parent" and "I don't know any other role but pupil." You note that you are good with groups, or you get nervous when you have to speak up; you are good on details, or you can't remember a thing under pressure; you are a person who remains cool under fire, or you tend to get very emotional when people are pressing you for answers; you think well on your feet, or you think of the right response after the meeting or when you're falling asleep.

As you plan for the first contact or meeting, make a list of your strong and weak points. Then write out what you need to do to help correct your weaknesses:

- You are nervous about speaking up, so write down your questions and demands.

- You can't remember a thing; again, write it down (everything you will want to say and use at the meeting or on the phone).

- You tend to become emotional or lose control; bring with you someone on your side (your personal advocate) who can help you stay on target or take over for you when you need moments to calm down.

- You're afraid you won't give the right response; the person you ask to accompany you to the meeting, if well informed by you, can help. Furthermore, your advocacy is not a one-shot deal. You will have contact after contact with the schools and other opportunities to use your "right response."

Your preparation probably includes role playing. Try to think in advance of what the school people might say to your requests, including the worst. Let your fantasy loose. Make up your own responses and rehearse them: If the principal says...then I'll say...and if he says ...I'll tell him...and then I'll bring out the evaluations . . . .

By preparing yourself for the worst, you may not need to use all of your practiced responses, but you will be in control when questions or statements are made because you are likely to have answers ready and actions at hand.

As part of your role rehearsal, include ways to close the meeting or telephone call if you feel it is becoming unproductive. Yes, you can end a meeting by requesting an evaluation, asking that another person attend the next meeting, "remembering" that you have a doctor's appointment, or just saying that you need time to think about the important issues that have been discussed.

A very important component of productive assertiveness is your understanding that advocacy for your child is a long-term job, and you are making the full commitment to that job. This commitment will affect and strengthen your manner and delivery when you are dealing with school people. You are embarking on a journey that can bring good services to your child through his or her school years. You will find that there are ways (people and methods) to strengthen your weak points. And, as you gain in strength, you will become a better advocate.

To complete your preparation for productive assertiveness, you need to begin keeping your records (see Chapter 5 for more details). Develop your file by collecting information about your child's past and present programs; beginning a list of school meetings and calls, with space to record results; listing your concerns and requests; and having a notebook or clipboard to take with you to meetings. Your home file can be fancy or simple; a shoebox or shirt box can do nicely. The important thing is that you have your notes and records where you can find and use them. Prepared in this way (you have reviewed and collected the needed information, assessed your strengths and weaknesses, and crafted practical responses), you can now attend your first meeting with some confidence. You arrive on time, organized, and with a list of questions and issues. The way you present yourself (calm and businesslike) tells the school staff that you are serious and there to stay as long as your child needs services.

Productive assertiveness is necessary for the first step in working with school systems, but it is neither a first step nor a stage. It is a quality you will develop and use in all of your dealings with the school system. You will maintain the ability to be productively assertive by keeping up-to-date information and resources and by rehearsing for situations that may look difficult. Productive assertiveness is not loud, but it is persistent and even relentless.

When parents have initiated the process of working with the school system by asserting their children's rights and needs, they will find available to them three methods of dealing with the system.

Collaboration

Collaboration is the ideal method to develop good education plans for students with disabilities. In this process, school people accept the parents as legitimate and equal partners in planning services and respect and value the information and concerns that parents present.

To be an effective advocate in this case, you need first to value your own ideas and questions. You are not a "mere parent." You are a valuable source of information about your child. Second, you need to be informed (through your own efforts) about your child's past evaluations and educational plans and of his or her performance in the current school placement. When you are informed and confident, you will no longer be timid about contributing to the development of good services.

In speaking up at meetings, present your information and requests in simple but specific language:

> **Not:** *Lindsay needs more services.*
>
> **But:** *Lindsay's progress in speech has been slow. Can we increase sessions for the speech-language therapist from two times per week to every day?*

or

> **Not:** *Michael can't read.*
>
> **But:** *Michael's reading doesn't seem to be improving. Wouldn't he benefit from computerized reading programs?*

Your request is clear and straightforward. The teacher or therapist may agree with your concern or respond with another suggestion. Their responses should also be simple and specific so that you both know you are talking about the same thing; the professionals should avoid jargon. At certain times, jargon may be used to put parents down by reminding them that they lack professional training. In the collaborative setting, however, jargon may be a momentary lapse, and a simple request from you for a clearer explanation will remind the professionals to use everyday language. Because professionals do talk to each other more than to parents, a confident parent can overlook these occasional lapses as long as the professionals are making an effort and the messages, if not clear the first time, are understood on the second try. When you have asked about more speech training and you hear things you may not understand, such as *apraxia, syntactical, CVCs,* and so forth, it's time to ask for a translation, and don't stop asking until you receive a satisfactory explanation in words you can understand.

Because collaboration is a process of sharing, you will want to remain open to suggestions from the school professionals, as in the following exchange:

> **Teacher:** *I understand why you want more speech sessions for Lindsay, but I have been working on an idea*

> *that might be better. The speech therapist has*
> *agreed to spend an hour in my classroom to set*
> *up programs that I can do with my kids. I had*
> *hoped to work with Lindsay and Mitch, who has*
> *similar speech problems, every day.*

Mrs. Sullivan: *You mean that she will continue twice a week*
with therapy and that you will work every day
with Lindsay? That's more speech work and less
time out of the classroom. Sounds reasonable. I
want to hear more . . . .

This parent and this teacher are sharing and developing new ideas, and Lindsay can be the beneficiary. This kind of give and take is the mark of collaboration. There is no put-down, no pressure, no freezing of roles ("I am the teacher; you are only a parent"); there is rather an openness, a sharing of ideas, and a common goal of improved services for the child. There may be disagreements, but differences are expected and respected.

Happy is the parent who can advocate through genuine collaboration; sometimes parents find themselves in a process that looks like collaboration but is co-optation in disguise. You begin to sense that you are giving in or giving up more than you are getting. (Remember, the successful advocate is one who gets more for her child than she gives up.) It may be that the school people wanted to collaborate from the beginning, but pressures to keep costs down have increased within the system, and, in spite of their good intentions, they feel they must hold back on new or increased services. Or it may be that subtle attempts at co-opting parents were there from the start and have increased to a level at which you find yourself thinking, "Just what is going on here?" When that question comes up, take some time to assess the situation. Is it just smiles and handshakes, or is it the services you want?

When collaboration fails or turns out to be nonexistent, you will shift to a process that involves not only information and assertiveness but that also requires the continued use of strategies and the constant presence of someone who is willing to back you up at meetings, either as a witness to the proceedings and a silent supporter or as a contributor of suggestions.

Negotiation

If the mark of a good parent advocate in collaboration is the ability to share information and remain open to suggestions, then the mark of a successful parent advocate in the process of negotiation is the skill to obtain more than you give away through the judicious use of strategies and compromise.

"But wait a minute," you might be thinking. "We're talking about education—my child's and that of other children with disabilities. It's hard to believe that school systems play these games with parents. It's their job to educate, after all."

Remember the discussion of the system and the pressures within it: the school budget, the limited number of specialists, and the limited amount of time teachers or administrators may have available for you and your child. Children with disabilities may well be a priority of the system, but they may be priority number 3 or 4 or even 10 or 20.

How can children with disabilities become a high priority in a school system? Through parents who bring their children's needs to the educators' attention in the way that squeaky wheels get the grease. Look at the families you know: Some children are getting better services and more attention because their parents are relentless. After enough parental squeaks and a growing awareness on the part of the system that the squeaking won't go away until something is done, services, like grease, are usually applied. Negotiation determines how much "grease" is used.

Negotiation is always a serious game that parents must play for high stakes (their children's futures) and at some cost (their energy and time). But it is a serious game for school people too, especially when their jobs or advancement in their careers may be in jeopardy. They may need to prove to someone in a higher position that they are tough-minded, tight-fisted, and fiscally responsible in their negotiations with parents and that in fact they do not just "give everything away."

Although you will find yourself negotiating with school people in a number of ways, such as arranging time to visit the classroom, setting an appointment to read your child's comprehensive record, and finding a mutually convenient time to meet with your child's teacher, the most intensive and challenging negotiation will usually happen in the meetings when the IEP is developed. This is the time when all your preparation and rehearsal will pay off.

To be an effective negotiator, you must begin by bringing to the bargaining table those qualities that parents use to achieve successful collaboration: a willingness and determination to share the information you have; a readiness for honest disagreement, discussion, and compromise (as long as it leads to a plan that benefits your child); and a strong belief in your ability to make a valuable contribution to your child's IEP. But for negotiation, you must be stronger in these qualities—more informed, more assertive, and more confident. You must be prepared to be more critical in your judgments about the other members of the team and, on occasion, suspicious of the motives that led to the program proposed by the school staff. You must make a case for improved or new services and be ready to work hard to convince people, some of whom may not be all that interested in what you have to say or may even resent your "interference."

Being a negotiator, however, does not mean that you arrive at the meeting with a list of service demands from which you will not budge even one inch. After all, your plan or list of services may not be the best one for your child. You at least need to hear the ideas, suggestions, and criticisms of the school people before you can make a rational decision to accept or reject their recommendations. Therefore, remain open to suggestion and even disagreement as long as the process is an honest one, meaning that everyone is at least trying to understand what the other person is proposing. When a proposal is rejected or accepted, it should be done for educational reasons, not because of the old myths or because the school is holding the line on the budget. Negotiation is harder than collaboration. For this reason, you need your advocate to know something about the law. This could be a knowledgeable friend or neighbor or a professional advocate who may also be a parent. We'll talk more about this in Chapter 5.

You may find negotiation necessary for only one issue in developing the IEP for your child. In that case, you may reach an agreeable compromise or even win your point and find yourself thinking, "Negotiation isn't so bad after all. I got something good for my child just by speaking up. This negotiation stuff can really pay off."

However, you may find yourself in a situation where the school staff are giving nothing away and you must argue every step of the way for the tiniest concessions. You start thinking, "This is exhausting. How will I make it through the meeting? Negotiation is hard work. It would be easier to give in." Still, even when negotiation is very difficult, by the end of the meeting you may have convinced the school people of the need for certain services.

Let's look at some examples of parents in negotiation. All of these parents have come to the meetings with a prepared list of services their children need, ranked in what they see as the order of importance. They first listen carefully to what the school people have to offer. (By letting the school professionals present their ideas or plans first, the parents may find that most of the services on their lists are also priorities for the school staff.)

"We Could Try It"

Colin Dwyer listens carefully to the school staff's presentations. He is pleasantly surprised by the agreement between his list and their plan.

Mr. Dwyer:	*I'm impressed with the services you have laid out. You seem to really know my daughter and what she needs. Heather has made a lot of progress in school. Through your efforts, she is almost totally included. I have only one concern I want to raise: She is 2 years behind in math.*
Principal:	*She has made progress in every other area. We don't want to push her too hard.*
Mr. Dwyer:	*I don't want to push her either. But if Heather had some extra tutoring, she might catch up and be in regular class all the time.*
Resource Teacher:	*She's in the resource room 1 hour each day and gets her math instruction there. That should be adequate.*
Mr. Dwyer:	*I had something else in mind. I would like her to be in a regular class with a special tutor after school.*
Principal:	*The teacher has a full work schedule and can't be expected to tutor after school.*
Mr. Dwyer:	*I realize that, but couldn't some other person be hired as a tutor?*
Principal:	*That means more money, and you know how tight money is.*
Mr. Dwyer:	*I understand the pressures on you. But in 2 years Heather goes to middle school, and it would be nice if she could go as a regular student. Listen, I think what you're offering is great, but I also think this small addition could*

> **Resource Teacher:** *make a lot of difference. Couldn't you arrange for the tutor?*
>
> **Resource Teacher:** *I'm not convinced that Heather will improve with tutoring.*
>
> **Mr. Dwyer:** *But you're not sure it won't work either. How about a trial of a few months?*
>
> **Principal:** *We could try it for a few months, I suppose. But in 3 months we'll review it and . . . .*

Note that by letting the school people lead, Colin Dwyer found that he had only one point to negotiate. He was pleasant (congratulating the school staff on the plan), assertive (keeping to the issue of the tutor), and willing to compromise (agreeing to a 3-month trial).

"It Isn't Needed"

Eileen Doyle has to work a little harder in the negotiation process. After listening to the school people present their plans, she realizes that they are talking about last year's program, which, to her, is clearly inadequate—there are no special therapies, the class size is too large, and physical education meets only once a week. She realizes that the situation requires a strong effort on her part when the school staff tell her that the meeting is already half over and that she must sign the IEP today.

Although her first response is panic ("The program is just awful and they want me to sign now! Help!"), she takes a long look out the window, and her personal advocate reminds her that time is on her side. She relaxes. The IEP is too important to rush. She then speaks up in an assertive manner and tells the administrators calmly what she feels her child needs, what is right and wrong with the program, and why. Her composed, assertive manner tells the school people that she, too, expects to be a reasonable but nevertheless active participant in this process, that for her the task is a very serious one, and that her evaluations and recommendations will become part of the proceedings.

She goes through the proposed program point by point and asks for specifics:

> **Mrs. Doyle:** *You say Patrick should have gym, but you didn't say how often, how long, or who his teacher would be.*
>
> **Principal:** *It would be the usual number of times.*

> **Mrs. Doyle:** *I'm sorry Mr. Brennan, but I don't know what that is. Could you be more specific so that we could write it into the plan?*
>
> **Principal:** *Two or three times a week.*
>
> **Mrs. Doyle:** *Three times would be better. My son, Sean, who is in general education class, has gym three times a week.*
>
> **Principal:** *Yes, Mrs. Doyle, three times each week.*
>
> **Mrs. Doyle:** *Now, I'm not clear on the goals for Patrick's physical education plan.*

In this way, Eileen Doyle pursues the specifics of the IEP. She asks to see any recent reports she hasn't received; her advocate reminds her to ask certain questions of the teachers and specialists. The negotiating process is continuous, and Mrs. Doyle is working very hard. Finally, both sides are deadlocked over the issue of an increase in speech-language therapy:

> **Mrs. Doyle:** *Patrick needs speech-language therapy every day. His speech is his major drawback in all his activities.*
>
> **Principal:** *He already has speech-language therapy twice each week, which is more than anyone else in his class, and, frankly, he hasn't made much progress.*
>
> **Mrs. Doyle:** *That is only partly true. He may not be making more progress because he's not getting enough help to make a real difference. He needs more. Actually, speech-language therapy has clearly made a difference. Before he got any, he had no speech. With twice-weekly therapy, he is now speaking better and more often. It is reasonable to expect that more therapy will produce still more speech.*
>
> **Principal:** *We don't have enough speech-language therapists to serve all the children who need help. I can't offer you any more. I'm very sorry.*

Mrs. Doyle: *Yet we all agree that this is Patrick's biggest need!*

Principal: *I don't agree that five times a week will help more. And besides, I can't offer it.*

Mrs. Doyle: *It seems that we have a difference of opinion concerning Patrick's needs for speech-language therapy. Also, you seem to be saying that even if you agreed that he needed more, you could not provide more. How might we solve this? (Looks at the teacher.)*

Teacher: *I have a suggestion. What if the speech-language therapist continued to come twice each week but spent some of that time working with me to help me set up a language program for Patrick. Would that help?*

Eileen Doyle expresses her interest by pulling her chair closer to the educational bargaining table, asking for more specifics. The principal breathes a sigh of relief and leans back in his chair (he, too, finds negotiating hard work!) while the teacher outlines a cooperative language program between the therapist and herself. The parent agrees but with reservations: She wants weekly contact with the teacher or therapist to measure the effectiveness of this new approach. The teacher says that meeting every week would be difficult for her, so the parent suggests a weekly telephone call and monthly meetings. This suggestion is accepted. Eileen Doyle then wisely asks that the weekly and monthly consultations between her and the teacher be written in the IEP.

In this kind of bargaining, the school staff first offered something that was not acceptable. When the parent asked for more, backing up her request with a sound and assertive argument, they offered something else. Through negotiation, all parties reached a mutual agreement about the service to be provided. Eileen Doyle worked hard, and in the end got a program she believed was good for her child.

This example also shows that the parent, by remaining open to new ideas (in this case, the teacher's), was able to obtain a more beneficial program than the one she originally proposed, which now includes regular meetings with the teacher. Her child now stands to gain through more attention to his language development (from two people), more time in the classroom to be used for learning other skills, more group opportunities for improving language performance, and more and regular information sharing between parent and teacher.

"It's Not Our Responsibility"

Some parents encounter strong resistance to their concerns and requests for services. Sometimes the old myths are the cause of this resistance, and a lot of time and energy must be expended to counteract them. Other times, it can be honest disagreement between the parents and the school staff. When this is the case, someone at the negotiating table is likely to ask questions and want to explore your concerns. The most difficult times are those when the school budget alone (though sometimes presented under the guise of the school's lack of responsibility) is determining the process and you find that the conversation seems to be leading nowhere and discussion is being closed. These are the times when you, the parent, will need to remind the school staff of their legal responsibility under the law.

Norman Johnson's request for adapted physical education for his son, Omar, is being turned down. He is not sure whether the school people really believe that Omar is doing well in gym or are trying to avoid the cost of providing a special service:

> **Principal:** *I know you'd like Omar to have the program, but we don't believe he really needs more than he's getting right now. Besides, that's a special service.*

> **Mr. Johnson:** *I'm not sure I understand what you mean by "special service."*

> **Principal:** *It's an extra; it's not part of our regular program. If you want to pursue it on your own by finding some after-school program, that's up to you.*

> **Mr. Johnson:** *I have my copy of the IDEA regulations here. It says that adapted physical education is a school service. If Omar needs this service, he's entitled to have it. I observed the gym program: There are so many distractions that Omar is lost in there. He might as well have no gym program.*

Principal: *Well, if you think he'd benefit from more time in the classroom, we could. . . .*

Mr. Johnson: *I think you misunderstood me. Omar needs a physical education program designed to meet his needs. I feel that it is one of the most crucial parts of his IEP. To be quite frank about it, I would have a great deal of difficulty signing the IEP if it were not included. However, if you feel you do not have enough information and want to have Omar tested. . . .*

Principal: *Maybe we should take another look at Omar before we make any decisions about testing.*

Note that once Norman Johnson suspects resistance, he first makes sure that he understands what the principal is saying, then makes specific reference to the law, ignores the attempt at diversion (e.g., more time in the classroom), and finally makes it very clear that the IEP will not be acceptable without the crucial service. His suggestion that the school might look into further evaluation is offered from a position of strength because he is fairly sure from his observations of Omar that a qualified evaluator is bound to find that Omar needs additional help and that the school would be reluctant to pay for it.

Norman Johnson is going through the worst kind of negotiation—one in which money, and not the child, appears to be the prime concern. Because of his knowledge of the law (as well as his determination), Omar's father may bring about the needed change in his son's program. The negotiation process, however, is not completed until the specifics of the agreement are written in the IEP and signed by both the school and the parent.

The three parents in the examples will finish the process when the IEP is presented to them in full detail, describing the plans that they have worked out with the educators at the meeting(s).

Most parents will use negotiation in dealing with the system, and most will achieve a reasonably successful IEP for their children. There will, however, be a few parents who, in spite of good or even extraordinary negotiating skills, will not be able to achieve a beneficial program for their children. These parents have a more demanding job ahead of them.

Productive Confrontation

When parents find themselves in a situation in which they are being asked to accept or sign an IEP that is presented to them without their full participation in its development, when every request for an improvement in service is rejected (e.g., "There's no money," "Your child is getting too many extras already"), or when, after a cordial meeting with much discussion, parents receive an IEP that does not match the agreements made at the IEP meeting and does not meet their child's needs, then parents must be prepared to move beyond the negotiation phase by rejecting the educational program. Negotiation fails when both sides say no. The system says, "No, you can't have anything more or any of the important things you have asked for," and the parent says, "No, I cannot accept the program as it is written for my child." Parents must then be ready to confront the system with its failure and to show their commitment to obtaining needed services for their children.

School systems sometimes say no to intimidate parents. Parents must be prepared to deal with that no in a productive way. Accepting the school's refusal is not productive, not from the point of view of your child's future. Therefore, you must let the school staff know that you do not accept the program. The first step could be a call to the special education director or principal to say that you intend to reject the school's program and that you are prepared to do so in writing, but first you want to check out the possibilities for reconciling differences before appealing to a higher authority. If there is no chance to renegotiate or if you have unusual difficulty reaching the administrator, then you must reject the IEP in writing, stating your reasons for rejecting the program while at the same time being clear in your letter about any areas of agreement.

Sometimes your verbal or written rejection is enough to bring more cooperation from the school professionals. They realize that you were not intimidated and you are not bluffing. (Remember, you should never, never bluff about your child's future. Say what you'll do and then do it.)

When negotiation fails, you must be prepared to move to productive confrontation, an often long and drawn-out, but necessary, process. It is discussed at length in Chapter 8. It is a last resort to use when other means have been tried and have failed.

Perhaps you are worn out at the thought of doing still more work and planning when you have just finished working so hard in order to do a good job of negotiating. An important consolation is that all of the work you've done and information you've gathered will be essential in working through the process of productive confrontation. You have likely narrowed down the issues of disagreement to one or two issues. Your new skills and self-control under fire will help you through the next phase.

In this chapter, you have begun to understand how parents like you may have been manipulated or pushed into isolated, co-opted, or reactive roles. Most parents didn't get there by themselves; they had some help from the system. This "help" came in the form of statements that we can label as snow jobs. There is one important difference between snow jobs and myths, which snow jobs sometimes resemble. Myths are things that people actually believe; they are ideas that must be challenged and changed. Snow jobs, however, are strategies designed and used by some school professionals to make their jobs easier by excluding certain students from needed services and even from school. Snow jobs are common enough that you should be prepared to deal with them.

SOME POPULAR SNOW JOBS

When people in school systems face parents who are asking for services for the first time, some school staff may say things that are intended to discourage the parents from making their requests, and a few school people may actually believe what they are saying. Some of these statements may be dishonest, insulting (to the child and/or the parent), and even illegal. Naive and trusting parents may take the statements at face value and creep quietly home, perhaps never to ask again. But informed parent advocates know the standard snow jobs and learn how to recognize new variations; they can reply to distasteful and illegal statements by using IDEA for support.

"Children Like Yours Can't Benefit from Inclusion"

The law requires that students with disabilities be provided with a learning environment in general education or as close as possible. This does not mean a separate wing or a separate building, eating lunch at their desks, or having all education in a segregated classroom. Nor does it mean plunking a child in the middle of regular class where no one understands or can support his or her needs. The law requires that the student be placed in the least restrictive environment so that schools can include students in ways appropriate to the students' needs (including appropriate supports and assistive technology).

Some schools have made great strides in including their students with disabilities partially or fully with typical students of the same or approximate ages. Most of the progress is being made in preschool and primary grades. Schools are less successful at the middle school/junior high and high school level. Other schools are struggling with the law and will need your help in determining to what extent and with what supports your child can be included. Still others are resistant and even offended by your expectation of inclusion. They may strive to maintain "business as usual" and may even recommend placements outside the local schools.

If your child is being excluded from contact with students without disabilities, you may need to educate your school system to its responsibilities under IDEA, including the importance of support services, assistive technology, and modifications with the right amount of help and supervision. You might want to remind them that Section 504 requires schools to share their policies about supports, modifications, and adaptations for students with disabilities with parents. Maybe your son or daughter can participate in the general education computer class if the program is modified to match his or her skills and needs or a larger keyboard or touch screen is provided.

When the schools try to put the responsibility for their failure on your child because he or she doesn't meet their expectations of the kind of student they like to serve, you, as the knowledgeable and committed advocate, should place that responsibility right back where it belongs—on the shoulders of the school system—because you know your child can learn and you know which supports and services can benefit him or her.

"We Don't Have Any Children Like This"

This statement (or a variation) is sometimes made with a sign of distaste: The implication is that your child's disability is too severe or that he or she is too different or even too grotesque to be served by the system.

A school superintendent told one parent with a partially ambulatory child with physical disabilities and high intelligence, "Your child is a basket case and doesn't belong in a public school." This child later went to a private school with typical students, did well, and graduated from college. Clearly, he could have succeeded in a public school if some supportive arrangements had been made.

Hearing such statements is a devastating experience for parents. If you have any reason to expect that unfair and insulting remarks about your child may be made to you, be sure you take someone with you when you go to meetings and take notes. It is amazing how much language gets cleaned up when there's a witness present. You may still have to deal with attitudes and excuses, but the personal insults will be reduced.

Keep in mind that IEP means an *individualized* program. You write the IEP for one child. The school does not need another "child like this."

"The Classrooms (or Facilities) Are Not Accessible"

Not only does this statement violate IDEA but also it stands in violation of Section 504 and the Americans with Disabilities Act (ADA), which both guarantee the civil rights of people with disabilities.

Remember the administrator who told a parent that her child would repeat the third grade? The parent suspected that her child was being held back because he used a wheelchair, and the fourth grade was on the second floor. Clearly the fourth grade was not going to move to accommodate her child. The fourth grade would continue to remain on the second floor with no accommodation being made for this child. The "caring" principal spoke of moving some books from the upstairs library to the first floor (but moved a mere handful). Nothing substantial was moved to the first floor. When Sanjay's class was promoted to the fourth grade on the second floor, he was left behind in the third grade for yet another year.

Accommodations can be made (most classrooms can be moved; art and music are portable; and books can be boxed and moved to accommodate students with disabilities), renovations can be started (ramps, lifts, new doors, lavatories accessible to persons with disabilities, and, if necessary, elevators), or a combination of accommodations and renovations can be undertaken to meet the needs of students with physical disabilities without extraordinary expense (e.g., relocating a classroom is cheaper than installing an elevator).

If your child could benefit from the programs (general and/or special education classes) in your local school and is being excluded because the facilities are inaccessible, you have the right and the obligation to insist that programs be made accessible. A strong and outspoken parent advocate can bring about the needed changes. However, the law does allow the school, if your town has more than one age-appropriate school, to move your child out of his or her neighborhood school to another school in town. Schools that are not inclusive can use the threat of a disruptive move to discourage parents. You still have the option of using your political allies to fight this battle.

"Children Can Be So Cruel"

This statement is usually coupled with the recommendation that your child be placed somewhere else, not in the local school. What school people are suggesting here is that they would really like to protect your child, but they have no or little control over all of the other students in their school. This is nonsense because school systems have numerous rules to regulate the behavior of their students (e.g., when to arrive, talk, eat, or move; what door or stairway to use; what to wear, given the public school push for uniforms). Furthermore, the purpose of the schools is to educate, not only in academics but also in values and behaviors (arrive on time, sit at your desk, answer when called on) as well. When school administrations make a strong commitment to students with disabilities, other students become more supportive and accepting of their fellow students with disabilities. Programs that include students with disabilities have already demonstrated that typical students can become supports and friends to their fellow students with disabilities and thrive. School systems (and society in general) have for a long time protected students with disabilities and prevented them from having contact with other students and, in doing so, have done a disservice to all students.

You can remind the school people of their obligation to educate all students and to foster through education an understanding and acceptance of students with disabilities. You can also say that you will be watching closely to see what efforts they make and how successful those efforts are, that you understand some of the difficulties they may face, and that you will help by finding films and speakers (yourself included, if this is something with which you feel comfortable) to present to both teachers and students, but that you cannot accept the "cruelty" of students as an excuse for the system's continued partial or total exclusion of your child.

"We Don't Have the Money"

In lean times this sounds like a good excuse. But even when the economy is good, this statement has been made to parents as a way to avoid providing a free appropriate public education (FAPE) for students with disabilities. Even when there was full funding for after-school programs (usually sports programs) for typical students (mostly boys), there were no funds "available" for extended day programs for students with disabilities, nor was money set aside to support students with special needs in existing after-school programs. A few creative schools found acceptable roles for students with disabilities (e.g., manager roles for sports, in charge of equipment) and other supportive and valued roles.

Schools need to think outside the box. Money is not always the answer or the only answer. You have already read about moving classrooms to the first floor instead of putting in an elevator, using walking and swimming to meet one student's needs for physical education, and using school personnel in more creative ways. Providing a teaching assistant to a classroom at the same or less cost as the transportation to a distant regional segregated program is another.

Even before IDEA was passed, lack of money was not a legal excuse for denying education. Most parents didn't know this; they thought they and their children were getting favors if any services were provided, and if their children were at home or in state institutions not receiving education, they more or less accepted the situation.

If your child is not in an educational program, you have the right and the obligation to insist that your child immediately receive services. The school is in violation of the law until your child is placed in an appropriate program and is in flagrant violation if they know your child is without a program and are doing nothing.

If your child is in a program that is not meeting his or her needs, you should request a new IEP that will include services to meet those needs. If the school people do not agree with you on those service needs, they must argue with you in educational terms, not in financial ones. Do not accept lack of money as an excuse for denying services.

"Your Child Would Benefit More from a Workshop Outside the School"

Parents of young adolescents, even preadolescents, have heard this copout. School systems, which may have been inclusive in the early grades, seem unable to provide inclusion in middle and high schools. But thanks to parents who want their children in their community schools, schools are learning.

Vocational training may be a very good goal for your child, but it should happen in the schools, which is where education happens for most kids. Sending students outside the system to sheltered workshops that lack the varied programs offered by schools (e.g., physical education, speech, academics) withholds access to appropriate tools and learning environments and denies students with disabilities the right and opportunities to learn, work, and socialize with typical students of their own ages. You may tell the school people that you appreciate their interest, but right now your child belongs in school. You may wish to save specialized vocational training for the time when your child turns 18 and has a few years of special education services left.

"Your Child Is Ready to Graduate"

This is good news for a parent, unless the adolescent still has educational needs that have not been met. The school may in fact be trying to push your child out for reasons that do not include his or her well-being. Graduation usually means the end of the special services and academic assistance that your child may still need. If you know that your child needs more education, do not accept graduation on the school's timetable—when he or she is 18 to 20 years old. IDEA covers students through age 21.

If your son or daughter is in a general education class and wants to graduate with his or her classmates, you and your child will have to make the decision together. This can be a difficult challenge for the both of you. Your child could still participate in the graduation ceremony with his or her classmates, but without the diploma and certificate of completion, perhaps with some substitute paperwork acknowledging the student's efforts or progress. The school can provide this participation, however grudgingly. If your child can benefit from education up to 21, you must continue to press for services, such as more computer literacy or vocational training.

Do not make your decision solely on the school's recommendation for graduation. As always, base your decisions and recommendations on your child's needs and what you both see in his or her best interest.

THE SNOW JOB CHALLENGED

Most parents may not have to deal with school people who make statements like those we've discussed. But if you are subjected to snow jobs, you must speak up. Tell the speaker that the statement is wrong and that it is not an excuse for excluding students from school. If you believe that the school person is in error and misguided, show him or her how to understand the needs of children in another and more valid way. Provide your school staff with information from resources available in the appendixes. If you find yourself dealing with the occasional school person who intends to put you down or drive you away, let him or her know you find the comments offensive and a poor excuse for denying service. You may even wish to put your under-standing of what was said in writing, making sure that your report of the comments is accurate, and send the letter to the person who made the remarks. In most cases, you will get back the "I'm-sure-you-misun-derstood-my-comments" letter, which will usually deny the remarks, tell you what the person "really" said, and indicate that the school is aware of the difficulty and already taking steps to correct it. Your let-ter can do more than correct the school staff's offensive or erroneous remarks; it may bring you a written promise of improved service for your child. Whichever way you choose to deal with school people, let them know that such statements will not put you off because you are serious about getting an education for your child.

In order to effectively combat the people who may put your child down, you want to strengthen or even develop some basic skills for dealing with school people. The next chapter will help you to apply skills you use in your daily life to the specific task of communicating with the school system.

5

Using Your Everyday Skills
"Hey, I Can Do That!"

checking yourself out • how good is your school system and your child's program • secretaries are gatekeepers • the polite social lie • importance of private practice • communicating by phone and e-mail • sample letters and how to use them • reviewing your own letters (all of them) • the advocate's advocate and other resources • going up the ladder • appearances can help

"Mrs. Mendez is very busy. I don't know when she can return your call."

"I know that you have been waiting for your child's IEP. But we have many students to serve, and we will get around to it as soon as we can."

"Your child's record contains professional reports that are too technical for you to understand. We would be happy to interpret them for you, but we cannot give you copies."

When parents hear statements like these when they try to get information or services from school people, they feel helpless. They need to know what to do to get the response and action they are looking for.

At this point, you understand some things you may not have understood or were not aware of before. You now know more about possible problems in getting services from school systems than most people, even those inside the system. You know the common myths and snow jobs, and the various ways school systems can deal with parents. Although all of this information about possible pitfalls and stumbling blocks will be useful, it may make you feel a little timid or reluctant about setting forth to right what is wrong with your child's education program. Remember that you will probably not have to deal with all of the problems detailed in this book. Your child's program may already be a good one, or it may need only a few small changes. As an informed and confident parent, you are in a better position to be a good judge of the quality of the current program and can therefore feel more secure about your child's educational program.

Informed? "Yes," you may be thinking, "I may now know more than perhaps I wanted to know or was prepared for. But confident? How can I be confident in dealing with all of these experts who always have a fast answer to give me? I don't have the skills to keep up with them."

This chapter demonstrates that you do in fact have skills that you regularly use in your day-to-day living, but that you, confused by the myths and lacking knowledge about the system, didn't apply in your interactions with school professionals. Furthermore, this book helps you to strengthen and refine those skills in ways that will prepare you to deal effectively with people at every level of the educational system.

Perhaps you do not think of yourself as someone who deals with systems or people who provide services, but you do it often, maybe even every day. If you manage a household (or live in one), are employed or run a business, have friends, make purchases, pay bills, belong to a club, or, in short, interact with other people in routine and sometimes complex ways, you are already using many of the same skills that will help you to obtain your goals when dealing with the educational system.

CHECK YOURSELF AGAINST THIS LIST OF SKILLS

The following checklist will help you see that you have many skills you can employ in obtaining your goals with the educational system.

Even if you have not done everything on this list, it is likely that you have done most of the items. When you did these things, were you successful? Did you get the appointment changed or the right item in the color, size, or working order you wanted? Even if you didn't get what you wanted, you learned something, such as that old receipts and check stubs are necessary, that you should have asked for the store manager, or that taking a friend with you for moral support can be helpful.

LIST OF SKILLS CHECKLIST

1. Verbal communication skills: Have you ever used the telephone to accomplish any of the following tasks?
   - ❐ Changing or canceling an appointment
   - ❐ Registering a complaint
   - ❐ Persuading someone to change his or her opinion or intention
   - ❐ Selling or buying something

2. Written communication skills: Have you written a letter or sent an e-mail doing any of the following things?
   - ❐ Sharing news or information
   - ❐ Requesting information
   - ❐ Saying thank you
   - ❐ Registering a complaint about a product

3. Planning ability: Have you planned any of the following things?
   - ❐ A menu
   - ❐ A party
   - ❐ Shopping
   - ❐ A trip or vacation

4. Ability to keep long-term commitments: Have you ever signed any of the following kinds of contracts or agreements?
   - ❐ Purchasing an appliance on time
   - ❐ Buying a house
   - ❐ Taking dancing or driving lessons
   - ❐ Serving on a committee or board of any kind

5. Self-confidence and assertiveness: Have you ever returned a product because it had one of these flaws?
   - ❐ Not as advertised
   - ❐ Defective
   - ❐ Delivered too late
   - ❐ Wrong size or color

6. Interpersonal skills: Have you ever had to work with one or more people in any of these situations?
   - ❐ Planning an event or activity
   - ❐ Reaching a decision together
   - ❐ Resolving an argument
   - ❐ Solving a problem

Learning something or knowing better is a kind of success because you now increase your chances for success in the future. This may be a small satisfaction when you feel you have failed, but with more opportunities, thought, and time, you can become a "pro" at getting satisfaction.

"All of this may be fine for buying a bathrobe or for getting an adjustment on a telephone bill," you might be thinking. In those cases, you are dealing with salespeople or service people. But we are supposed to be talking about education, and, after all, educators aren't sales or service people—or are they?

Educators are most definitely service people. Their job is to deliver a service to your child for up to 21 years, a service that should benefit your child and that you can approve and support. Keep in mind that everyone who works in the school system, from the superintendent to the custodian, was hired to perform a service for the children of your town or community. As for being salespeople, some parents who have had bad experiences can tell you about the "bill of goods" they were sold by school staff. So the skills you have used with salespeople may be appropriate to use with some school professionals on certain occasions.

"But how will I know if a service is the right one for my child?" you may ask yourself. "It's easy to know when a vacuum cleaner isn't working, but education is more complicated. I'm no educational expert." You begin to know if the educational program or service is working by asking yourself these questions about it:

- Has the IEP been explained in a way I can understand?

- Is my child's IEP being followed?

- Is he or she getting the special help in the amounts promised?

- Is he or she making any progress?

- Is he or she progressing at a satisfactory rate?

- Is he or she making progress outside of school (e.g., at home, in the community)?

- Does the program have drawbacks or limitations (e.g., too many stairs, too few school hours, too little inclusion)?

- Does my child want to go to school?

You may have some "I don't know" answers to these questions, but that's okay because now you know where to start looking. Your job is to find the answers to the best of your ability. In doing so, you will probably develop your own questions for school staff. You may end up with many "yes" answers, in which case you can relax a little and feel good about your child's service. If too many of your answers are "no," then you should get ready to go over the IEP again, either to be sure it's actually in operation or to get it changed if it's not meeting your child's needs. (While you are doing this, remember to be alert to myths that could hinder your effectiveness. If necessary, review Chapters 3 and 4 again to give yourself confidence and to remind yourself that you are one kind of expert—an expert in information about your child.)

Yes, it is much easier to judge the effectiveness of your vacuum cleaner than your child's school program. But by observing your child and looking at his or her performance and school history over the years, you will begin to make judgments. Perhaps they will be weak and tenuous at first, but they will become stronger as you gain confidence in your own natural ability to evaluate your child and his or her progress in school.

"But," you may be thinking, "if I am convinced that my child's program is insufficient, I'm afraid I'll get emotional when I ask for things for him. After all, my child is much more important to me than anything I would buy."

Of course you will feel a lot of emotion. Recall what was said in Chapter 3: Your feelings for your child make you a concerned and committed parent. Without them, you would be a poor advocate and an even poorer parent. When you use and control your feelings, they can be your best asset.

Consider how you react in your everyday experience to a defective product or service. Have you ever found that when you became angry about it you also became determined to get satisfaction? Your controlled emotion may have kept you going through numerous telephone calls, letters, and trips to the store. Emotion can be the carefully stoked fire that keeps you going to the finish line. You can control and channel it into successful dealings with the school system.

Unlike your everyday purchases or services, education goes on for a long time. Only when your child reaches the upper age limit for special education do the services end. At any time during your child's school years, you can request a review of his or her program and, if necessary, a new or revised program. Your skills will be put to good use, for you will deal directly and formally with the system at least once a year, during the IEP annual review, and you should have a number of informal dealings throughout the year, particularly with the teachers and specialists. You may be working with the system over months as you advocate for the right plan for your child. So let's look at the skills you have and see how to use them to meet your child's needs.

USING THE TELEPHONE

Most people use the telephone every day to make personal and professional appointments, call friends and acquaintances, order services or products, or have bills corrected. They call physicians, politicians, radio stations, and garages expecting responses within a reasonable time. Yet nowhere are parents as timid or apologetic as they are apt to be when calling representatives of the school system. They will tolerate being put on hold, waiting for a return call, or even getting no return call at all with a humility that is astonishing. Even on the telephone, they exhibit the behavior of the old school pupil who is willing to wait indefinitely without complaint. When they do finally get through or get a return call, they are apt to be more grateful than the situation warrants. And if they make complaints, they use language so apologetic and weak that their complaints are hardly recognizable. For example, a weak complaint to the special education director might sound like this:

> *"Oh, Ms. Danielson, you are really good to return my call. I'm sorry to bother you at school when you are so busy. I hate to trouble you, but Josh's bus isn't coming to pick him up until 45 minutes after school starts. Can anything be done to get it here a little earlier? I'd be so grateful if you could help."*

Parents who talk like this are usually afraid of rocking the boat. Yet if this parent doesn't start being more assertive, Josh may end up spending as much time traveling to and from school as he does in school, especially if he leaves school early so that the bus can be available at the regular closing time for the typical students. (Yes, some parents accept the early return, as well as the late pick-up.)

How would you talk to the telephone company if they continued to overcharge you? You would certainly not apologize for their error. You would probably make it clear to the company representative that there was an overcharge that you expected to be corrected immediately. In the same way, Josh's parents should make it clear that there is an error—Josh is being deprived of the full school day to which he is entitled—and that an immediate correction by the school system is expected and necessary.

If, like other parents, you feel intimidated by school staff and act humble and apologetic, you can begin to change by making a firm resolve to be more assertive. (Remember that assertiveness need not mean aggression or rudeness.) Of course, resolve alone will not make you assertive. Timid behaviors are habits that have grown strong over time; to undo them you must practice new, assertive behaviors.

When contacting your child's school, keep in mind that secretaries and administrative assistants are important people. These individuals are the "gatekeepers" to the school administrators you want to reach. Always treat them with courtesy, and they may help to get your messages through more quickly and more clearly.

The best place to start is in private rehearsal. Imagine the telephone call you want to make or recall one you made earlier with the changes you would make:

1. What do you want to get as a result of the call? (e.g., "I want Josh picked up on time.")

2. What difficulties or roadblocks might you expect in making the call? (e.g., "The special education director won't be in. They'll put me on hold and forget about me or the director will tell me my request isn't possible. She might get angry, or maybe I'll get upset or angry.")

3. Anything else? (List other concerns or expectations you can think of.)

4. Now, think of things you can say (you can write them down, too): first, to yourself (e.g., "Josh has a right to a full day; I will speak up without hanging back or being timid; I will not be put off; the issue must be dealt with right away."); second, to the person you are calling (identifying yourself again, stating the problem, stressing its urgency, and stating your expectation that he or she will fix it); and third, to the secretary or receptionist who answers the telephone (say who you want to talk to and who you are; if the special education director is not available, state why you are calling and stress the urgency, and say where you can be reached and when).

Now think of what they may say to you and how to deal with problematic responses (it's fair play to imagine the worst possible responses, just in case you get them). First consider what to say if you can't reach the person you are calling right away:

Secretary:	*The special education director isn't in. May I take a message?*
Mrs. Golden:	*Yes. (Provides information: name, telephone number, and problem) When can I expect her return call?*
Secretary:	*I will give her the message as soon as she's out of the meeting.*
Mrs. Golden:	*Please tell her I will be waiting for her call.*

or

Secretary:	*The special education director is out of town today but will be back tomorrow. I'll give her the message first thing in the morning.*
Mrs. Golden:	*Thanks. Please tell her I will be waiting for her call then at this number. . . .*

or

Secretary:	*The special education director is a very busy person. I don't know when she will have the time to call you.*
Mrs. Golden:	*Please tell her I am waiting for her call. If I do not hear from her today, I will call again first thing tomorrow morning.*

Then consider the range of possible responses (best to worst) from the school person:

Special Education Director:	*Hello, Mrs. Golden. This is Ms. Danielson. I didn't know Josh was being picked up late. Of course he should be picked up on time. I'll speak to the person in charge of transportation as soon as we hang up. If there's any problem, I'll get back to*

you; otherwise, expect him to be picked up on time.

or

Special Education Director:	*We've been having a problem organizing transportation. Can you give me a few days to see what I can do?*
Mrs. Golden:	*Yes, but this has already gone on for a few days (weeks). I'll call you at the end of the week if things haven't improved.*

or

Special Education Director:	*Look, Mrs. Golden, we don't have enough buses to get everyone to school on time. We give first priority to the regular kids who can really benefit from school.*
Mrs. Golden:	*If you need to stagger the bus schedule, it should be done fairly so everyone has a full school day.*
Special Education Director (growing more irritated):	*We can't change the whole schedule for one kid. Josh's class doesn't do much anyway.*
Mrs. Golden (controlled):	*Ms. Danielson, when I called, I thought we had a transportation problem. Are you telling me the program is poor as well?*
Special Education Director:	*No, I'm not. I'm telling you I can't do anything about the bus.*
Mrs. Golden:	*Can you tell me who can? Can the school superintendent do anything?*
Special Education Director:	*I don't know. Excuse me. I have another call coming in.*

It might help Mrs. Golden to know that transportation is part of Josh's IEP. If she calls her state's Parent Information Center, she could learn that, by law, for every day that Josh is late for school, he is entitled to compensatory education for the time he missed. Once Mrs. Golden makes that known to the special education director, she's likely to see some action in getting Josh to school. If this doesn't move the special education director to action, she can continue to go up the ladder, informing the superintendent of the law's requirements for compensatory education.

These examples, along with your own, give you an idea of the range of possible responses, good and bad. Being prepared to deal with difficulties makes it possible to better manage them when they arise. As you imagine these and other examples, think them through and act them out: "If she says this, then I'll say that," or "What if she says. . . . Hmmm! What will I say then? Oh, I know. . . ." and "If things get out of hand, I'll find a way to end the conversation and call later when I'm feeling calmer."

When you rehearse a potential situation, you are developing those new behaviors that you need and will use later on. Practice (alone or with the help of a friend or family member) will strengthen the assertive behaviors you want in your package of advocacy skills. With a little bit of private practice, you may feel you are ready for a live public performance. With any notes you need in front of you, you pick up the telephone and perform what you have rehearsed.

The telephone is a good place to start being assertive with school staff because you only have to be concerned with what you say. You don't have to worry about how you look, where you should sit, or if anyone is noticing that your knees are knocking or that you have bitten your nails to the quick. Your attention is focused only on what you say and they say. Also, you can close the conversation and make a fast exit if you become too nervous: You can invent an excuse, a *polite social lie,* such as your boss has just come into the office or the doorbell is ringing. You can have more excuses at hand and you shouldn't use the same one every time unless it's true.

In your first performance, you may or may not get what you want. Keep in mind that this is only the first step in your new approach to getting services. If you didn't get what you wanted, you have some material to review and evaluate:

Were you able to get past the secretary? Why not? Did you stress the need as strongly as you should have? What can you say next time that will make a stronger case? Did the other person's statements leave you angry and speechless (or intimidated)? What will you say next time? Did you follow up in writing so you will have a written record of this conversation?

You now have some idea of what treatment to expect when you call the school system, so you can decide what you will do in the next call. Now you're back to rehearsal and practice again, perhaps in front of a mirror. You are developing a routine of strengthening your new assertive behaviors in a series of stages:

- Expectations

- Private practice

- Live performance

- Examination and evaluation of your performance and that of the school professional

- Keeping a log of calls and responses

- Keeping hard copies of letters and e-mails

Repeat this routine every time you deal with the school system, and you will find new ways to improve your performance and increase your effectiveness.

Whenever your child has a school-related problem—his or her educational needs, including transportation and lunch, are not being met—you should be ready to pick up the telephone and call the school. You also use the telephone to make contact for sharing information, scheduling meetings, and, in later calls, reminding people that the problem still remains and that you are waiting for them to take action to solve it.

It is up to you to make certain that your child's needs are not neglected. If you had an elderly, ailing parent living with you when your heating system went off because of a power failure, you would watch the thermometer like a hawk and inform the power company that there was a person in your home who was at risk because of the situation. You would not be likely to wait without complaint for very long. Now, although the periods of reasonable waiting time for the power company to restore service and for the school to develop a beneficial program for your child differ in the crucial amounts, time is a real issue. Delays of weeks or months can be imperative for your child's welfare. In a very real way, children with disabilities are at risk if they do not receive the basic educational and support services they need. The telephone is one of your tools to keep school personnel on their toes; use it with them just as you do with others in your daily round of activities.

If you are put on hold and abandoned, do not fade away because the school staff are too busy or not interested. Instead, hang up, call back, and tell them you were on hold for 10 minutes; ask that they please put you through to the person you called. That is, treat them the same way you would treat the department store personnel when you are having a bill adjusted.

If you get upset during a telephone call, always keep in mind that you can terminate the call at any time. Being aware of this can sometimes help you stay calm long enough to complete the call. But if you feel you are working up to saying something you will regret, get off the telephone, but not by banging down the receiver. Instead, use a polite social lie because you may have to see this person again and you don't want him or her to have any real criticism of you that will interfere with developing a good program for your child. Always save the polite social lie only for those cases when you feel you must remove yourself from a situation in which you are about to become either aggressive or intimidated. It is an excuse given to the school system to buy you time to regain your control or confidence. In many cases, school people will suspect, if not realize, what you are doing and may even welcome an end to a conversation that promises to become unmanageable. You, of course, should never lie or distort information about your child: That is one of your most important contributions to the IEP process and must not be tampered with. But using a social lie to prevent an argument and maintain cordial relations with school staff can be a wise strategy in some circumstances. You can call back later when you are calmer and/or have more accurate information from your Parent Information Center or another source outside the school system.

If you are waiting for a return call, you need not hover over the telephone all day for several days just on the chance that someone will call back. On your first call, state the times you can be reached; for example, before noon or after 2:00 p.m. (after all, you may have to leave the office or go out to buy groceries). If your call is not returned, call back, tell them you are still waiting, and ask to be put through or given a reason for the delay and a time when the call will be returned.

If you are not getting through after a reasonable time, ask the person who is answering the telephone whether it would be helpful to write a letter to get to speak to the person you have been calling. If the question by itself is not enough to bring the desired person to the telephone, send an e-mail or sit down and write the letter. That will often bring results because requests you make by letter are stronger and harder to ignore than spoken requests.

USING E-MAIL

Many people use e-mail and expect that to work as well as the telephone. In one sense it is better because you can keep your own copy of the e-mail. Make sure the subject line adequately states your issue (e.g., Josh Golden's Transportation, Tomorrow's Meeting, Still Waiting for the Speech Evaluation). The contents of your e-mail should be direct, short, and formal. The down side of e-mail is that school staff may receive dozens of e-mails each day and may feel that they do not have time to open all of them. Among the ones left waiting for the next day or later could be your e-mail. If you are known for short e-mails, you increase your chances of your e-mail being opened more quickly.

SAMPLE E-MAIL

From: Golden 67@globalcast.net
To: E.Danielson@your town.gov
Sent: (date and time)
Subj: Late Bus Today

Dear Ms. Danielson,

Josh was picked up at 10:30 today. I expected him to be picked up at 8:05.

Please call me by the end of the school day. My number is 555-4321.

Sincerely,

Sarah Golden

If you do not get a response and there is some urgency to reach that person, make the telephone call and state that you are sending (or have sent) an e-mail about the burning issue. The combination does show an urgent need for contact.

The telephone should be your usual means of contact with the schools. In most cases, it will bring the desired results or at least an improvement in the situation, which may be satisfactory. You increase your chances of getting results by sharpening your everyday telephone skills. But when you know that you have made a reasonable effort to contact and share information with the schools, and using the telephone and/or e-mail isn't doing the job, you then turn to another basic and more formal skill—writing letters.

WRITING LETTERS

Letters are another basic tool, a more formal one that is generally used less frequently than the telephone and e-mail. Most of you will probably need to write only a few letters in your career as an educational advocate for your child; some of you may never need to pick up the pen. However, for a few of you, the pen, your computer, or even your old typewriter will become crucial instruments in getting services for your child.

If you write letters as part of your regular job or for social or volunteer activities, writing letters to school people may present little difficulty. However, many parents seldom have the need to write formal letters except for the occasional letter of complaint to a business or shop. Furthermore, letters to school staff may involve more than straightforward complaints, although complaints will generally be the reason you write such letters.

You may think to yourself, "Writing letters to the school system! Who? Me? I'd make a mess of it. I wouldn't know what to say." Your concern is understandable. But is a little of that concern coming from the old school pupil whose writing in English class came back red-penciled, corrected, slashed, commented on, and graded? You didn't worry about being graded on the telephone; instead, you were concerned about what you said and what response you got. And because you are no longer the school pupil, you can worry less about things like penmanship, creativity, fancy language, and form; instead, you are more concerned with facts—who, what, when, and where—and with getting the services your child needs. The kind of simple, direct letters you may have written to the gas company or the Better Business Bureau will serve as well for the school personnel.

Sample Letter 1 is short and simple, but it does the job. It gives the information about the problem (transportation), the parent's past efforts to have the problem corrected (including the number of telephone calls and dates), and where the parent can be reached. It also states what the parent wants in this case—the bus to come on time. Of course, when writing letters to school staff, remember that you should keep a copy for your own records.

SAMPLE LETTER 1

October 13, 2010

110 Main Street
Your Town, State 00000
555-0123

Ms. Bette Danielson
Director of Special Education
Local School
Your Town, State ZIP code

Dear Ms. Danielson,
Josh's bus is coming to pick him up 1 hour after school starts. He is missing a lot of school and he should be in school for a full day.

I have called you six times (September 22 and 29, and October 1, 7, 11, and 13) and was not able to reach you. I left messages with your secretary but you have not called me back.

Will you please arrange to have Josh picked up on time and call me so that I'll know everything has been taken care of? You can reach me at work (555-1023) from 8:30 a.m. to 3:30 p.m.

Sincerely,
Sarah Golden

Sample Letter 2 is another simple letter that can be written when telephone calls have not done the job. This letter, also short and simple like the first sample letter, reminds the principal of previous conversations in which the parent tried to get the school people to do their job (to set up the meeting to develop the IEP) and of the time that has gone by without any action by them. It also requests action from the principal. Mr. Hunter could have included the specific dates on which he talked to the teacher and principal about getting the IEP process started. Doing that might have been a little more impressive and businesslike, but this letter has enough information to do the job.

SAMPLE LETTER 2

January 5, 2010
12 Broadway
Your Town, State Zip code
555-1234

Mr. Colin Larsen
Principal
Local School
Your Town, State ZIP code

Dear Mr. Larsen,

My daughter, Ellen, does not have an individualized education program yet.
I spoke to her teacher in October about setting up a meeting. Then I spoke
to you at the end of November and you said you would set up a meeting in
December, but it never happened. Now January is starting and Ellen still has
no IEP. Please set up a meeting right away so that Ellen can have the program she needs and to which she is entitled.

I recently learned that the law requires that each special education student begin school with an IEP in place and that any day without an IEP in
place is a day of noncompliance. This opens the school to meet the requirement that compensatory time must be given to those days without an IEP.

I will be waiting to hear from you.

Sincerely,
Basil Hunter

Sample Letter 3 is an example of a letter that follows telephone
calls or meetings when a school person has said something that the parent believes to be in violation of the law. This letter is a request for confirmation, meaning that the parent writes what he or she thinks the
educator said and asks that the educator confirm or deny the statement.

SAMPLE LETTER 3

April 20, 2010

3636 Park Ave.
Apartment 2B
Your Town, State ZIP code
555-2345

Dr. Gregory Simon
Superintendent
Local School District
Your Town, State ZIP code

Dear Dr. Simon:

When we met in your office on April 7 to discuss the location of my son Russell's program in the far wing of the third floor of Greenwood Junior High School and my request to have the program transferred to the main building of the school, you said some things that bothered me. I understood you to say that it would be impossible to move the class because all of the other classrooms are being used by the regular students and that they need to be able to change classes quickly.

Did I understand correctly? Are you planning to keep Russell's class so isolated? Please let me hear from you as soon as possible since I am very concerned about Russell's program.

Sincerely,
Dolly LaVigna

The request for confirmation is a tricky letter to write. It should be used only to advance your cause and not just to vent your anger or distress when you suspect that you or your child has been insulted. (Often a parent's direct looks during meetings will put an end to careless comments.) When you write this kind of letter, you are in fact giving the school person the opportunity to deny, rephrase, or qualify his or her statements and to reassure you that efforts are being made to resolve the problem. Because your letter is a record of statements you think you heard, the educator is often eager to write his or her "you-must-have-misunderstood-me" letter, also for the record. That return letter usually includes a statement of the school professional's efforts to correct the situation. What may have been an unpleasant situation for you now can be turned to your advantage. The administrator's written intention or promise, signed and dated, can be used by you as leverage to improve your child's program. You can hold the administrator accountable for his or her own statements, which are now a matter of record: The return letter, carefully preserved in your file, is that record.

Some parents will need to write a letter rejecting the IEP. These parents may have done a marvelous job of advocating, but they were unable to reach agreement with school people about the IEP because the school people did not share the parent's views, were not able to write the program's goals in precise language, or resisted the parent's requests because of budgetary reasons. Sample Letter 4 is an example of a letter rejecting the IEP. In this letter, Mr. Jordan makes it clear that he is rejecting the IEP and backs up his rejection with some specific complaints about the program. He indicates that he is willing to work with the school to try to reach an agreement; he wants to negotiate further, rather than move immediately to confrontation. His letter not only informs the school people but also stands as a record of his quick and interested response to the IEP and of his willingness to pursue the issue to some mutual agreement.

SAMPLE LETTER 4

June 1, 2010

123 Elm Street
Your Town, State ZIP code
555-1234

Dr. Winnie Baker:
Although I agree with the class placement for my son Aidan, the extra support of a half-time teaching assistant, and the daily use of the computer for his classwork, I am rejecting Aidan's IEP, which I received in yesterday's mail.

The program does not match the items we agreed on at the meeting. For example, Aidan should be integrated into the regular gym three times per week and in the regular language arts program daily. The objectives for Aidan's math program in the resource room are fuzzy. The plan does not meet Aidan's needs.

What is the next step? I can meet with you during June or July to see if the program can be corrected and we can come to an agreement.

I will be waiting to hear from you.

Sincerely,
Matthew Jordan

cc: Parent Information Center

None of the four sample letters are fancy or long; they are short, clear, simply worded, and to the point. Remember, the best letter is the shortest one necessary to do the job. Also, short letters are often the first ones to get read. When school people receive letters several pages in length, they may glance at them and set them aside until they have more time.

There are, however, some basic, simple mechanics to writing a businesslike letter to schools. Your address and telephone number (or number where you can be reached) should always be included on your letter so that the school staff can easily contact you. Dates are important, so always put a date on your letter. When you need to review your file on your child's educational program, you will want to know when you did what, or how long it took the school to do something about the problem. Next year or even later this year, you may not remember in which month you wrote the letter.

The school person's full name, title, and location at the top of your letter is not only polite and businesslike, it is information you need for your records and future activities, and that you can share if necessary with people you may want to ask to help you deal with the school, such as representatives from parent organizations or legal advocacy organizations. You want to make it easy for them to advocate with you. By sharing your letters, they will not waste time trying to track down school people.

But what if you don't know a person's full name or title? Call the school and ask for it:

> **Mr. Jordan:** *Would you give me Mrs. Baker's full name please?*
>
> **Secretary:** *Do you mean Miss Rachel Baker at Southern Junior High School?*
>
> **Mr. Jordan:** *No, I am talking about the Mrs. Baker who is at the high school where my son is a student.*
>
> **Secretary:** *Then you must mean Dr. Winnie Baker.*
>
> **Mr. Jordan:** *I think so, but this person is chair of the committee for my son's IEPs.*
>
> **Secretary:** *That would be Dr. Baker, who chairs all high school IEPs.*
>
> **Mr. Jordan:** *Thank you. What is her official address?*

Don't be afraid to ask how the name is spelled; some names have very strange spellings. And don't be timid about taking up people's time to get the information right. Your correctly addressed letter will expedite the process. A letter addressed simply to Mrs. Baker could go to the wrong person or get lost in the school system. Dr. Winnie Baker will not only be pleased to see you know her correct name and position but also will know that you are a businesslike advocate.

Remember, the information in the letter is just that—information. It is not opinion, rumor, or hearsay. You will deal in facts, dates, people, services poorly given or denied, and what you want from the school system. You will write in simple, clear language to prevent misunderstanding and keep the letter short to encourage the recipient to read it immediately (because you are in suspense while waiting for an answer). If you are not sure that your letter says what you want it to say, read it to a friend or relative in person or over the telephone. Discuss it. If it doesn't express what you meant to say, enlist the other person's help to get it right. Just don't fuss excessively or forever; a simple letter will do the job.

The closing of your letter should include your signature and your name (typed or clearly printed under your signature). If you want to be called at work, include your work number. In short, make it very easy for school people to know who you are and where to reach you. Your carefully composed letter provides no excuse for delay in contacting you.

Should your letter be typed or written? After you have reread the rough copy of your letter and made your corrections (perhaps you deleted or revised a sentence that sounded sarcastic, included some important dates, or restated your request more strongly), you may find yourself worrying about legibility and neatness, especially if you don't type. Good typing is better because it's prettier, cleaner, and easier to read, but it is not essential. If you do not have access to a computer and spell check, perhaps you have a friend or child who types; enlist his or her help in preparing the letter. But if your collection of available family and friends consists of bad, worse, and awful typists, a carefully handwritten or hand-printed letter is far better than a typed letter full of errors and crossed-out words. One parent of limited resources (no computer or access to a computer) tore a page out of a spiral-bound notebook and wrote her letter with the required information. On her next grocery trip, she photocopied her letter, curly edges and all, and then sent it on. It did the job. As always, you want the school people to understand the problem immediately and act on it.

Your Copy of Your Letter

Whether you type or handwrite your letter, always keep a clear copy for yourself. This means a printed copy from your computer, a reproduction on a copy machine, or even a copy using carbon paper if you still have any on hand. When you are dealing with the school people, you need to know what you have said and when you said it. You should not rely on the school system to provide you with that information.

Just as you get and keep a receipt as a record of your purchase when you buy something, you should also keep a record of your correspondence with the schools. Your copy of the letter done on a copier or computer is a receipt to keep as a record of your request or complaint. No matter how rushed you are to get the letter out, never mail it without keeping a clear copy for your personal file, one sharp enough to make another clear copy to share with other people who want to assist you in your advocacy efforts. (See the section Using Your Allies in this chapter.) All of your letters, sent and received, will become an important part of your records.

Certified Mail

Certified mail means that the post office makes a special event of your letter and gives you a record when you request a certified receipt, in the form of a postcard, of when the letter was delivered and who received and signed for it. Some people use certified mail for every letter they send to school systems and agencies. However, certified mail not only requires more of your time, energy, and money but it also sets a certain tone. It implies that the school personnel will only take action when they are tracked down or pushed. Unless you have strong reason to expect resistance, the first letter can go out by regular mail; it will usually receive a response. But if you do not get one after you've waited a reasonable time, placed a follow-up telephone call reminding them you are waiting, and have sent a note or e-mail (copy to file), you may want to send out a second letter by certified mail. (See the section Special Records later in this chapter.)

In general, the more collaborative your relationship is with the school, the more you will use the telephone, e-mail, and regular mail; the more strained, complicated, or adversarial your relationship is, the greater the need for certified mail.

Formal Copies to Others

When the school system is slow to take action, you may want to let the school know that you are sending copies of your letters to others interested in helping your child get school services. There is a standard format you can use that will indicate on your letter that you are doing this (see Sample Letter 4). In the bottom left-hand corner of your letter, show that you are sending "carbon copies" (cc's) by writing:

cc: Parent Information Center

Rep. Mark Forsyth

Mrs. Valerie Perske

Here, the parent is sending copies to three places. You may wish to send to only one or you may wish to send more, depending on how many people you think should know about the action you are taking. In addition to "carbon copies," you can also send "blind copies," in which the names are not listed in your letter.

Do not make the mistake that Kim Chen made. He sent one copy to the state department of education. The department did not feel the urgency an advocacy group would have and filed Mr. Chen's letter for some unspecified future review. Mr. Chen waited for enforcement that never came.

Formal copies can often help to move resistant administrators to action. However, if you have a good relationship with the school people, you may want to hold back on using carbon copies. Like certified mail, they imply that the school people need some pushing to do their job. You can always make copies of your old correspondence later and send them to whomever you choose. For your records, you should note who has copies of your letters.

KEEPING RECORDS: YOURS AND THEIRS

"What do I know about keeping records?" you might be saying. "I'm not a clerk or an accountant. As for a file, the few pieces of paper I have could fit in a standard envelope with room enough left over to hold all of my household bills!"

In fact, just about all of you keep some records. Don't you save your canceled checks (or copies), paid receipts, and tax forms; write appointments on a calendar; have a photo album or baby book; or even save old tickets stubs from games and events you've been to? If so, then you do keep records of events and activities in your life.

"But they're not in a file or a filing system," you say. Are they in a drawer, a shoebox, an album, a bowl, or an envelope? Can you find them when you want them? Then you already have a filing system that can do the job for you and your child. But you need to know what you should be keeping and collecting for your child's special IDEA file.

Records You Already Have

Think about whether, over the years, you have collected any of these things:

- Notes from teachers, either on pieces of paper or in books that go back and forth from school to home

- Notes from specialists both inside and outside the school system

- Notes in your log/notebook you have taken before, during, or after your visit to your child's school or your phone conversations with the school people

- Notes from anyone that describe your child's achievements and failures, progress, or lack of progress

- Samples of your child's school work or creations from past years

- Reports from camps or recreation and community activities that describe your child's skills and needs

- Reports and evaluations from doctors and other medical specialists

- School reports, including report cards, evaluations, and education programs for your child

- Letters that the schools have sent to you—notices of meetings to develop your child's education programs, notices of suspension or exclusion of your child from school, and denials of your requests for better services and placement

- Copies of letters you have written to the school system—letters of complaint or request

- Letters (or copies) written on your child's behalf by outside professionals, advocacy organizations, or lawyers

Many of you will have some of these records, a few of you who are already active in your planning and advocacy may have practically everything on the list, and some of you have nothing except for a few of your child's schoolwork papers. That's okay: You can now begin to save and to collect the various papers, evaluations, and official documents you need. Make a list of what you have and prepare to add to it. Some of the basic items for your file are letters (or copies of letters) that you have received or written, copies of special education laws and regulations, and materials on your rights and your child's rights from advocacy, parent, or legal organizations. How useful will all of this information be to you? If you are lucky, you may use very little of it. However, even lucky parents can't predict which information they will need. If you have to work hard to get the school system to comply with the law in providing services to your child, you will need every paper you can get, so save everything. When the time comes, you will be glad that you have created a record file that is as comprehensive as you can make it. After all, in managing your bills, you have hard copies of your canceled checks because you know that if the gas or electric company makes a mistake in billing you, your canceled checks are the information and evidence you need to prove you have paid your bill. Information is help and power. Here's how to get more.

School and Agency Records

Schools and other agencies (e.g., hospitals, clinics, camps, special services) have stacks of records. Sharing records between agencies is a common practice. Parents are often asked to sign a release for a "mysterious" document—an evaluation, test result, or report—to allow one agency to send a record to another. The document is "mysterious" when the parents are not given an opportunity to read and review the information they are being requested to release to some other agency or to the school. When parents cooperate by signing releases without seeing the documents, they are acting out of ignorance, allowing the professionals to share and reproduce information that may be harmful through impressions or errors or insulting to the child and also to the family. In order to be a responsible parent and advocate, you must know what information is being given out on your child, and that means you read the records.

In the past, a number of assumptions and prejudicial statements were entered into students' school records, such as "antisocial child," "hostile parent," "father may have a drinking problem," or "student lacks skills and should be tracked for lower level vocational program." Statements like these were based on educators' impressions, often with very little (if any) evidence to back them up. However, the statements stayed in the students' files, and often teachers looking at the files decided that a student or parent was a troublemaker and treated the person accordingly. This type of treatment had an effect on the students' programs and progress. Parents never saw these statements, so they were unable to fight back.

IDEA gives parents the right to read reports, correct the official record by having the school amend the record or by placing a statement prepared by the parents into it, limit the access of other people to their child's records, and have copies of the records (for which the parents may have to pay). Students over the age of 18 are also entitled to read their school records. Not only do these rights guarantee that parents can have the information they need to be good advocates, but they have also caused those educators who used to write biased and occasionally libelous statements into records to become careful about what they write. With the coming of the Education for All Handicapped Children Act of 1975 (PL 95-142) (the basis of IDEA), a lot of records were cleaned up. Chances are you will not see judgments about "cold, disinterested parents" in your child's file nowadays. If you do, you must have that file corrected so it will be factual and accurate.

You may find errors in professional evaluations as well. One parent reported that her child's last medical evaluation stated that he had multiple evaluations when he had only one and that the child could do only the most rudimentary arithmetic when he had excellent math skills (this misinformation resulted from the difficulties of a stranger assessing the child in a strange environment). Read everything.

Some schools may resist your efforts to read and copy your child's records. You must keep repeating to yourself and to them, "I have a right to these records." If you are timid, rehearse what you will do and say before you go to the school. If the school people resist, go back with a copy of the regulations or a statement from your state department of education notifying you of your legal right to read the records. If they continue to resist, write a simple letter to the superintendent, describing your efforts and asking him or her to make the records available to you.

Eventually you will be sitting in the school office with the complete (cumulative) record in front of you. (Make sure you have the complete school record for your child and not a summary record, which is a partial record.) You have brought your list of what you already have in your own file and are about to review the school file to see what is in there and what you will want for your file. You will take notes on some documents; you will see others that you want in your file or that are too long for you to read and understand in the time you will be in the school office. In reviewing the file, you may realize that some of the documents are missing, such as an old speech evaluation, the teacher's reports from 2007, or a letter from you that you asked to be included in your child's file. Make a note of the missing item(s) and inform the school staff that the file is incomplete. You make your list of the school file. Now you have two lists:

Home file	**School file**
IEP 2009	Teacher reports 2008, 2009
IEP 2010	IEPs 2009, 2010, 2011
Penmanship papers 2008	Intelligence test results 2008
Camp Summertime Report 2008	Speech-language therapist's evaluation 2008
Telephone notes 2010	Psychologist's report 2007
My letter on transportation problems 2010	
Notes on missing items	

When you have finished, decide what you want: perhaps the 2011 IEP (you should have had a copy anyway), the results of the intelligence testing, and the evaluations of the speech-language therapist and psychologist. You might also want a teacher's report from 2008 to show your spouse because you think it contains some statements that should be removed.

When you approach the principal or his or her assistant to ask for copies, you may encounter some resistance:

"I'm afraid the person who does the copying is tied up now. Perhaps another time."

"Now, Mrs. Carroll, what do you want these reports for? They are full of professional language that you can't really understand. I'll tell you what you want to know about your child."

"We can't be spending the taxpayers' money to reproduce all of this stuff for dissatisfied parents." (You may want to remind the principal that you are also a taxpayer and that there was a time when many parents were paying taxes to support general education while their own children with disabilities were denied educational services by the school system.)

"This teacher's (or psychologist's) note is a personal communication. It can't be copied or even removed from the file."

First, respond with reasonableness to these attempts to limit your access to your child's records:

"I would like to make an appointment to read the record. I could be available on. . ."

"I can wait a reasonable time for the copies and will be happy to return tomorrow or the next day when the copies are made."

"I will pay a reasonable cost for the copies."

"I would like to make a reasonable effort to read the reports and prepare a list of questions on what I don't understand."

"The professionals' notes in my child's file are part of her record, and therefore I am entitled to copies."

By presenting yourself as the informed, committed, and businesslike advocate, you will get the copies of the records you want. You may have to resort to your telephone and writing skills to get them (adding telephone notes and copies of your letters or e-mails to your growing file), but your persistence will pay off.

Medical records from hospitals and clinics may be hard to get. In all states, patients have the right to information. However, your physical or other health professional may resist giving you access to the full medical record. You should persevere, especially if you believe that your child's health status is relevant to his or her educational program. Some medical professionals are comfortable only when they are sending information to other professionals (e.g., from the clinic to the school) because of their own "mere parents" myths. This practice is a put-down, but remember that once the information or report is in the school file, you have the right to see it and have a copy.

When you have begun to collect the various records we have discussed, the shoebox you had in mind for the job may be looking smaller and smaller. How will you organize all of these papers into a manageable file?

Organizing Your Records: The Best Method

Any container (e.g., large manila envelope, shoebox, small carton, drawer, file box) that will hold the papers you have collected with room for more is fine for the job. But if setting up a fancy system helps you feel businesslike and confident, then do it. The key to a well-organized file is access—your records are in one place and you can put your hands on just the paper you want in a few minutes. Then what is the best way to organize your file for this kind of access and efficiency?

The best filing method is the one that works for you. Remember, it's your file and you are the one who will be using it. You can set it up alphabetically, by year, or by category (e.g., schools, specialists, camps). If you are good at remembering names, you can file from *A* to *Z*; if you remember times and events better, you can file by years. There is no one system for filing. A log (a bound, loose-leaf notebook or special file on your computer) is essential to your system; it will help you remember whom you contacted, when you contacted them, and what you and they said. Any time you deal with the school system or other agencies, make an entry in your log. Your entry should include these items:

- Date

- Name of person you contacted (by telephone, e-mail, letter, or visit)

- Person's agency and position or title

- Topics discussed, promises made, and deadlines for action

It will also help to keep the names, titles, and telephone numbers of people you are and will be dealing with on the inside cover or the first page of your log. These should include the following:

- Your school superintendent and school principal

- Your special education director

- Specialists who are working or have worked with your child

- Resources for information and support

You may not have all of these when you start; you will be adding as you continue your work on your child's behalf.

You may not need or even use all of the information you collect for your files. But you are prepared to deal with almost any issue that may arise. The prepared and informed parent is the effective advocate.

Special Records

If, in your advocacy efforts, you are constantly meeting resistance or indifference, you may want to resort to certified letters. Because the postcard or computer notice that serves as your record that the letter was delivered can be easily lost, staple or tape it to your log or folder as soon as you receive it.

Photographs are a special kind of record. Very few of you will ever need to take pictures, but there are a few cases in which they are necessary, and they are very powerful records. If your child has been physically abused (e.g., bruised, bitten, otherwise injured), if your child is on medication and beginning to look downright sickly, or if your child is roller-skating despite the school's insistence that his motor skills are poor, you should seriously consider taking a photograph of your child's condition.

This can be a hard thing for parents to do in cases of abuse. They naturally prefer to take happy and attractive photographs of their children, and they want to forget how their children looked when they were abused. Usually, however, parents can't forget—they keep their mental pictures—but they can't use their memories as hard facts. Pictures are especially necessary when the children involved cannot communicate and therefore cannot provide testimony on their own behalf. If you ever find your child in such a situation, take pictures, as heartbreaking as that may be, and you will have strong evidence to prevent a reoccurrence for your child and other children.

One parent regretted the fact that she had taken no photos of her son who has emotional disturbances and brain injury when she had to remove him from camp. He had "acted out," and, in being "restrained" by a staff person, sustained multiple bruises about the head and face. She was concerned that an unqualified staff person who had injured her son was allowed to continue to work with people with disabilities, but she had collected no evidence to back up her complaint.

Another parent of a child in a state institution was able to bring about a review and change of her child's medication simply by showing pictures of him before the medication was started and afterwards, in his deteriorated state, to a physician outside the institution, who took action to get the child off of the medication. The child's appearance and health immediately improved.

Pictures, videotapes, and audiotapes of happy events and activities can be important evidence in making a case for your child's skills. For example, if the school staff insist that your child's motor skills are poor, pull out your snapshots (or have the meeting set up for your videotapes or DVDs) of your child roller-skating or cross-country skiing. If they minimize your child's language skills, play audiotapes you have made at home that demonstrate your child's competence. When you have clear evidence of your child's capabilities, use that evidence.

Releasing Records and Signing Forms

You have been concerned so far with gathering documents, but you also need to be concerned about how your child's records are used and to whom they are released. In the past, parents were denied access to their children's records when practically everybody else—credit bureaus, police departments, mental health clinics, and even professionals doing research—could request and get confidential information about your child. IDEA has put an end to that. Not only do you have the right to read or copy your child's records but also you must give your written consent for other people (except for school employees) to have access to your child's file.

You should never, never sign a blanket release for your child's records. You must make sure the school asks for a release every time that they are sharing information and that you know what the information is and to whom it is going.

Even in the case of school employees, you and your child are protected by law: The school must keep a list of personnel who have access to your child's file. Make sure you see this list. You may want to ask why certain individuals are on it. You may find out for the first time that a particular specialist is seeing your child. You might want to ask why the psychologist is counseling your child with learning disabilities when the school has been reluctant to provide a learning disabilities specialist to help your child with her academic needs; you may find that your school has assumed your child's emotional needs are a priority when you feel her academic needs should come first. The information may be new, startling, and occasionally disagreeable. But the informed advocate is in a position to be a better advocate.

When you are asked to sign a release for your child, you should know several things before you sign:

- Who wants the records

- For what purpose(s)

- The content of the specific record, report, or evaluation being released

Before you sign any release, you should know what you are signing away. The only way to know is to read the record. You may even want to ask for a copy of the specific record for your files.

Remember, you do not have to sign the release if you feel that releasing the information will not benefit your child. When you are careful, even stingy, about confidential information about your child, you are merely protecting your child's rights. If you have in the past signed what is called a *blanket release,* giving permission to the schools to release any or all information to a number of people or agencies, don't be alarmed. You can fix that by writing a note to the school system withdrawing your permission to release records and explaining that you feel you did not understand the seriousness of the release form. A letter, rather than a telephone call, is needed here because the school has a written record of your earlier permission; you want them to have a written record of the withdrawal of your consent. Because of IDEA, few school people will ask you to sign a blanket release because they know that it is a very weak piece of paper and that they would have a hard time defending their actions if the parents chose to complain. Should you be offered such a blanket release form to sign, politely refuse and inform the school person that the law requires informed consent before records are released, which means that you need to know the specifics before you agree or refuse to sign.

Never, never sign anything unless you feel that you fully understand the agreement. A written release is one form of agreement; the IEP is another. When you are asked to sign the IEP, check to make sure that all of the information you have agreed upon is entered into the form. Do not accept the "trust me and we'll fill the blanks in later" approach. Signing a half-empty IEP is like giving a blank check signed by you to the school staff who will later write in the amount, which is almost guaranteed to be fewer or less adequate services for your child. You should insist that the agreement be complete and that you understand it before you sign it.

Even if the IEP is completely filled in at the meeting and you think you are satisfied with what you see, you will want to take home a copy to read again without the pressure of the meeting before you sign. In some cases, the completed IEP may be mailed to you. When you have your completed copy and have carefully reviewed it, then if you approve, you sign where it says "I accept the program." You don't like the program? Then sign where it says "I do not accept the program." If you are not sure about the IEP, tell the planning team you want more time to think about it. School people are usually eager to close the deal, and most will try to get you to sign on the spot. Don't do it! This is an important decision, and you are wise to take your time. The law is on your side.

These concerns about releasing and signing documents are serious ones. Your responsibility to your child is to do your homework, speak your piece, and take the time you need to make the right decisions. This section on records is an important one because records are the rock on which you build your case for better and more beneficial services for your child. Making the case for your child is hard work, demanding that you bring both emotional and physical energy to the task. You shouldn't have to do it alone. In fact, don't do it alone! Allies and resources are available to you that you already know, and you will seek out more in the course of your advocacy career.

USING YOUR ALLIES

In your everyday life, you use allies regularly. When you had to take your child to the hospital emergency room and were shaking so badly you couldn't drive, you called a friend or neighbor who drove you. Or, when you impulsively signed the contract with the door-to-door salesperson, you called the Better Business Bureau or a consumer protection agency for information and advice on what to do because you were unsure about whether you were being cheated. Another time, your trash still wasn't being picked up after many calls to the town hall, so you called your town representative, who took care of it. And when you were having trouble assembling the Christmas toys for your children, you called a friend who came over, read the directions with you (or for you), and together you managed to do the job.

In much the same way, you can call on individuals and organizations who will give you the help and support you need to be a strong and effective parent advocate. Use their information, skills, talents, interests, and power to get the right program for your child. But who are these people and what can they do for you?

The Advocate's Advocate

Perhaps the single most important ally you have is the person you choose to be your personal advocate, your special buddy. Ideally, the person you choose to be your personal advocate should have these qualities:

- Cares about you and your child
- Agrees that your child has the right to an education that benefits him or her
- Is willing to commit some time and energy to you and your child
- Can work in a collaborative way with you
- Is willing to learn something about your child's needs and IDEA

- Can speak up when necessary
- Knows his or her personal strengths and weaknesses

Having all of these qualities may be a tall order for most of the people you know who come to mind:

"My neighbor seems really sympathetic, but I think she feels special education is just baby-sitting and a favor."

"My brother would be terrific, but every time we try to do something together, it ends up in an argument."

"If only my friend Sonia were here instead of in another state, she'd help me."

Three strikes? Not really—perhaps that neighbor can be converted to a strong believer in special education through your convincing arguments.

Keep going. Who else is there? Other neighbors or friends? Your clergy (or a recommended member of his or her congregation)? Professionals outside of the school system who have worked with your child? Ask yourself if they would have enough time available to help you and at what financial cost. Mentally explore all possibilities: You are looking for someone who you can trust and who cares about your child. Parents assume that when they go together, that serves the requirements of advocacy. But unfortunately, they are almost treated as one unit and are poor witnesses to any disagreements with the school system. One advantage is that some school systems do still seem to feel that a man's time is more important than a woman's. Father may get more attention but no improvement in the plan.

Okay, now you've done the review and you think you've come up with the right person(s), or you've come to the conclusion that there is no one to help you. No one? Well, you wouldn't be the first parent to walk a lonely road. But before you give up, ask yourself if you are being too critical. If you are convinced that you are not demanding absolute perfection, then you must begin to look for help outside the circle of people you know.

Organizations (perhaps you are already a member) do exist that may be able to help you find an advocate. These are generally parent or citizen groups organized around a specific disability or across a range of disabilities. You may already have some material about these organizations in your house. If not, search on your computer or look in the yellow pages of the telephone book under social services; contact any organization that looks promising. The first one may not be the right one; tell the person at the other end a little about your problem and ask him or her to refer you to an organization that can help you. When you do reach the right group, explain your problem and tell them that you need help in getting a suitable education for your child. They should respond in one or more of these ways:

- Taking your name and other information

- Transferring you to a person who could take your case

- Setting up an appointment for you to meet an advocate

- Recommending a person or agency in a nearby town who can help you

- Giving or sending information in everyday language to help you understand your rights and your child's

You might be thinking, "But these are strangers, and you said it was important that the parent's personal advocate should care about the parent and the child. How can strangers care?"

These strangers can be the friends you haven't met. Most of the people who work (volunteer or paid) as advocates for students with disabilities have a strong emotional, professional, and moral commitment to getting good educational services for all students with disabilities. They will care about your child because he or she is a member of a class of children who in the past may have been deprived or forgotten. You can rely on them to help you.

Your organizational advocate will want to meet with you to discuss your child and your school system and to review the records you already have. The advocate may bring you information about the law, a copy of the law, the regulations, or how-to handouts. He or she may also plan to be with you at the IEP team meeting and other important meetings after that.

In some cases, such as instances in which parents live in sparsely populated areas or when the organization is overloaded and understaffed, you may have to do most of the work on your own. That need not mean you are completely alone. You can work out an arrangement where you keep in touch with the organizational advocate or advisor by telephone. Ask to call before meetings to get advice and after meetings to report and ask for more advice; offer to send documents (e.g., IEPs, evaluations, correspondence) to your long-distance advocate for review and comments. Even with problems of distance and understaffing, if the school system is acting in flagrant violation of the law, the long-distance advocate may put in an appearance at a later meeting. Just when all hope seems lost, the cavalry arrives.

The day of the first IEP meeting arrives. You have an arrangement worked out with your long-distance advocate over the telephone, but you still have to go to the meeting alone. Enter the "warm body advocate." This is the person who may lack many or most of the qualities you look for in an advocate. He or she is a well-meaning friend or relative you have asked (or perhaps even begged or pressured) to come with you. You have made it clear that your warm body advocate only has to be there, look alert, and nod once in a while when you are talking and that he or she doesn't have to say anything except possibly, "Hi! I'm Fran Santos, and I'm here to help my neighbor, Marsha Brant."

To the school people, your friend is seen as a witness to what goes on in the meeting. Your friend in fact may be a very poor witness, but the school people don't know that, and past statements such as, "That kid doesn't belong in a public school" become "Well, now, fitting your child into the program presents some difficulties. It may take a little time." For the parent who has ever been on the receiving end of cruel statements, this kind of improvement makes it possible for the parent to at least function at the meeting.

Occasionally, even the warm body advocate comes through. Your friend may tell you after the meeting that the principal wasn't listening to anything you said or that the physical education teacher seemed interested in everything you said about the things Linc does around the house. Halfway through the meeting, your warm body advocate might even burst out with, "How can you say Linc is only good for 10 to 15 minutes of work when I watched him yesterday rake and bag leaves for 2 hours?"

Just having a friend at a meeting is a source of support, but if that "warm body" turns into an observer, a source of information, and a champion for your child, you may find that you have created an advocate.

Your personal advocate can do the following things:

- Listen to you talk about your concerns, fears, strengths, and weaknesses, what you want for your child, and what you think your child needs

- Help you sort out all of these things into the important and not-so-important (set priorities), into the realistic and the not-yet-manageable, and into solid data and areas that need more information

- Serve as a spokesperson and a source of information about your child, either through direct personal knowledge or indirectly through reading your records

- Be a coplanner with you as you develop a plan of action

- Be your witness and source of personal support as you go through the process of getting a good school program for your child

We will talk more specifically about the role of your personal advocate when we get into the IEP process in Chapter 7. What you need to know right now is that you don't have to do the job alone. Help is out there. Getting help may mean that you have to reach out aggressively to other people, perhaps setting aside your pride or your timidity. When you find your IDEA buddy or personal advocate, you will feel the load lighten and the job begin to look manageable.

"What if my buddy is like me? It could be like two of us going over Niagara Falls in a barrel, instead of one. We wouldn't have enough information or power to change things."

Fortunately, you have available still other allies who you haven't considered yet and who are a powerful source of information and pressure.

ORGANIZATIONS

Both private and public agencies are out there that are set up to help you. They include parent and citizen organizations such as United Cerebral Palsy, The Arc (formerly Association for Retarded Citizens of the United States), and other organizations that operate on national, state, and local levels. There are also parent information centers in every state, operated and staffed primarily by parents and other family members; the major role of these centers is to provide information and training about IDEA to parents and advocates.

All of these organizations can be sources of information and pressure. Contact them by telephone, e-mail, or letter and say you need help with getting an appropriate education for your child. Tell them what you want to know and explain to them what you think your child needs. They will send you information about the law, about the nearest chapter of the organization, and perhaps about other organizations in your vicinity that can offer you information and assistance, such as developmental disabilities councils and protection and advocacy agencies, public interest law firms, and other special projects or advocacy agencies. When you have received and read the information sent to you by various organizations, you will begin to feel a little more assured about the job ahead of you. But other questions may start coming to mind, and your personal advocate may be raising questions too. Write them all down; don't be afraid they will sound dumb. You'll learn that the only "dumb" questions are those that aren't asked.

When you have collected a stack of information, pamphlets, brochures, and laws, start by reading the easiest materials (shortest, simplest language, and largest print), then read the ones that are a little harder. By the time you get to the most difficult ones (with the fine print), you will already have learned quite a bit about your rights and those of your child from your earlier reading. Read all of the materials; underline and mark them up. Later it will be easier for you to find just the line or phrase you want. Share the informational materials with your personal advocate. You want him or her to be as well-informed as you are becoming. Perhaps your advocate is better at reading and understanding the information than you and can help you to understand more. That's a bonus. Maybe he or she needs the material explained and you have to try to make those explanations. That's a bonus too. Every time you have to explain the law, you get better at understanding it and at talking about your child's rights.

Are there other ways that private organizations can help you?

Newsletters

Get on their mailing lists to receive their regular publications, which may contain up-to-date information on the law; notices of meetings where you can meet other parents who share your problems (and may have solved theirs); and notices of workshops, training programs, and conferences that deal with getting appropriate education.

Workshops and Conferences

These are opportunities for you to hear about special education problems and solutions. They give you a chance to have some of your questions answered and to make contact with people who can be a source of help, such as a parent who has a child like yours or an agency that is monitoring education in your town, county, or state, and wants to hear from parents of students with disabilities.

Advocates

The organizations may help you find a personal advocate to work with you from the beginning of your advocacy efforts or may offer to troubleshoot for you, should the going get rough. If later on you need a lawyer, they may also suggest some lawyers experienced in special education law.

Pressure

Organizations can serve as pressure groups to bear down on local or state departments of education when schools are in violation of the law. Your case could be the one they have been waiting for to swing into action. Or your letter to them describing your experiences with the school can bring forth the formal letter to you (or the school staff) stating that the school system is in violation of the law and that your child is entitled to the service you are asking for. (Send a copy to the school system, keeping the original for your file. Because school systems don't like to see their sins in print, they may finally come through with the desired service.) The organization may even send a representative to go with you to the IEP meeting or the mediation session ("I am Mrs. Whaley, representing the Statewide Parent Coalition, and I am here to assist the parents in this case"). Because organizations represent numbers of people (as opposed to your one or two), they can often put effective pressure on school systems.

Public agencies, such as your state department of education, are also supposed to serve you and provide you with information. State agencies are funded with public money to provide service to the public, but unfortunately they seldom put pressure on local school systems unless some outside group leans heavily on them. There are exceptions, of course, but they are rare. State agencies, like the school systems discussed in Chapter 4, tend toward business as usual and do little to help the parent advocate get the appropriate educational services. Do not rely on your state agency to pressure your school system. What you need from your state department of education, besides enforcement, and what you are entitled to get, is information. You can ask for and get copies of the state and federal laws, regulations, and departmental policy statements that go out to school systems. Call or write asking for specific information. This can be difficult when you are asking for agency policy statements because you may need to know the title, number, and/or date of the statement. If you are lucky, you will reach one of those dedicated public servants who work to improve service; this kind of person can be enormously helpful to you in tracking down the information and sending it out to you. Be appreciative. However, you may reach someone who doesn't care or whose hands are tied. You will have to use your skills or allies to get the information, such as a formal letter of request (stating your willingness to pay a reasonable cost, if necessary) or a letter or call from a private organization or your political representative.

Your state education agency may have already prepared some pamphlets on IDEA, which they are usually happy to send out. Get them if they are available; they have useful information in them. However, when you compare them with the advocacy pamphlets, you may find the state material has left out a few important (to parents) items of information, such as the parent's right to take a personal advocate to IEP meetings or the right of the child to have a second independent evaluation when the parents believe the first evaluation to be inadequate.

Know your agencies and what they can do for you. Don't hesitate to call on them when you need their help or information; public agencies are supported by citizens like you. You should consider joining organizations that try to help parents with children like yours. You can support them by membership, contributions, by being active (a little or a lot), and ultimately by offering yourself (the successful parent advocate) to serve as personal advocate to a parent who reminds you of yourself when you didn't know what to do or where to go.

Elected Officials

Politicians are another resource available to you. "But what does my representative (or councilman or assembly person) know about IDEA? And why should he or she be interested in what happens to my child?" Your representative may know very little about IDEA; he or she may even know nothing about it. A few will be knowledgeable, but chances are they were educated by other parents like you who called for help and support. The point is that elected officials don't have to know anything about special education to help you: They can provide the needed push—the pressure—that gets you what you want. Their political power is your leverage. When you are having trouble getting a copy of the IDEA and state education regulations from the state education agency, you can call your state representative's office and explain, "I have called and written the state department of education for regulations and received nothing."

You will be asked for specifics: what regulations and who you talked or wrote to. You will also be asked your name and where you live to find out if you are a voter or potential voter from the representative's district. The office will usually call the state agency for you.

You may even get a follow-up call that day from the official or an aide telling you that the state agency has been contacted and a copy of the regulations is in the mail, and that if you do not receive it in a few days, call back. You, of course, should warmly express your appreciation for the official's or aide's help.

But why did the state agency respond to your elected representative and not to you? They were quick to respond because your representative belongs to the group (legislature or assembly) that every year approves the budget the agency needs to operate. The agency wants to keep the people with the power to make appropriations decisions happy. But why did the representative respond to you? After all, you are just one person. To the representative, however, you can be a very important one person: You are a member of the community who is a voter, a potential supporter, and a person who can tell other people in the community what a great person he or she is. Some of your elected officials may have a natural concern and sympathy for your problems, but all are concerned with votes. If an official is unable to help you, it may be necessary to contact one in a more influential position. Perhaps you feel your child needs a specialized private school placement, but the school people refuse to write it into the IEP because there is no money in the budget. You have called a member of your school board and your state representative, but they weren't able to help. Why not call your congressional representative? He or she is working to get federal dollars into the communities in his or her district, including yours. It may be that your town is depending on that official to obtain a federal grant for a revitalization program. A call from that office to local officials who want to please him or her may set the wheels in motion and get the program you want for your child.

When you are encountering roadblocks in getting appropriate education and you feel that a little push will clear the way, use political people to help you get the appropriate services. When you call their offices, identify yourself as a constituent of the district they serve. Give them the information they need to help you—the law, the section of the regulations with which you are dealing, the names and positions of the school staff, and a clear explanation of what you want. By the time you reach the point of calling your elected officials, you will probably know quite a bit about your rights and your child's; share this information freely.

By all means, talk to the official's aide, who may be the most knowledgeable person in the office. If you insist on talking to the official, you may find yourself in a three-way conversation in which the official keeps calling on the aide for help before answering any questions. Deal with the most knowledgeable person in the office. Let your official do what he or she knows and does best—make telephone calls to public administrators and agency heads to get things moving. Don't expect your official to go or send someone to meetings with you or help you develop an IEP. Use your official to give the system a shake when a little shake will put the gears in motion. Use your power over the official carefully. Don't threaten. The official knows that if you're dissatisfied, you aren't going to beat the drum at the next election. Maybe the official made a real effort to help you but it failed, and maybe you will want to come back to use his or her services another time on another issue, so keep the door open. Express thanks for the time spent with you.

Whether you got what you were after, you did help to educate your official about the problems in education. He or she will be more knowledgeable when you call the next time. Some people call their officials regularly: They tell them how they want them to vote, ask them to have street lights fixed and vacant lots cleaned up, and complain about tax bills, high-rise buildings, and police protection. These people expect action, or at least an explanation, and they almost always get one or the other. If you and your child can be helped by your elected officials, don't be afraid to call them, and remember that it can be hard for an elected official to ignore a concerned and caring parent, especially when he or she wants to look good to the voters.

Special People

Other people can serve as sources of help, information, or power. They are the professionals who have worked with your child outside the system, the "good guys" in the school system, and the lawyers and paid professional advocates you may have to hire if you and the school people cannot reach agreement on your child's IEP.

The professionals outside the system who know you and your child are most certainly a source of information. Before you decide to use the outside professional, make sure he or she can find the time to attend the IEP meeting and that you two are in reasonable agreement. Everyone can have small differences, but you should both agree on the basic and priority items that you want in the IEP. Call or make an appointment with your outside professional to discuss these issues. When you feel comfortable with the statements the outside professional intends to make (you understand the jargon-free explanations and you feel the reasons are good), talk over your concerns about the upcoming IEP meeting. Sharing these concerns gives your professional a chance to plan in advance how to support you at the IEP meeting.

Your outside professional can also bring a little power to the meeting. As a professional, he or she has the status that comes with specialized training and expertise, which can impress the school professionals. If your professional is widely known in the field, his or her name and presence add more weight to your side. If he or she works out of a prestigious institution (e.g., a university or a medical school), there is more pressure on the school people to acknowledge the expert's recommendations and make some attempt to meet them. Your outside professional's appearance at the meeting tells the school staff that he or she thinks your child's case is important enough to justify taking time from a busy schedule to be there. This presence stamps your child's case "IMPORTANT." Because you may be (or may end up) paying for the professional's time, his or her presence also indicates the seriousness of your commitment: Not only are you willing to invest your time, energy, and emotions, but you are also prepared to spend some hard cash to see that your child's interests are protected. (You are paying only for the specialist's time at the meeting, and not for the educational services to which your child is entitled by law. With your efforts, these will be included in the IEP.)

Your outside professional is one of the special resources you use. In most cases, it would be impossible to use this professional as your personal advocate because of the time and cost required for planning and meetings. However, the information, the support for you, and the status he or she brings to even one IEP meeting can strengthen your case.

The "good guys" in the school system who are trying to help you get the services your child needs are also a hidden resource. They can offer you information and behind-the-scenes support. They can tell you what they feel your child's priority needs are. Teachers and specialists can be an invaluable source of information about the system, as well as about your child. Think what a help it would be to you at the IEP meeting if you knew that the reason for holding back special services was because of the budget. And you thought it was because your child could only handle so much intensive therapy! Properly informed, you will now insist on and hold out for more.

"But my child's teachers and specialists don't give me inside information like that. I get the party line." Although some teachers will only preach the gospel according to the school budget, some teachers do regularly share information with parents, and others would like to but fear the wrath of other school professionals if they are discovered helping parents ask for more services.

How do you find, develop, and support the school personnel who give you inside information or make individual recommendations? First, you find them by sharing one-to-one on a personal level your information and concerns. When they realize that you are being open in asking their advice, they may directly voice their own limits and concerns, or perhaps, momentarily caught up in their own emotional concern for your child, they may let slip information such as that there is a ceiling on special services. The good advocate considers these personal statements from inside professionals as privileged communications, not to be publicly expressed; you reassure the insiders that you respect their confidence and that you are grateful for their demonstration of trust and concern. The good advocate supports his or her inside resources by protecting them.

When you get inside information, how can you use it without identifying its source? You ask yourself where else the information could have come from. Do you have any old reports, evaluations, or educational plans that contain or support the information recently given to you? Have you previously discussed with an outside professional the needs that are surfacing again? Another constant and reliable source is your own past and present observations of your child. Your confidential discussion with your inside professional may have triggered an old memory:

"A few years back, our family doctor said we should consider special visual testing for Ned some time in the future. Even though he tested 20/20, the doctor thought he might have some tracking problems; I just thought his poor recall was lack of attention." Or "That sounds like the article I read last month in *Downhome* magazine."

If you think about it for a while, there is usually some recent or past experience to which you can attach your new information so that you can use it and at the same time protect your inside resource. Not everything said in a one-to-one conversation needs to be confidential; in fact, very little will be. But whenever a school person says to you, "I shouldn't be saying this," or "This is in confidence," you should respect that confidence and realize that you are probably dealing with a "good guy" trying to share inside information with you.

"This is beginning to sound like cloak and dagger stuff," you are thinking. "Why can't it all be up front?"

In most systems, all will be up front, including the problems. In some resistant systems, however, you may be the only person without inside information, and to be an effective advocate, you need it. Consider your "SPIES" to be Special People Inside Educational Systems, special because they are willing to risk a little trouble to help you and your child.

Lawyers are another resource, usually an expensive one. They should be your last resort when your other resources have failed and you are going to a formal hearing. (You'll read more about hearings in Chapter 8). Do not think lawyers are necessarily a short cut to the services you want.

Educators are not at their best trying to think, discuss, and plan educational services in the presence of lawyers. They are likely to become even more careful of what they say for fear they will offend someone or violate someone's rights or some school policy; they are afraid of saying the wrong thing at the wrong time to the wrong person.

If you appear at your planning meeting with legal representation, the school staff are likely going to feel intimidated and call out their lawyer. Immediately the situation will become very structured, formal, and legalistic. Lawyer talks to lawyer, and points of law and procedure may predominate. You may find that your educational concerns may get less attention than you expected.

Because each side has its own lawyer to represent its interests, collaboration and informal negotiation become next to impossible. What might have been a working group (you and the school people) becomes an adversarial situation ("It's either them or us"), and any new options or creative alternatives that might have developed in the group process can be lost in a legalistic format.

This does not mean that you can't privately consult a lawyer experienced in special education law at any time. If you have reason to believe that the school staff are misinterpreting the law or denying your rights or your child's, you can check it out with your attorney. He or she may tell you to finish up the IEP and forward a copy immediately, offer to call or write the special education director and explicitly lay out the provisions of the law, or suggest that he or she attend the next school meeting "because these people need to know that you can't be put off by their misinterpretation of the law."

Give the educators a chance to do their thing before you call out the legal troops. Besides, you know your child best; you certainly know better than your lawyer which services will benefit your child most. When you and the school staff have completed the process, agreed on some services, and disagreed on others, you will have clarified the issues. If you find you must go to formal hearing, then the lawyers can come in to argue about those specific services you want and can't get using their legal expertise and special knowledge of IDEA. The time for lawyers is when collaboration and negotiation break down, and it's clear that you and the school staff have irreconcilable differences.

Using lawyers is discussed in Chapter 8. For now, you need to know that many parents have been involved in developing good IEPs without legal advocates, but that some parents have found it necessary to bring a lawyer into due process to get the desired and appropriate services. You should say to yourself: "I will do the best job I can, and I will use all of the resources I can find; but if my best efforts fail, I am prepared to go the whole route and engage a lawyer to help me."

This kind of self-statement will give you confidence when you are dealing with the system: You remind yourself that you have something to fall back on. Your confidence in yourself delivers a message to the system that you are involved down to the finish line.

Using the Ladder

As there was a ladder or hierarchy in the school system, so there is a ladder in using your resources in your educational advocacy. You start with you and your personal advocate. You don't begin with your lawyer or your elected official. You want to have issues cleared before you climb to the top of the ladder. Otherwise, those resources will be able to do very little for you and they may ask you to come back when you know what the issues are. Needing help without details is not enough.

USING SPECIAL PROPS

There are things you can bring, wear, or do at meetings with school people to impress them with your businesslike approach to achieving a beneficial education for your child. They are little things, but because every little bit helps, they are worthy of your consideration.

Your Well-Used Copy of the Regulations Can Look Impressive

Before you go to any meetings to plan a program for your child, you should have already obtained a copy of the regulations. As you read them, mark or underline parts you want to use to make your case. Reading the regulations (alone or with help) is part of your basic preparation. But when you arrive at the school with a well-worn copy, it is a signal to the school professionals that you have done your homework and are not likely to be put off with vague answers or promises. You may feel you don't know enough, but they don't know what or how much you know; they will become very careful in what they say, expecting that you will flip to Section "QRS" and explain their legal obligations to them. This may seem like a bit of gamesmanship, and sometimes it is. Remember all of the times you may have been confused or put off by jargon or faulty information, and enjoy the feeling of power and the benefits that can come from using your special props.

How You Carry Your Papers Can Be Important

Another prop you may find helpful in impressing school staff is how you carry your papers. One personal advocate who assists a number of parents relates that her briefcase alone impresses a number of school people, who often assume she is a psychologist, a lawyer, or a social worker and treat her (and the parent) with more respect. If you work or have worked in a field in which people carry briefcases, by all means use yours or consider buying one. However, if you don't have a briefcase, you can still impress them with a clipboard, large manila envelope, or loose-leaf notebook in which all of the papers you will need at the meeting are filed. This is appropriate for everyone. You demonstrate your businesslike approach in the way you prepare and handle your materials. Remember, you are trying to impress, not deceive. You don't have to tell everything, but your behavior and statements should be honest.

When you go to meetings, it can be helpful to dress conservatively; that is, in a businesslike fashion. This doesn't mean you should rush out and buy a three-piece suit or a dull dress you will never wear anyplace else. It does mean you should plan on leaving the sneakers and sweats; the loud sport shirt; or the flaming pink, ruffled, low-cut dress at home. If you don't feel at ease wearing a tie, don't wear one. If the brown skirt is too short or tight, wear something else. You'll have enough concerns at the meeting without squirming in your clothes. If you are still in doubt about what to wear, look around at people in the bank or at church until you see someone who dresses quietly and in a way in which you could be comfortable when meeting with school people. The clothes in which you present yourself can deliver the message to the school that you are a serious, no-frills parent advocate.

"What does it matter? I'm still the same person without a briefcase and not dressed up. These aren't the issues. My child's education is what counts."

You are right; these are not the issues. But it is amazing what can impress people. School professionals, like most people, are impressed by appearances. And although none of these special props by themselves will do the job of getting the services you want for your child, they can help to establish you as a serious, businesslike person. You will need and use all of the support you can get to do the job, with grace when possible and with props and pressure when necessary.

You have ahead of you just one more task to complete in which you will practice your newly refined skills and prepare yourself for the IEP process. You are about to take a critical look at your child's program in action.

6

Getting Inside Your Child's School
What It's Like for Your Student

Open House Day is not the real deal • the school's responses • the entry letter, if needed • the role of the trusted professional • some days are better • when your student says, "no way" • visit preparation by the unobtrusive observer • environmental considerations and classroom content • don't forget the lunchroom • wrapping up • teachers are different • now you are as ready as you will ever be for the big event: the IEP

"I don't have to go to school to find out how my child is doing. I get the reports."

"The principal won't even answer my telephone calls, and you expect him to let me visit the classroom?!"

"What do I know about evaluating a classroom or a teacher?"

If you find yourself raising objections like these, you must first understand that in order to be a good parent advocate, you have to know what kind of program your child is in now. Your child probably has an IEP, which the law requires; various reports or report cards may have been sent home to you; and you may be having regular talks with the school social workers, psychologists, specialists, or teachers.

Have you seen the program in action, or is your knowledge just secondhand, transmitted by various school staff? Although the information you receive from school people is useful and important, the only way to have firsthand information is to visit the classroom so that you can judge for yourself whether or not the program might benefit and increase your child's rate of progress. Remember, that's what IDEA is all about: an education that is appropriate and beneficial for your child.

If your child cannot tell you about school because he or she is too young (preschool or primary school-age) or has a disability that results in a difficulty in communication (e.g., aphasia, autism, cerebral palsy, intellectual disability), then it is especially important that you see what goes on in school.

But who are you—a mere parent, an outsider, an intruder—to attempt to evaluate what goes on in your child's school? How can you, a layperson, presume to assess the effectiveness of the teacher in your child's classroom? Remember the discussion of myths in Chapter 3: Teachers do have special training and skills that must be acknowledged; however, the range of special education needs, disabilities, and teaching methods to correct or improve a child's performance is so broad that an individual teacher cannot be expected to have all of the answers or even to have asked all of the right questions about a given child. You can assist the teacher by at least asking some of the right questions about your child. Indeed, many teachers have been helped by parents' questions and reports. You are the overall expert in the area of information about your child. In addition, you are often the pipeline through which information flows to the school when it is making its evaluations of your child (and your family). It is your right to request that information about the classroom and your child flow back to you.

THE RIGHT TO VISIT THE CLASSROOM

Visiting your child's classroom (general education or special education) is your right and not a privilege or special favor granted by the school system. As an equal partner under IDEA, you have the explicit right as a parent to visit your child's classroom during the school day if you first notify and schedule with the school office. The information gained during the visit(s) is essential to your full participation in the IEP process. A general rule of thumb is that your visits can be arranged at reasonable times upon reasonable notice even in those states that do not have a law on visits.

Many parents have never asked to visit their children's classrooms; if they have visited, it was on a school Open House Day when all parents are invited. Open House Day does not give you a realistic picture of what your child's school day is like because the teacher talks to many parents, many people are coming and going, and the day may be arranged to show children doing their best work or favorite projects.

Parents may be reluctant to ask to visit the school for fear of intruding. Some school personnel may strengthen this idea (e.g., "We would like to have you visit, but it would disrupt the class"). You need to recognize that some of the fear of intrusion is another response stemming from your own school days (e.g., "Where is your class?" "Are you supposed to be in the hall now?" "Do you have a pass?"), which you need to overcome. A well-prepared, businesslike parent who has come to quietly observe and who will talk with the teacher after school (in person or by telephone) is hardly being intrusive. The students will notice you when you enter the classroom, but will soon return their attention to their work and their teacher.

Remind yourself of why you are not an intruder:

1. You have the implicit right to visit and observe your child's program (explicit in most states).

2. You are a mature adult whose presence in the classroom will not interfere with the educational process.

3. You have the responsibility as the natural and long-term advocate for your child to see and evaluate what kinds of teaching and services your child is actually getting in his or her daily program.

You are now ready to approach the school system with your reasonable request to visit your child's classroom. You can begin with an informal request. If you are meeting with the teacher for a parent–teacher conference, if you will see the teacher or principal at a PTA meeting, or if you are dropping by school to leave boots for your child on a stormy day or a cake for a sale, your on-the-spot request is casual and friendly. The happiest and most promising response you can get is "Yes. Let's arrange a convenient time. We like to know that our parents are interested in their children's education."

When you receive this type of response, you can arrange a mutually convenient time with the teacher when you can see the activities in which you are most interested (perhaps reading, speech-language therapy, or gym).

However, you should be ready for a range of responses when you ask to visit. These responses can range from simple surprise to suspicion ("Why do you want to visit?"), reluctance ("It might disrupt the class"), or downright resistance ("Parents are only allowed to visit during Open House, which is scheduled in 6 months," or even "Parents are not allowed to visit").

Surprise may not be a problem. You may in fact be the first person to ask to visit the class at a time other than the annual Open House visiting day. Your expressions of parental interest in your child's education may be enough to result in arranging a time to visit.

This is not the time to express concerns (if you have them) about any shortcomings of the program. Remember, you are at the evaluation stage; you want to look to see what is happening. After you have seen the class in action, you may then have some criticisms, recommendations, or praise, which will be grounded in actual on-site observations by you.

Suspicion may or may not be resolved by your expression of interest in the school program and an obligation to follow your child's educational career through regular observations. If you feel the school's suspicion is merely the visible tip of their deeper reluctance, then you may need to say that it is your understanding that visiting is a right that parents have, and ask if the school has that same understanding. Usually, this is enough to lead to an arrangement for visiting.

Statements such as the following may demonstrate *reluctance:*

"We don't encourage parents to visit."

"Parents tend to disrupt the work of the students and teachers."

"I'm sure a talk with the teacher would give you all of the information you need and allay any fears you might have."

Such statements are usually intended to intimidate or at least convince you to stay away from the classroom. You must respond by restating your interest, your right, and your ability to observe in a classroom without it being a disruption. When your statements do not lead to the desired arrangements (however reluctantly the school makes them) and you are beginning to feel you are up against a stone wall, you are probably right.

Resistance is the name for that stone wall, and it is apparent in such statements as "Parents are not allowed to visit classrooms," or "There is one day a year set aside for all parents to visit. That is the only day we can allow visitors." These are put-downs, designed to keep you away and in your place. It is amazing how many parents accept these "rules" without question. But you know better: You know that an advocate without information is a weak advocate, and that important information is on the other side of the classroom door. No wall is insurmountable; with the proper tools (e.g., appropriate assertiveness, script, partner), you can get to the other side of the wall.

If you are one of the unlucky parents who, in this first informal encounter, finds the school staff's surprise or suspicion becoming reluctance and resistance and feels increasingly uncomfortable, insecure, and distressed, know that you can stop this exchange at any stage by simply saying, "Today I am pressed for time, and I will call you back in a day or two to finish this discussion."

If you are pressed to stay because the school person wants to settle the discussion in his or her way, embellish your excuse with a polite social lie, such as, "I am already late for my dental appointment."

Leave right away and go home or out for a cup of coffee or whatever appeals to you. You deserve a reward, both for hanging in during a difficult session and for knowing when it's time to get out of a situation because your effectiveness is being undermined. It's very important that over your cup of coffee, you write down all you can remember about the interview:

- What you said (including when you will call)

- What school staff said

- How you felt (e.g., intimidated, nervous, insulted, overwhelmed)

- What the issues were

- What additional information you need

- Which people you may need to help you (you might want to review the section "Advocate's Advocate" in Chapter 5)

Date this account for your files, which you are now keeping faithfully in your notebook, file, laptop, or handheld device, always resulting in a hard copy.

Go over your information on the interview: Were either you or the principal fuzzy in your statements? Practice privately. Next time at least you will be clearer. Were you nervous or too easily intimidated? Private practice or rehearsal will help here, too. You might even want to practice in front of a mirror.

Did you need more information about your rights? If so, there are sources you can consult. Contact the local school board and the state department of education for information. Ask for the name and number of the law that allows you to visit your child's classroom, ask to be sent a copy of the policy that defines your right (you might have to pay a reasonable cost for the copying of the policy/law), or ask the officials for their response affirming your right in writing if you feel you need it. If the answers you receive are vague or noncommittal, then ask if there is a policy or law that prohibits your visiting, and request a copy of it if it exists.

Is this becoming a situation in which you need an informed advocate? Can your friend who was the PTA president help you? Is there an advocacy or parents' group that can give you the information you need? Would a call to your state representative, assembly person, or city councilor help you to get the information you need from the school board or department of education? Your politicians can be powerful and valuable resources. Use them if needed. You may, however, wish to save them for the times when other resources seem to be failing. But they can usually get the information from public agencies mailed out to you within days.

Remember, you said to the school staff that you would call back in a day or two. It is a cardinal rule that you follow up on your promises to call; this will convince the schools that you mean business. Does the collection agency stop with one request? After all, you are collecting on your rights and your child's future. Before calling back, you need a little more planning, including some rehearsal. When you rehearse, try to think of the range of possible outcomes or responses and think of several that are best for you. Here are some examples of what can happen when you return the call:

Mrs. Ling: *This is Mrs. Ling. I promised the principal, Mr. Sallas, that I would call today.*

Secretary: *I'll see if he's available.*

Mr. Sallas: *Yes, Mrs. Ling. You caught me at a bad time the other day. I don't see why we can't arrange a time for you to visit. Ms. Mancini, your child's teacher, will call you and set something up.*

Mrs. Ling: *Thank you, Mr. Sallas. I appreciate your helping to set up my visit.*

You may be thinking, "Why didn't you say so the other day and spare me the grief?" but now you can afford to be generous and polite—you are going into the classroom.

Another example you rehearse may be a less-satisfying outcome of your effort:

Mrs. Ling: *This is Mrs. Ling. I promised Mr. Sallas I would call today.*

Secretary: *Sorry, Mr. Sallas is in a conference now and can't be disturbed.*

Mrs. Ling: *What is a good time to reach him?*

Secretary: *I really can't say. He's a very busy man.*

Mrs. Ling: *I see. Would it be better if I put my request in writing?*

Secretary: *That may not be necessary. Let me give him your message and I'm sure he will return your call if he can.*

Mrs. Ling: *Thanks. I'll be home (or at this number) from 1:00 to 4:00 p.m.*

You wait until almost 4:00, but there is no call. You can use the polite social lie here as a way of showing that you will not give up, while sparing people the accusations about not calling:

Mrs. Ling: *Hello. I'm sorry; I was out of the house (office) for a few minutes and was afraid Mr. Sallas might have missed me. Is he available to talk with me now?*

Secretary: *Sorry, he's out of the office again. Perhaps you could call again tomorrow.*

Mrs. Ling: *Uh-huh. Any special time?*

Secretary: *I can't really say. Try in the early afternoon.*

You have been writing in your records the dates, content, and numbers of your calls. Repeat the calls one more day, but if you are still unsuccessful, you should begin to compose your letter (a sample letter follows).

But suppose you finally get the principal on the telephone. (He has realized after four to six calls that you are really not going to go away; your message is being received.) You may be told the following:

Mr. Sallas: *Sorry I did not get back to you, Mrs. Ling. What can I do for you?*

Mrs. Ling: *I would like to know when I can visit Kim's classroom.*

Mr. Sallas: *Oh, yes. I suppose we could arrange something.*

Or you might be told something like this:

Mr. Sallas: *This is against our usual policy and I would like to check with the school board. . . .*

Or something like this:

Mr. Sallas: *I told you the other day that we do not allow parents to visit.*

You can imagine even more conversations than are presented here and be prepared to continue to make your request until the issue is resolved. At some point, with a resistant principal, you should consider putting your request in writing. Here is the sample letter from a parent whose telephone calls to a school principal have been ignored or resisted.

SAMPLE LETTER

October 28, 2010

12 Park Street
Your Town, State ZIP code
555-0789

Mr. Alfred Sallas
Principal, Local School
Your Town, State ZIP code

Dear Mr. Sallas:

On October 5, I asked you to set up a time for me to visit Julia's classroom, and you told me that parents are not allowed to visit. On October 7, I called your office twice. You did not return my call. On October 8, 12, and 13, I called again, without success. When you did return my call, you said you would check with the school board. That was 2 weeks ago. In the meantime, I have checked with the state department of education about visiting rights, and they sent me a copy of the public law that says that parents do have visiting rights.

Please write or call me to set up a time to visit my daughter's classroom.

Sincerely,
Jack R. Fontanez

You will probably first send this letter only to the principal. You have, of course, kept a clear hard copy of this letter for your files. When you feel that he or she is practically immovable, then you can share your correspondence with your resources later or even sooner (see "Formal Copies to Others" in Chapter 5). Usually this kind of a letter does the job and you can begin to plan for your visit.

If there is a school policy that actually prohibits your visiting, you must look for other ways to find out what goes on behind the classroom doors. Is there a trusted professional outside of the school system who has worked with your child in the past and who would be willing to visit the classroom? It would be hard for a school to refuse admittance to a professional person who has worked or is working with your child. If such a person agrees to visit in your place, sit down beforehand and share your questions and concerns with your friend. Perhaps you could read this chapter together.

Another problem may arise around visiting the classroom: Your middle school or high school student might say, "No way!" If you can't negotiate with your resistant child, this does not stop you. You will have to resort to your trusted professional or professional advocate.

One way or another, you or someone will be on the other side of the classroom door at a time agreed upon by the teacher, at which point you will get some of the information you want.

THE CLASSROOM ASSESSMENT: AN APPLE FOR THE TEACHER

You begin to gather information about the teacher when you arrange with him or her to set a time for your visit. Although this might seem like a great deal of arranging, it will be easier now because the front office has stamped approval on your right to visit. Be prepared for the same range of responses (e.g., acceptance, surprise, suspicion, reluctance, or resistance) as you were with the principal. You will, in almost every case, be able to work through the problem exchanges through negotiation and compromise and by being flexible and expressing consideration for the teacher's scheduling difficulties.

Explain to the teacher (by telephone or after school) when you can come, how long you want to observe, and which activities you would like to observe (perhaps for this first visit you don't really care; you just want to see the classroom in action), and tell him or her about any questions you may have about the educational program.

Present the teacher with a list of times you are available. If you can come any time, then say so. If you have other responsibilities that limit your availability, the teacher should respect your needs and activities. If you must take time off from work to come to the class, make it clear that you may have to make arrangements that are difficult for you, but that you are willing to do this because you are very serious about your responsibilities to your child.

Try to pick a day when you will see a representative sample of the program. Some days are better than others for visiting. Avoid Mondays, especially after vacations; Fridays; days after a holiday; Halloween; Valentine's Day; and so forth. On these days you probably wouldn't see a representative sample of the children's or teacher's performance.

Within your schedule, ask the teacher what days or times she thinks would be best (i.e., more informative or most relevant to your concerns). The teacher may state his or her own preferences. If you can make it and if you feel the preferred times will give you the information you want, then accommodate the teacher (demonstrating your flexibility). In doing this, you can present yourself not as a threat but as a cordial person and possibly a future ally.

Compromise may be necessary. For example, if you would like to see the class for 2 hours and the teacher would like you to visit for only half an hour, you may be willing to accept the half hour if you can arrange to visit at other times as well. Or you may have trouble taking time off from work and, considering the difficulties, a minimum of an hour makes more sense. Seeing the activity you want to see may be more important than the length of time you are there, however. You and the teacher should work out a mutually agreeable length of time.

The accepting teacher will ask you what you want to see; the suspicious or reluctant teacher will ask why you want to observe and may probe for your complaints. You should try to reassure the suspicious teacher by saying again that you are interested in your child's program and that you may have some questions only the teacher can answer based on what you see in the classroom. The suspicious/reluctant teacher may merely be a nervous teacher who is uncomfortable being observed, or he or she may have received a message from the reluctant principal that this parent is trouble. The way you present yourself can do much to allay the teacher's concerns and even fears. The more comfortable the teacher, the more representative her performance on the day you visit, and the better the information for you.

If you find that your talk with the teacher is deteriorating and you are losing control or not making your best case, remember the polite social lie and remove yourself from the situation. If necessary, you can call back at another time to make the final arrangements. Keep notes on all conversations for your file.

Preparation for Your Visit

The time is set. Perhaps arranging your visit was easy, or perhaps you feel like you've been through the battle at the Alamo. Either way, you now need to prepare for your visit and ready your props.

First, reread the most recent IEP. You do have a copy, don't you? If not, get one fast; you are entitled to a copy and you need it. On the IEP, mark the areas of your greatest concern; then make a list of the things you want to observe (e.g., reading program, teaching materials, how the teacher uses his or her attention to criticize or support the students). Review any notes you have in your records, such as the teacher's comments on your child's behaviors, abilities, and performance in school and your child's past progress or lack of it in certain areas.

Do not neglect the lunchroom, which will tell a lot about the degree of inclusion your child is experiencing. Is he or she sitting alone, with other students with disabilities, or mixed in with the typical students? Unfortunately, teachers are rarely in the lunchroom, so they may have little idea of how inclusive the setting is or if there is any social interaction at all.

Gym can be another important place to observe if your child has sensory or motor difficulties. Too much going on? Too noisy? Expectations without accommodations are difficult (e.g., a rapidly changing schedule of learning new competitive sports that may demand a level of motor organization that is more challenging for your child than the other students).

Your notebook is at the ready for the observations you will make during your visit. Your notebook is important for two reasons: It will be difficult for you to remember all of your important impressions and questions if you don't write most of them down, and your notebook also gives you something to do and another place to look in the classroom if you are feeling nervous or tense (and you proba-bly will be).

Plan and practice your behavior before the visit: how you will enter the classroom (e.g., quietly, cordially, on time), how you will take signals from the teacher (e.g., where you sit or stand, whether or how you should respond to the students' questions, when to ask your ques-tions), and what you will do if you become tense (e.g., do relaxation exercises; read your notes; draw a map of the classroom, which is good information and, unless the teacher indicates otherwise, is a great place to start).

When you and your materials are ready, read some fiction, take a walk, or do whatever it takes to relax you. Remember, this is just your first assessment visit; you may not understand everything you see and you may not have all of your questions answered. If you need more visits, you know how to arrange them now. Reward yourself for good planning.

Your Entrance

You arrive on time with your notebook under your arm, and you enter the classroom quietly with a pleasant expression on your face and a nod to the teacher. If you feel tense or even angry, think about something pleasant, however remote, if that's what it takes to put a small smile on your face. The way you enter should suggest the careful and cooperative observer, not the avenging angel arriving at last, and not the nervous and emotional parent. The way you move into the room and your glances to the teacher should tell the teacher that you want to take direction from him or her on what you should do in the classroom.

You note the teacher's response to your entrance:

1. You get a cordial glance and a nod to a chair set up for you at the side or back of the room, and the teacher continues the lesson.

2. You are invited to the front of the class and the teacher intro-duces you to the students. (If you are offered a chair at the front of the room, let the teacher quietly know you feel you would be less of a disruption sitting in the back.)

3. You are ignored and left to decide where you will sit, stand, or lean.

These are your first observations. You are not making judgments now; you will make them later when you have all of your notes and obser-vations to consider and evaluate—after your visit.

Classroom Setting

Begin your observations by noting the physical arrangements in the room; draw a simple map. If you are a bit tense or uncomfortable, this is an easy way to begin. It may help to relax you and possibly the teacher, too, as he or she sees that you are interested in the total environment and are not there just to criticize or pounce on his or her style or performance.

Your attention to the setting is not just busy work, however; you will gain important educational information from your map. You note several types of things:

1. First, the location of the classroom:
    *   Isolated: Is it in a noisy area or a separate wing distant from general school activities?
    *   Inclusive: Is it an inclusive classroom, alongside or mixed in with the general classrooms, or close to general-use rooms, such as the cafeteria, gym, music room, and so forth?

2. Then, the room's general characteristics:
    *   Large or small
    *   Sunny (or well-lit) or gloomy
    *   Warm or cold
    *   Well-kept or deteriorating
    *   Quiet or noisy (perhaps it's too close to the cafeteria or gym or the furnace, and no one else wants the room)
    *   Anything else that seems important to you

3. Finally, the teacher's organization of the room (how the teacher makes the best use of what he or she has):
    *   Location of the teacher's desk: Is it in the center in front of the room between the students and the blackboard, or is it located in a front corner where the teacher can easily move to the blackboard and to the students without being constantly in the students' line of vision?
    *   Location of the students' desks: Are they in the traditional arrangement of students in rows facing front, small groupings of desks, a circle of desks reminiscent of kindergarten, or individual desk arrangements?
    *   Are any special areas of the room set aside for individual instruction, quiet reading and learning tasks, free activities, or crafts?

- Location of equipment and materials: Are things located where they are used and accessible so that there is a minimum of wasted and possibly disruptive movement? For example, if the free activities area is at the back of the room, are there games and books there, too, or must the student walk through or around other working students to find a game? Are the materials and equipment easily available to the teacher? Can he or she pull out what's next and needed quickly?
- Is there anything else that seems important to you? Any single characteristic of the classroom may not be all that important, but the total picture is. Is the room generally pleasant and well organized? Have you noted many good things and perhaps a few minor deficiencies? Is the teacher making the best use of what he or she has?

Perhaps you are just a bit nervous about evaluating the setting (i.e., falling into the "mere parent" trap). How can you, the nonprofessional, assess a classroom planned by the professionals? The answer is that you do it the same way you assess any setting for people. A classroom is a place where people live and work; the people are students and the work is learning. And you know about people and work: Do you run a household? Do you manage or work in an office or shop? Then you know that a dark room can be depressing and hard to read in, that you can't do a good job if you can't find your tools, and that it's hard to concentrate on reading or writing in a noisy room or office. Use what you know and apply it to the classroom.

You will begin to notice other things based on your own everyday experience. You may see a classroom that looks neat—everything is stacked in orderly piles—but the teacher can't seem to locate the materials readily. Neatness and organization are not always the same thing. Your teacher's classroom may look a little disorderly, but you see that he or she knows exactly where everything is, and his or her lessons flow smoothly. Use your judgment.

Look at the way students are seated, as well as the arrangement of the room. You may notice a student at the back of the room who is squinting at the board and wonder why that student is not seated near the front of the room. Or you may see a student in the middle of a group who can't seem to attend to the paperwork, and you think that student might do his or her work better if his or her desk were placed at the edge of the group. You may surprise yourself at how much you do see. Of course it would be inappropriate to comment on those other children. If your own child has a hearing or attention problem, you may be happy to see your child seated near the front of the room, or distressed that he or she is far from the teacher and probably hearing or processing very little. (Make a note to discuss this with the teacher.) Trust yourself to make good observations and to ask important questions. Your judgments, based on what you know, can be very sound.

General Activity

Now that you have some good notes on the physical setting, use some of your valuable, everyday experience and your good ideas to assess the way the teacher works and interacts with the students. This is harder, but in a short time, you will be making observations that you will feel are reliable. Here are some important questions:

1. Is the teacher generally supportive and friendly to the students? (The behavior of both students and teacher will give you the answer here.)
    *   Note the teacher's tone of voice, frequency of smiles, and how and when she gives attention and touches the students. (Touching depends on the student's ages: Younger children appreciate and generally respond to being touched by a friendly, caring teacher, but older students may not like being touched at all, and sadly, some schools have policies on not touching students of any age.)
    *   Do the students seek out the teacher's attention?
    *   Do they like to do things to please the teacher?

You know your own child, your other children, and their young friends, so you have a basis for evaluating the teacher and students' interactions!

A word of caution is needed here about individual teaching styles. Every teacher is different from every other teacher; each has a unique style. Some are outgoing and effusive; others may seem serious or even a little stern. Some will seem very loose or casual in the way they run their classrooms; others will run a tight ship, and you may even feel they are a bit rigid. If you have questions or concerns about the teacher's fairness or caring, watching how the students respond to the teacher will give you some of the answers.

2. Is the teacher in control of the classroom?

- Does he or she have a schedule to stick to and in which the students can finish the assigned work without teacher pressure or nagging?
- How does the teacher deal with disruptions? (Are the disruptive students getting most of the attention, or does the teacher help the students to improve their classroom behavior by giving them attention when they are engaging in productive behaviors such as cooperation and diligence?)
- Has the teacher established classroom rules, such as how the students are expected to enter the room, the proper way to get the teacher's attention, and when they will be allowed to have free time?

3. Is the teacher generally skillful in teaching the students?
   - Does he or she know how to break down learning tasks into steps, however small, to help a student learn a task?
   - Are the teacher's directions clear enough so that the students know what is expected of them?
   - Does the teacher prepare work that the students can do in the allotted time with a good chance of doing it well?
   - Does the teacher go to a student who is beginning to look like he or she needs help and offer it before the child falls behind, gets lost in the lesson, or becomes disruptive?
   - Does the teacher circulate among the working students to give a word of praise, a pat on the back, a helpful new direction, or a correction?
   - Does the teacher prepare students by telling them the lesson will be over in a few minutes and, when time is up, end the lesson on a good note?
   - Does the teacher offer or plan to give extra help later to the student(s) who needs more time and help from the teacher?

4. In guiding individual work, is the teacher able to be organized, consistent, and yet flexible?
   - Are the individual sessions obviously planned, with the teacher giving clear directions (e.g., oral, written) and the help the student needs?
   - Is the teacher able to present different directions when the student is having difficulty understanding the first ones and to offer physical help (e.g., "I'll guide your hand in writing this letter") to one child while offering verbal help to another (e.g., "This should look like a circle we didn't finish. That's a nice letter C.")?

- Can the teacher end a session that isn't going too well with some feeling of competence or success for the student (e.g., "These letters are really hard. Just make me a nice letter *A* and we will be all done.")?
- Can the teacher plan to correct, modify, and improve the session for the next time?

What a lot of questions to be asking yourself while you are trying to observe the class in action! How can you possibly watch everything and remember all of these points? You can't watch everything, and even if you could, you couldn't see everything during one visit. But you will see enough—enough to realize that the teacher is a caring person and a skillful teacher, enough to be concerned about the teacher's competence or motives, enough to raise your own questions to the teacher when you and he or she sit down to talk about your visit, or enough to know you want a return visit to satisfy unanswered questions.

The questions presented here are your practical guide to getting the information you need to make good decisions about your child's program and educational future. As you use them to help you observe, you will begin to develop your own questions and your own valid comments. The questions become easier when you draw on your own daily living experience to understand the classroom. For example, the last time you made something only to be told what was wrong with it is like the experience a student has when the teacher says, "This problem is wrong" and doesn't praise the nine problems done correctly. You know the feeling that comes when efforts go unrewarded, and you know that there's a better way. The more you draw on your own experience to understand the experiences in the classroom, the better observer and critic you will become. It may take more than one visit, but on each visit, you will see more and you will see more clearly.

Materials and Curriculum

Up to this point, we have discussed observations you can make about the teacher's style and ability to work with all of the students. Now we want to look at what is taught (the curriculum) and how it is taught (the materials and methods). It will be difficult for you to make good observations in this area except as it affects the one student you really know well—your own child. For example, you know that your child remembers everything he or she sees but very little of what he or she hears, or that he or she can tell you a terrific story but can't write it down because he or she can't hold a pencil well, or can't spell, or that he or she does things well with his or her hands but can't do simple arithmetic. This is the kind of information you have circled on your child's IEP and in your notebook. Use your notes to help you remember all of these points as you watch the teacher work with your child and as you watch your child working alone with the materials.

1. Are the materials presented to your child close to his or her level of skill?
   - Is the material at the right age level? (For example, if your 12-year-old child with an intellectual disability is just starting to read books, are the books he or she is given interesting to young people, or are they "baby" books?)
   - Does the teacher use materials that take into account your child's learning style and strengths? (For example, if your child is good with his or her hands but poor at math, does he or she use blocks, a number line or some other objects, or even a calculator to help solve simple arithmetic problems?)

2. Does the teacher adapt the prepared or purchased materials to your child's skill and interests?
   - Is the material presented in the amounts and the form that your child can use? (For example, the arithmetic problems may be at the right level, but the print is so small or there are so many problems crowded on the page that your child is making errors that he or she would not make were the print larger or were there fewer problems and more space on the page.)
   - Does the teacher involve your child by using special topics your child cares about? (For example, does the teacher use writing and reading assignments about your child's own experiences, arithmetic problems that are about planes or baseball or movies, and books about teenagers or celebrities?)
   - If your child falters, can the teacher rephrase the question to help him or her answer successfully?

3. In individual tutoring sessions with your child, is the teacher prepared with alternative materials and ways to teach?
   - Can the teacher provide the on-the-spot prompts, cues, and assistance that your child needs (e.g., a letter to trace, a physically guiding hand, a new verbal or written instruction)?

- Does the teacher let your child drop back to an earlier skill level to end the session pleasantly and successfully?
- In an individual session, can the teacher take the responsibility for a difficult lesson and say, "This is too hard," or "This is too much work," and add, "You've worked very hard. Let's stop now"? Or is the teacher determined that your child will do all of it, no matter what? Even the best materials will not work if the lesson is too long or the student is under too much pressure.
- Does the teacher provide short practice sessions for your child's special difficulties, either in a tutoring session or for independent desk work?
- When your child is doing work that is difficult on his or her own, is the teacher aware, close by, and regularly monitoring to see that he or she is doing the work correctly and not making mistakes that will have to be unlearned and that will interfere even more with progress?

4. Is the teacher helping your child to develop feelings of competence and independence?
   - Can your child answer most of the questions the teacher asks verbally or in written tests?
   - In group sessions, does the teacher make sure to call on your child when there is a strong chance he or she knows the answer, or are the students called on randomly?

5. Can your child do most of the independent desk work without a lot of help from the teacher? Is the independent desk work an opportunity for learning, or is it busy work? (For example, does your child, who has poor writing skills, spend most of the time laboriously copying from the board while the computers are reserved for the "brighter" students?)

By looking at the materials and by watching the teacher and your child work, you will know if your child's special needs are being met and new and active learning is taking place.

If, during your visit, a specialist (e.g., speech-language, reading, physical therapy) enters the room to work with the class, to take a student from the classroom, or to return a student, watch the interaction between the teacher and specialist.

- Is the specialist welcomed?

- Do the teacher and specialist exchange questions and information?

- If the specialist works in the classroom, do the teacher and specialist work together or does the specialist work alone with a single student?

- Do the teacher and specialist arrange a time to talk to each other?

How specialists and teachers work together affects the progress of their students. This is something you may want to discuss with the teacher when you meet after your classroom visit.

During your classroom visit, be prepared for a few surprises. It may be that your child, who seems so dependent on help at home, behaves quite independently in the classroom and even initiates activities on his or her own. Sometimes you will see new strengths (and weaknesses) your child has when you see him or her outside the home.

Should you suspect early on in your visit that the teacher is nervously watching you take notes, you may need to limit your notetaking to the most neutral features of the class and room (e.g., location, schedule), which you can share with the teacher. If there is reason to think this is the case, bring a recorder with you as an alternative that you will use as soon as you leave the school specifying the high (or low) points of the visit. This will minimize any loss of information.

THE FOLLOW-UP INTERVIEW: USING YOUR PERSONAL SKILLS

After your first visit, you will have some good notes, a lot of information, and a lot of questions to ask the teacher. You will also have some idea of the kind of reception you can expect from the teacher when you sit down to talk. Did your entrance into the classroom bring you a friendly nod and a place to sit, or were you ignored? During your observations, did the teacher occasionally include you with a smile or a comment, or did you never make contact? Did the teacher seem relaxed, nervous, indifferent, or even hostile? Use your experience with people in general (and your past experiences with the particular teacher) to guide you in your approach to the teacher.

You will be presenting concerns, questions, and information to the teacher. Because you want the teacher to accept your comments as valid and to openly share with you his or her concerns and knowledge, you might begin by trying to put him or her at ease. Teachers get nervous too. You may be the first parent to make an independent visit, your motives may not be clear to the teacher, or the last parent to visit the classroom may have found fault with everything, perhaps even the teacher's taste in clothes.

During your personal interview, you will be able to tell if the teacher accepts or rejects you and also if the teacher is friendly, bored, or suspicious; you will begin to know whether the teacher is confident, overconfident, or insecure and whether the teacher is competent, inexperienced, or inept.

The friendly, accepting, confident, and competent teacher is the ideal. If you have found such a teacher, your work will be easy (at least at this level of the system). Some of you will have to deal with the other extreme—the rejecting, suspicious, self-satisfied, or inept teacher. (Keep in mind that even this teacher, reluctantly or indirectly, does provide you with important information about your child's program and future.) Most of you will deal with teachers who have good skills and some weaknesses. If you work carefully and thoughtfully with your child's teacher, you can make that teacher your ally in getting good educational services for your child.

Making the Teacher an Ally

Unless your visit to the classroom was a total nightmare, you begin your interview by telling the teacher you enjoyed visiting the class and talk generally about the good things you saw in the classroom. Sometimes this will be easy:

"That was a terrific math lesson. It looked like all of the students were interested and working hard."

"You certainly manage to get my child to do a lot of work. I'm impressed."

"You are so well organized that everything seems to just flow in this classroom."

Other times you will have to reach to say something positive:

"What a nice room you have here."

"You certainly have your hands full."

"I'm very interested in what you were doing during the writing lesson."

This is not the time for you to deliver the total and absolute truth, and certainly it is never the time for you to tell the teacher how you think the class should be run. Nor is it yet the time for you to present your most serious concerns and criticisms. At this moment, you want to establish a good relationship so that you can obtain some solid information from the teacher and begin to share some of your own.

Be sympathetic to what the teacher has to say. If excuses are offered, they may be valid:

"My aide is out sick today."

"The speech-language therapist didn't take one student today, and, on the spot, I had to prepare extra work for him."

"I don't know why the kitchen next door is so noisy today. It was impossible to teach the reading lesson, and I had to change the schedule from reading to crafts."

Be understanding and use the excuses as an opportunity to set up a second visit when conditions may be better.

Next, begin to ask your questions. It is a good idea to present your concerns and observations in the form of questions, such as, "What was Malik doing with the blocks during the math lesson?" The teacher may tell you that Malik can do his math better when he can use the blocks as an aid to solving the problems. This may be a good answer, but perhaps it looked to you like more play than work was going on.

You may think that the teacher needs to do a better job of monitoring and providing individual help more often, but now you think about how to phrase your concern before you speak:

Mr. Saleh:	*Knowing Malik's difficulties, your approach makes a lot of sense. He did well at first, but did you notice that he seemed to slow down a little bit toward the end of the lesson?*
Teacher:	*Malik is not a good worker.*

or

Teacher:	*I meant to get back to him halfway through the lesson to give him the help he needs.*

The first statement tells you that you may have trouble working with this teacher; the second statement tells you that the teacher understands your child's needs. You should express your support for the good teacher's intentions and performance: "It must be hard to be in so many places at once, but I'm glad you understand Malik's short attention span."

Ask for explanations about materials and methods:

"How will this picture book series help Tyler learn to read?"

"I notice that you have Nicole sitting at the front of the room. Is that to help her pay attention better?"

"Why does Pedro do his reading in that little box (carrel)?"

Because you are a parent and not a professional, you can ask all of the "dumb" questions you want. So don't hesitate to ask for further explanations, and, if necessary, ask your question another way. Does the teacher answer you in jargon? A good teacher can explain to you in terms you can understand. Is the answer better or clearer the second time around? If so, the teacher is trying to communicate with you but probably needs more practice dealing with parents, and you, of course, are a willing subject.

Present your concerns as questions:

"Brian is so active. Is it possible to give him more opportunities to move around?"

"At home, Sheryl's speech is hard to understand. Do you think she needs more speech therapy?"

"Do you think Jeremiah has a visual problem? Should he be tested?"

Questions are generally less threatening to a teacher than statements (which may seem critical) or demands. You are not presenting yourself as Mr. or Mrs. Know-It-All Parent; your questions imply that you value the teacher's responses and the special information he or she can give you. If you are presenting yourself as a sympathetic, interested, and concerned parent who is not there to accuse and who can be trusted, you may get some good and useful answers, such as the following:

"Yes, I do think Sheryl needs more speech therapy but . . .".

"Jeremiah definitely needs visual testing, but, when I have asked, my requests have been turned down."

You can then let the teacher know that you appreciate his or her honesty and that you will ask the administrators for the service, but that your request will not put an extra burden on the teacher. You need not identify the source of your information or question. Your request will be, "My child has a serious disability and needs more. . . .," not "Ms. Newsome said that. . . ."

As you establish yourself as a supportive person to be trusted, you may find the teacher asking you questions, such as the following:

"Do you think Austin would do better if he sat near the board?"

"What are Heather's special interests that I can use to make her reading more rewarding?"

"Does Nick need a lot of help in getting dressed at home?"

"Is Desmond as shy and quiet with the neighborhood children as he is in school?"

Now the teacher is looking to you as a source of information about your child. Show your pleasure and appreciation by giving the best answers you can without appearing to criticize the teacher. If you don't have the answers ready, tell the teacher you will watch your child more closely at home and get back with the information later by note or, better yet, by telephone. This could be the start of productive and frequent communication between you and the teacher.

A good teacher wants and needs the information you have about your child. Your information, suggestions, and questions may stimulate the teacher to new ideas about how your child learns best, just as the teacher's (or specialist's) ideas and reports may lead you to find new ways to help or deal with your child at home. A good teacher and a good parent can make a formidable team.

If you and the teacher have a good relationship and good communication, you are likely to have a greater impact on your child's educational program. You will have opportunities to shape the teacher's behaviors, not only with you but also in the classroom with your child. By telling the teacher what you saw that you liked, there is a good chance that the teacher will do more of what you liked (teachers enjoy praise too, as long as it's genuine). When you praise, you can offer little suggestions or questions that may further shape the teacher in the direction you want; for example, "I see Daryl's written work is getting much better. Is that because you are giving him extra help? It's working great and Daryl seems a lot happier." The teacher feels good, and you will get more of what you want.

Several strategies can help you become a more important resource and ally to the teacher. For example, you might ask the administration to get the occupational therapist (or the visual testing) both you and the teacher want for your child. Because the teacher wants to work more closely with the speech-language therapist (and you agree on the importance of that teaming), you could ask to have written into your child's IEP that the speech-language therapist will meet regularly with your child's teacher and provide a plan for language activities to be done in the classroom by the teacher. Or you could speak up to the administration about giving more gym time to your child's class. You can use the teacher as your private resource, and you can become the teacher's special resource.

The effective collaboration of parent and teacher can happen when mutual respect and trust are established. Sometimes this can happen quickly, but it usually takes several productive and pleasant meetings. An inexperienced or insecure teacher may need a lot of your support; an established and competent teacher may need to see that your observations and suggestions are carefully considered, relevant, and valid. You need to know that the teacher is sensitive to your ideas and your child's needs. You and the teacher can become educational allies in the service of your child.

Years ago, I worked with an extraordinary teacher to develop school and home programs for my son. Although at that time I had no special education training or experience, the teacher treated me as a collaborator, with weekly calls to the home to share ideas, discuss areas of progress (or lack of it), brainstorm, and jointly develop new techniques or treatments. Given the state of special education at that time, it was an exhilarating and astonishing experience for me, which led to great benefits for my son. Teachers can become your partners. It can happen.

But what do you do when you have presented yourself as a concerned and interested parent who wants to support the teacher and you find that you are dealing with a rejecting or disinterested teacher?

Dealing with the Reluctant Teacher

The reluctant teacher is probably the one who made it difficult to make arrangements for visiting the classroom, or he or she probably ignored your entrance to the classroom or introduced you in such a way that you were made to feel like an intruder who was being granted a special favor. He or she did not look at you during your visit, or, if you did receive glances, they were not warm ones. You may feel that you have been on the receiving end of indifference at best and, at the worst, anger or hostility. Be aware that a nervous teacher also may not welcome or look at you. But you know how to recognize nervous people: For example, they may lose their place in thought, speech, or action; or they may drop things. Some pleasant and supportive glances from you may help to put this teacher at ease.

Occasionally you will meet a reluctant teacher who, on the surface, seems to do all of the right things: greets you, indicates where you should sit, and smiles at you. But you feel the smiles are cold, and the teacher is the original iron hand in the velvet glove. You mentally note these feelings and plan to check them out during your personal interview with the teacher. Your feelings are important: They are your antennae that signal you that something is going on. Respect your feelings, but do not act on them until you have more information. To be on the safe side, be careful not to judge a teacher on the basis of one experience.

When you sit down with the reluctant teacher to discuss your concerns and observations (in the form of questions, of course), there are some things to watch for that will tell you that you are probably dealing with a reluctant teacher and that will help you assess the potential difficulty in working with this teacher. First, you are likely to hear that your child's lack of progress is due to his or her faults and disabilities:

"He's lazy."

"She's incapable of doing the work."

"His paperwork is always messy."

Or, you might be told about your inadequacies as a parent:

"You must talk to your child about her behavior in school."

"Do you ever do things with your child?"

"You should spend more time on your child's homework."

"I wish you would not try to teach your child at home. It only makes my job more difficult."

You may have expected as much from this teacher, whose only previous contacts with you may have been to inform you by note or telephone that your child had a fight during recess or ruined a schoolbook. But even when anticipated, this kind of cold and insulting reception is very hard on parents. You must remain cool, take notes, and continue to ask your questions.

Second, you are likely to hear jargon from this teacher in response to your questions. Attempts on your part to get answers you can understand will likely lead to still more jargon, and continued efforts to gain clearer communication will bring forth statements such as the following:

"It's very complicated, Mrs. Ramirez."

"Why not leave the teaching in the hands of the professionals?"

Why, you may ask, are you even talking to this creature who seems bent on putting you down and insulting you and your child? What can possibly be gained by going through this process? What you can gain is information! However unpleasant, you are still gaining valuable information about the teacher, the classroom, and your child's educational future. You are making worthwhile observations about the teacher's style, personality, inability to deal with parents and students, or inability to communicate what he or she does. Your direct questions haven't been answered, but you intend that they will be, if not by this teacher, then during the development of the IEP, by the special education director, or by someone else who has the capacity to speak plainly.

When you feel you have as much information from the reluctant teacher as you need or feel you can handle, you can end the interview with a "Thank you for your time." (You need not wait to be dismissed.) Go home and finish up your notes, which should include some direct quotes. For now, congratulate yourself for having done a good job of collecting information that you will put to good use when you approach the administration to plan for your child's educational future.

Dealing with the Incompetent Teacher

At some point, some of you may encounter a teacher who is a nice person and who is devoted to the students but who is simply not a competent teacher. You will learn to recognize this teacher by your child's lack of progress and, during your visit, by the absence of beneficial educational activities in the classroom. This teacher may smile a lot and run a beehive of activity, but the activity is basically busy work. You realize that your child is doing the same work that he or she was doing last year or even the year before. You see the students start tasks that they never get to finish; the teacher works without a well-organized plan; the educational goals set for the children are too low, too high, or vague; or there are too many free activities. The teacher may be very kind and the children seem happy. What more could you want for your child? You want an education, and you want one that will benefit your child.

When your observations and discussion show that you are dealing with an incompetent teacher, you are really in a difficult position: Who wants to complain about a fond, well-meaning teacher and happy children? It will help you to remember that public education for children with disabilities is time-limited. Your child has only so many years in school, and those years should be used to maximum advantage before they end.

In your personal interview with the teacher, carry on your discussion in terms of your child's needs. Never personalize the discussion by commenting on the teacher's inadequacies. It may be that the principal or special education director already knows. In some future discussion at an IEP meeting, your theme will be only that your child is not making progress in his or her present classroom and may need to be considered for another placement. Even then, you should not make statements about the teacher's lack of competence, but instead focus on the program's inadequacies. Your observations and assessment of the teacher's competencies will probably be both valid and useful, but be careful about how you share this information. You are on more solid ground when you are talking about your child's needs.

Most of you will deal rarely, if at all, with the extreme types of teachers we have just discussed; many of you will deal with teachers who are sometimes overworked, overwhelmed, inexperienced (on the job or with parents), or involved in a temporary personal crisis. You can bring these teachers along by your interest, support, information, and concern.

Learning about classrooms and teachers was the last step in your basic preparation for the big event, participating in the process of developing an appropriate IEP for your child. Everything you have read in this book has been leading up to the moment when you, the knowledgeable and practiced parent, sit down at the working table with the professionals to plan your child's educational services. The IEP process is the heart of IDEA.

The next chapter takes you step by step through that process, helping you to identify potential problems and to use your information and skills to your child's advantage. If your child is approaching preschool age, Chapter 7 tells you how to "help" the school system find your child if the school has not contacted you as required by IDEA.

If your child is in school but does not have an IEP, you will learn how to start the IEP process. What looks like a problem—no IEP—can be an advantage. Because you will be starting from scratch, you, as an informed advocate, can work to ensure that the first IEP is a good one.

If your child has a poor or inadequate IEP, you will learn how to obtain a better one.

7

Getting the Right IEP

when not to sign • getting the process started right for your child • setting up the meeting • preparing yourself and your advocate (who's who, records, rehearsing together) • some have to go alone • a sample meeting • talk is cheap, get it in writing • your 20 questions • getting more • the IEP evaluated • extended school year • discipline code • to sign or not to sign • dealing with your frustrations • moving on

---

Mrs. Russell found a copy of her son's IEP in his backpack with instructions to sign and return it immediately to the school principal. When she called the teacher to ask what she should do, the teacher told her to sign it because it would save time, as the IEP was based on some informal discussions they had had a few months ago. When Mrs. Russell expressed her concern that there was no written objective for physical education, she was told, "We'll work that out after the school year starts."

Janetta Fox, when mailed a copy of the IEP, refused to sign the IEP and insisted on a meeting. She dreaded the meeting, but at the last minute she found an advocate to go with her. After greetings and social chitchat, this first meeting turned out to be too short, so she and her advocate asked for a second meeting. Next time, she will be sure to ask how much time has been set aside for the meeting before the meeting starts. She plans to stay until she has an IEP in hand.

As soon as Nick Fraser was diagnosed as having learning disabilities, his father requested an IEP meeting. Although he had to take time off from work, he was able to arrange a day when his workload was light. When he received a copy of the IEP agreed on at the meeting, he found that the extra math tutoring he had asked for had been omitted. He asked for another meeting but the special education director told him the omission was an error and a corrected copy would be put in the mail. Mr. Fraser will wait a few more days before calling again.

———◆———

Now it is your turn to start actively participating in the process of developing an IEP to meet your child's unique needs. Perhaps you have already been through an IEP process that was arranged, orchestrated, and completed by the school system and in which you put yourself and your child's future totally in the hands of the school staff. It was all quite friendly. The IEP was wrapped up in less than an hour, and maybe it wasn't so bad. But now you may want to take another look at your child's completed IEP as you read this chapter and consider whether you have need or justification for requesting a new IEP.

Maybe you have just received the IEP in the mail and haven't signed it yet. Make sure you read this chapter before you sign. You should have received a copy of the IEP at the meeting. There was a meeting, wasn't there?

Or possibly you have received a notice informing you that the meeting is being held this week (or next), and you are in a panic because there isn't enough time to prepare yourself. Relax. There's time. That notice is not a court summons requiring you to appear at the appointed time. IDEA gives you the right to negotiate a mutually agreed-upon time and place for the meeting. IDEA does this to accommodate parents so the meetings don't jeopardize parents' jobs. Rarely is an IEP meeting held in the home, but it has happened. Usually, finding a mutually agreed-upon time means that the parent ends up accommodating the school system by taking time off from work. However, if the school staff tell you they can only meet during the school day because of teacher contracts, you may have to remind them that IDEA supersedes school agreements. Don't be afraid to ask for another week or 2 or more if you feel you need it to prepare to be the well-informed advocate. If you haven't yet visited the classroom, this might be a good time to ask the school people to arrange a visiting time for you, before the meeting. If there are reports and documents you want, now is the time to ask for them so that you have at least 48 hours to review these materials before the meeting, adding that you don't wish to create a need for a second meeting just because you are uninformed.

As you become involved in the process, you will probably feel nervous. In times past, you may have been content to sit on the bench while others played out the game, but now that you know something about how the system works—and about your skills, knowledge, and rights—you realize that dealing with the system this time is a whole new ball game and you will be an active participant. Your nervousness is okay when you are knowledgeable and prepared for your part. It is the same with a good athlete or performer before the big event. However, if you are paralyzed by fear, you will need more relaxation and some more rehearsal.

A moderate amount of skepticism is okay, too. By now you know that you should ask questions and that you are entitled to answers that make sense to you. Your former total trust of and reliance on the school staff may be replaced by an unwillingness to accept everything on faith. You want to know why particular recommendations are appropriate and how they will meet your child's needs. This does not mean that you substitute total suspicion for your former blind faith, or that you are looking at every school professional's statements as potential traps leading to an inferior education plan. It does mean that before you agree to the IEP (or any of its components), you expect to be convinced by explanations you can understand that your child will benefit from it. When you are not convinced that a recommendation is a good one, your skepticism impels you to get further justification for the recommendation or to develop another more beneficial recommendation.

Pessimism, however, is not okay. Some parents will say, "They didn't pay much attention to me last time. Why should they want to include me now?" They will if this time you are more knowledgeable and more assertive than you were before. If you go to the meeting expecting to be ignored or put down, that's what will happen; it is hard to be assertive when you are expecting to fail. Your pessimism can contribute to an inferior IEP. By the end of the meeting, you will prove to yourself that you were right ("They didn't pay attention to me this time, either"), but being right is small satisfaction to parents who want better services for their children and don't get them. Set your pessimism aside and go to IEP meetings with some confidence in your abilities and with some realistic expectations of success. You will achieve at least some of your goals for your child and maybe a better plan than you thought possible.

Many parents, at the point of entering the IEP process, still hang back, saying, "Do I have to? Can't the school people develop an education program without me? After all, it's their job." Of course they can develop a plan without you; some school staff would even prefer to do it without you. But it won't be the best plan or maybe even the right plan for your child. The school staff (and your child above all) need you as an active participant to help develop the plan best suited to meet your child's needs. If you have more than a little stage fright, go back and reread or skim the earlier chapters to remind and reassure yourself of your importance in this process. Commit yourself to working through the IEP—no more hanging back. Set your pessimism and extreme nervousness aside, and get ready for the meeting.

ARRANGING THE IEP MEETING

Chances are your school system has already held or is calling an IEP meeting for your child because it is the school's responsibility under IDEA to identify preschool and school-age children with disabilities. However, some children may still be "undiscovered," either because they are very young or because they have fallen through the system's cracks. As your child's agent, it is up to you, the parent, to see that he or she is "discovered" by the school department as soon as possible.

Here are some examples of children with unidentified disabilities and some suggestions for bringing them to the attention of the responsible school systems:

1. Your child is in an early intervention program and will be turning 3 in just a few months. It is time to talk to your case manager or your child's early intervention teacher (both of these professionals are required under IDEA to assist in the upcoming transition to preschool and the need for an appropriate IEP). You, the case manager, teacher, or others involved in the care of your child can make the referral to your local school system. Allow enough time to talk to the school and to work on the IEP. You can expect the early intervention staff to participate in the IEP meetings because they will be serving your child until his or her 3rd birthday and because they will want to make sure that your child continues to receive the kinds of support services (e.g., speech, occupational, physical therapy) they have provided.

2. It is becoming increasingly obvious to you that your preschool-age child will require some special services. You call your local

school system to refer your child for services because you suspect that he or she has a disability and that he or she at least needs to be evaluated and have an IEP developed. You begin. Record in your log the date you contacted the school system, the method of contact, and the content of the conversation or a copy of your letter. Depending on your child's age, he or she could be placed in a preschool or a typical kindergarten for diagnostic services while the IEP is being developed.

3. Possibly your child has been a student in a general education classroom but is doing poorly and you suspect that he or she has an undiscovered disability. If this will be the first contact you have made with the school system, you might want to start with a phone call. But if you have repeatedly mentioned your concerns to the teacher and the principal and have not gotten any response (and you've noted such calls and conversations in your log book), you should send a letter. Explain in your letter that you have reason to suspect that your child has a disability and that you understand that it is the responsibility of the school system to evaluate such children and to develop an IEP as soon as possible. In your letter, you should request that a meeting be scheduled without delay. If you believe that your school system has made an oversight or has been careless, then send your letter by regular mail. But if you suspect real reluctance or resistance on the part of the school system, you should consider certified mail.

4. You believe that because your child is in a private school, he or she is beyond the responsibility of your public school system. This is wrong. If you have a child with a disability, it is the responsibility of your school system to evaluate your child and develop an IEP and monitor its implementation whether in a private school or a home school program. If the school system is paying for the private placement, it is accountable for ensuring that your child has an appropriate educational placement. Even if you have elected and are paying for a private school placement that has not been approved by your school system, you still have the right to request an IEP meeting for your child. The IEP assessments could uncover new and valuable information about your child. This new information may give you reason to consider placing your child in public school (or it may further convince you that your decision to place your child in a private school was the right one).

In some communities where school systems provide services to private schools such as parochial schools, you may find that your child is entitled to some publicly supported special education or related services. A home-schooled child is also entitled to related services.

Send your request for an IEP meeting to the public schools, stating your child's present placement and your understanding that he or she is entitled to an IEP, including evaluations.

5. When IDEA first became law, there were many children living in state institutions with little or no services. Because of IDEA, that has changed dramatically. Many state institutions have closed permanently. But there are still children in extended stays in hospitals or who are homebound because of extensive illness or in juvenile correctional institutions. If your child is in such a program, you may believe that he or she is outside the responsibility of the public school system and/or that he or she is receiving services already. You are wrong on both counts. The school system is still responsible for your child's education program and must identify, evaluate, and plan for your child and ensure that the school provides enough services for your child to make adequate progress. To whom do you turn for those services? Your local school system. Prepare your letter to the director of special education in your town, informing him or her that your child is a resident of a health or state program and that you are asking the school system to initiate the IEP process. If the IEP is lacking because of these new situations, you can ask for a new one.

If there are other reasons the schools did not find you and your child (perhaps you recently moved into the community), help them. Although the legal responsibility for identifying your child is the school's, you are perfectly willing to help them find him or her. Again, send your director of special education a letter of introduction and ask that the IEP process be put in motion for your child.

Perhaps your child was identified, but the services are still wanting because the IEP process may not have been satisfactory or in compliance with the law. For example, your participation in the process was minimal or even zero because of one or more of these practices:

•   The IEP meeting was held on short notice.

•   The meeting was held at a time when you couldn't be there.

- The meeting was conducted in jargon and there was little opportunity for you to ask questions.

- English is not your primary spoken language and there was no one at the meeting to help you understand the discussion.

- You were not given the opportunity to read your child's records before the meeting.

- You were never properly informed (e.g., the IEP came home in the backpack with instructions to sign).

For these and other reasons, if you believe your rights to participate in developing your child's first IEP were violated, you should notify the school system in writing (always save a copy in your file) that you were not actively involved in the original IEP because of (state your reasons) and that you are requesting that the IEP meeting be reconvened so that you may rightfully participate, as defined by IDEA.

When you are notified of a date for the IEP meeting, you are entitled to negotiate that date. A cooperative school system will call in advance of the notice to discuss times that are mutually convenient and then send you a notice stating the agreed-upon time. A school system that is resistant or tends to manage parents by control or intimidation will send an unexpected notice. In this case, if the time is impossible or even difficult, you should respond in writing, stating the problem and requesting a more convenient time.

If you experience serious difficulty in arranging the IEP meeting, you and people willing to help you in your advocacy efforts must aggressively pursue the school system through letters and calls. Reread Chapter 5, especially the sections on writing letters, keeping records, and using your allies. A certified letter from you with a formal copy (i.e., you note a "cc:" at the end of the letter) to an agency or political representative may be necessary to bring about the desired meeting. Often a call from a citizen organization can help.

◆

When Mrs. Parsons finally enlisted the services of an advocate, she told the advocate, "Every time I wrote a letter to the school I sent a copy to the state department of education. Nothing happened. Aren't they responsible for overseeing the public schools in this state?" Her advocate told her, "Technically, but don't hold your breath. Now I am here to help you."

◆

Don't assume that a copy of your letter to your state department of education will result in action. It may have little effect or delay action. It's okay to send them a copy as long as you send a copy to an outside person or agency. But your state department of education is most useful as a resource for information about the specifics of the law and the state regulations.

Whatever was required of you in calling or setting a time for the IEP is entered in your log. Later your records will support you if there is undue delay or difficulty and you need to complain. These records also provide a check on your memory: When you review your log, you may find that you talked to the secretary and not, as you thought, the principal (maybe time to get on the telephone again and make sure you reach the principal in person). Or a convenient meeting time was in fact arranged 3 weeks after your request, not months later, as you in your impatience imagined. Once you have the meeting conveniently arranged so that you have at least 2 weeks' lead time (more if you need it), you begin your final stage of preparation.

GETTING READY FOR THE IEP MEETING

In the time remaining before the scheduled meeting, you have some important work to finish so that you can present yourself as an informed and active parent participant in the IEP process. If you have already been collecting information, visiting the classroom, and readying records, you can use this time to prepare yourself:

- Organize your records and your thoughts.

- Get copies of items not in your files, such as missing evaluations or more information on the law.

- Make your list of concerns, questions, and recommendations that you want considered in the development of the IEP. Put them in order of importance.

- Talk to your personal advocate about what the meeting will be like and plan what his or her role will be.

- Write statements you want to make to the IEP team.

- Write self-statements you will make to yourself for personal support.

- Rehearse your role in the IEP process, including management of any difficulties that you think could arise, and rehearse again.

If you discover, while preparing yourself for the meeting, that you have good reason for delaying or changing the meeting (e.g., you are missing some evaluations in your file, waiting for recent evaluations to be completed, or your personal advocate cannot make the scheduled meeting), do not hesitate to negotiate another meeting time. You are not trying to make life difficult for the school staff; to the contrary, you may in fact simplify their jobs by coming fully prepared. In the weeks before the IEP meeting, you should be prepared to share your expectations for goals and objective, other services, and options. At this time, ask the school to share the same with you. This avoids the problems that can come with surprises.

In these weeks before the meeting, give yourself sufficient time to do the work, but also allow yourself some time off for relaxation. All work and no play can make an uptight advocate. If you are overworked, you may be a less effective participant. Besides, you deserve some reward for all of the time and effort you have been putting in.

REVIEWING THE RECORDS

This is the time to make sure you have collected all of the information you need. One way to do a thorough review of your records is to make a complete list of everything you have in your log or notebook. List materials by year, by topic, or by whatever grouping is going to work best for you. (See the section Keeping Records in Chapter 5.) Make note in your list of what you consider the most important information for developing a good IEP and determine whether there are any missing documents. Plan to have the missing documents in your hands by the time of the meeting. If your file is too large to carry to the meeting, pull out the documents you expect you might want to use at the meeting. If your file is small, you can take it all with you. If your papers are only one-quarter inch thick and you are the parent of an older child, the file itself can make a statement about the lack of services, plans, and evaluations for your child: "Maryann has been in special education classes for 6 years now, and these are all of the reports I have collected. Surely we need to do more for her."

Not only might you pull out and mark the important documents, but you can also underline or highlight the sections that appear significant to you and make comments in the margins, such as "I don't know what this means," or "Taylor could do this several years ago." These are the records that you collected to help you work for your child; mark them up in any way that helps you remember the issues and communicate them to others—your advocate, the school people, or agency representatives.

As you go through your files, jot down issues and concerns to raise at the meeting; for example:

Teachers' reports 2008 and 2009: Reports do not agree. The 2008 teacher report has Randy more capable than the 2009 report. Speech report is also better for Randy and is similar to camp report.

Report from Camp Tall Trees, 2008: Raise speech and independent skills as areas of concern.

Speech Evaluation, 2009: Stress speech evaluation and camp report at meeting.

Listing items in this way helps you sort out your concerns and questions and enables you to use the information you have as support for getting the services you want. On their first try, some parents will find that they are listing everything as important. And they are right: Everything is important. But some things are more important than others. If you find yourself with an unwieldy list, don't think the job is unmanageable and give up in despair. Go through your "unwieldy" list and star the most important priorities for this year. Look for groupings of items that will support your priorities and make a mental note, as in the following case:

> *"This year I think speech-language therapy should have the highest priority. Now, let's see. The evaluation from the Children's Medical Center will help, and so will the report from last year's teacher. Here's something else. With these reports I can make a strong case for the service I want my child to have."*

As you go over your records in this manner, you will begin to see how useful they will be. You don't have to do the review in one sitting unless your records are very slim. This is not a test of your endurance. It can be helpful to set the records aside and come back later when you are fresh for the task. When you have culled your records for priorities and for back-up information to support those priorities, and when you have organized your thoughts and the list of services that you believe your child needs, you will have prepared the basics of a plan for the IEP meeting. Now share that plan with your personal advocate.

GETTING YOUR ADVOCATE READY

By now, based on the information you received in Chapter 5 on the advocate's advocate, you have sought and found a personal ally who will accompany you to the IEP meeting(s). Whether you have a strong or weak advocate, a long-distance advocate or one at your side, your advocate must be fully informed about and involved in the planning for the IEP. All of your preparation in reviewing the records should now be shared with your personal advocate. (Note: If, in spite of your efforts, you find yourself without an advocate, you should not ignore this section. You will find some special comments throughout on how to use this advice when you are the lone advocate.) Begin preparing your personal advocate by sitting down with him or her and going over the following:

- Your list of priority issues for the IEP

- Selected documents you have deemed important (If your advocate has the time, ability, and interest, you can invite him or her to read everything you have.)

- The people who will be at the meeting and your past impressions of them

- Any correspondence you have had with the school people (which may indicate that smooth or rough sailing is ahead)

- Information about IDEA and the state laws (if your advocate needs this)

- The role (specific statements and behaviors) that you hope the advocate can play to support your efforts

- Your concerns, questions, hopes, and fears about the upcoming meeting

You must be ready to share all of the information you have with your advocate. A sophisticated advocate may only want your list of priorities, a few selected documents, and your verbal report of your contacts with the school system. Your long-distance advocate may, after talking to you on the telephone, request that you send copies of one or two documents that he or she will review before advising you in a follow-up call. Your well-meaning but naive advocate may be overwhelmed by the information. Here, the rule is that you should give your advocate all of the information he or she can handle, and no more. When your advocate protests, back off, suggesting that maybe the two of you should just go over your priorities. Later, perhaps you can do more preparation; for now, you should respect your advocate's anxieties and concerns.

An experienced advocate will ask for more. Any advocate should be informed about what you hope to get out of the IEP meeting. Therefore, review your list of desired services, noting which are the most important and which are the least. Let your advocate know that, although you would like all of the services, you don't expect to win all of your points; you do expect, however, to get your child's most important needs met in the IEP. Explain why these services are necessary, talking about your own experiences with your child, including your observations and your attempts to help him or her. In this way, you show your advocate how the service is important. Also talk about which of you will take the lead and which gentle signals you will use to make each other aware of your concerns.

If in spite of all of your searching for an advocate, you realize you cannot find even a naive advocate and you have to go it alone, keep searching, but understand that the lone parent advocate can help him- or herself by playing out the situation, trying to put in words what he or she wants in the IEP. For example, "I want more physical therapy for Kathy." (Why?) "Because she needs it." (Not strong enough!) "This report indicates that she should be having it daily." (Specific reference, good!) "She has a more pronounced limp now than she had last year." (You're using your own observations to make a stronger case.) By rehearsing your requests and explanations to a fantasy helper, you can learn to criticize your own performance, improve your statements, and strengthen your arguments. Write down your good statements and arguments to use at the meeting, or they may be lost.

Share documents (selected ones or all of them) with your helpers in the way they can get the most out of them: mailing copies to your organizational advocate, letting your sophisticated advocate read them with or without you, or describing some of the most significant reports in your own words to your naive advocate. They will give you back useful comments and questions that will help you build your case. Don't underestimate the value of naive questions from an inexperienced advocate. Naive questions sometimes cut right to the heart of the matter: "If all of the reports you've been describing say that Chuck needs daily therapy, then why isn't he getting it?" You may decide that this question is the one to put to the school system. Give your advocates all of the information and papers they want and can handle, but don't overload them. Respect their comments, opinions, and ideas about the information you have shared with them.

At this point, it might be helpful to introduce your advocate to the cast of characters who will be participating in the IEP meeting. Perhaps your naive advocate is visualizing a meeting of Godzilla, King Kong, and Attila the Hun. It may be reassuring to him or her to hear your impressions of the school staff that you expect to be at the meeting:

> *"I found the special education teacher, Ms. Atkins, to be a little stiff and formal with me. But Laura likes her and is finally start-ing to read for pleasure. Ms. Atkins may not be very good with parents; at least I feel a little uncomfortable with her. Still, she impresses me as a competent teacher. Then there's the general edu-cation class teacher, Mr. Hale; he was as friendly as can be and told me what a great student Laura was. But Laura says he doesn't pay any attention to her when she's in his classroom. The special edu-cation director, Mr. Green, seems like a nice guy, but he doesn't push for new services. I think he's more worried about the budget than anything else. Then there's the school psychologist. . . ."*

When you describe the school staff to your advocate, they may begin to appear less intimidating to him or her. Your advocate may recog-nize their similarities to people he or she has successfully dealt with before. Perhaps she says something like this:

> *"You know, that Ms. Atkins sounds like Ms. Haag, the town's head librarian. She glares at you if you make the least noise in the library. But she knows that library inside out, and if I want to find a book, I go right to her and she finds it pronto. She may be tough, but she knows her business. If Ms. Atkins is as smart as you say, maybe she's the one we want to watch at the meeting to see if we are on the right track."*

As you and your advocate continue through the cast of characters, you both might begin to think of strategies. For example, you agree with your advocate that it might be helpful to watch Ms. Atkins to see if she agrees or disagrees with your recommendations. If she's the tough old bird you think she is, she may also intimidate Mr. Green, which could be used to your advantage. In your discussion, note which participants, in your opinion, will have the knowledge, the competence, or the power you need behind you at the meeting; when to call on each participant for information; and where hidden sources of support might be. The lone parent advocate will also find it helpful to reflect on the school's cast of characters, and where the expertise or power lies. As you go through your list, you make notes for yourself—expect some support from this person, resistance from that one, nothing from one or two others.

Both the school people and the task of developing a good IEP are now beginning to look a little more manageable and a little less frightening. You should remind your advocate and yourself that you are discussing your impressions based on your own experiences and information from your child. Any one of the participants may present him- or herself differently at the meeting and prove you wrong. This is not always an unpleasant experience. The general education class teacher, whom you may have expected to be a mere bench warmer, might tell the group that he has great difficulty understanding Laura's speech; for that reason, he feels he isn't giving her the help she needs and may ask about getting more speech-language therapy for Laura. You may be pleasantly surprised and immediately add your support to his recommendation. Thus you and your advocate should be prepared to shift gears and strategies when the occasion calls for it.

Your advocate will also need to know how easy or difficult it was for you to arrange this IEP meeting. This is the time to bring out your correspondence with the school system and tell your advocate what problems, if any, you met in arranging the meeting. Hearing about an accommodating school system could help your advocate relax a little; learning about the resistance you encountered might bring forth the response, "Sounds like we have our work cut out for us, but we can hang tough, too." Your review of your correspondence and experience can help your advocate to understand and be ready for what may lie ahead.

If your advocate is naive about special education, provide information about IDEA, but don't hand him or her complete copies of the law and regulations (unless requested), because reading legal language can be difficult and confusing. Instead, give him or her a few pamphlets that explain in simple language what IDEA is all about. (You can get these pamphlets from the parent information center in your state. Your advocate will want to ask you questions about the law and you should be prepared to answer them. When you can explain your rights and your child's so that they are understood by someone who doesn't know the law, you will be better prepared to state those rights at the IEP meeting, if that becomes necessary. (This is good exercise for the lone parent advocate, too. Even if you don't have a personal advocate, try to find someone who will listen for 5 minutes while you explain the law and then tell you how much he or she understands.) If your advocate asks you questions you can't answer, go through your materials and find the answers. If you can't find them, then call an organization that can help you. You and your advocate, to the degree that you understand the basics of IDEA, will be better advocates for your child.

Everything discussed above has been in the nature of information sharing. Now is the time for you and your advocate to do some concrete planning. Because you and your advocate will work as a team, you should plan your performance. First look at the strengths and weaknesses of each of you:

- Is one of you more forceful (or less timid) than the other?

- Which of you is more knowledgeable? About which area? (You, of course, know your child best, but a sophisticated advocate may know the law better.)

- Which of you is better at speaking up? At reminding everyone of what was said or lost? At carrying on an argument? At sizing up a group?

- Which of you can be calmer and cooler?

- Which of you (if either) has a face whose expressions are worth a thousand words or the face of a good poker player? (Each can be used to your advantage.)

- Which of you can engineer a graceful shift or exit when the discussion is going nowhere or getting rough?

For the lone parent advocate, a review of your strengths and weaknesses is essential. List them on paper: Look at your weaknesses and think of ways you can manage them. If you are nervous in a group, write down what you want to say beforehand, and plan to take notes during the meeting on what is said. If you are afraid of being pressured into something you don't want, write on a card or in your notebook things you can say, such as, "I think we need more information about Joanie's performance in this area. I don't want us to get bogged down here." At the meeting, you can add, "Could we talk about the computer training program, which is very important to me?" If you can engineer a shift in this way, you can temporarily reduce the pressure on yourself.

You must compensate for the lack of an advocate by even more careful preparation. As the lone parent advocate, you should prepare for the meeting by getting your tape recorder set up. This is essential so that you will not miss the information you would have gained with your personal advocate in attendance. This also helps you in keeping your long distance advocate informed.

The parent with an advocate must also plan strategies for the meeting. When you and your advocate discuss your individual qualities, you will start to get some idea of how active each of you will be. One of you may play the leading role, the other, the supporting role. You want to balance your styles, strengths, and weaknesses. For example, your advocate may not be at his or her best with strangers (seldom speaks up), but he or she has a memory that would stagger an elephant and has a good sense of whether groups are working well or doing poorly. Together you can decide whether your advocate will play the supporting role. For instance, at the meeting, your advocate might plan to sit at your elbow with the desired list of services in hand, poking you and making comments to you when things are going well or when you are getting a snow job.

Or perhaps your advocate is a salesperson by nature or profession: Nothing and no one fazes him or her. This type of advocate will do better playing an active role at the meeting. You might sit across the table from one another so that he or she can watch your expressions to make sure that he or she is saying the right thing, that you are not getting too anxious, and that between the two of you, you are able to see everyone's expressions and reactions.

In this way, each of you gets to use personal skills in the style with which you are most comfortable. Your combined assets can make you a more effective advocacy team. You know that it is impossible to predict everything that will happen at the meeting. But if you carefully plan your roles, statements, and signals (to each other), then you both will grow in your confidence that at the upcoming meeting something good is going to be planned for your child.

As you and your advocate wrap up your planning session, you may want to say something more about your hopes and fears for the upcoming meeting. You might also tell your advocate that your fears are a little less and your hopes a little more because you will have someone who is on your side with you and because you won't have to walk in alone. You and your advocate should plan to meet before the scheduled IEP meeting, perhaps for a quiet cup of coffee and definitely for some last-minute tips or coaching. You won't be reviewing material (unless you just got a copy of a long-awaited report) or making lists of items because you have already done that in your planning sessions. This is the time for you to reassure each other and relax as much as you can. When you leave for the meeting, you and your advocate go together and arrive together.

WORKING THROUGH THE IEP

Let's walk through a sample meeting with you and your prepared advocate. We'll look at everything from greetings and seating arrangements; through issues, responses, and dealing with jargon; to the conclusion of a carefully written IEP, which you accept, modify, or reject. We will also see how and when to cooperate, negotiate, and confront during the IEP process.

Setting the Stage

You and your advocate should arrive on time and greet everyone in a friendly and assertive way:

> *"I'm glad we could arrange this meeting because Harry has needed some changes and more services in his school program for some time now. I brought Mrs. Tate, my neighbor. She is interested in Harry's progress and has been helping me work on the IEP. I am fortunate that she could make the time to be here with me today."*

This kind of statement helps to put your advocate at ease and defines her position in the group. It is not a good idea to say things like "I'm so grateful to you for arranging this meeting, and I hope it's okay for Mrs. Tate to come with me." This kind of timid, hat-in-hand entrance sets you up as a weak parent and puts Mrs. Tate in the position of being an intruder. Approached in this way, the school system has already done you two favors: They "gave" you a meeting and they let an "outsider" sit in. Your participation in this meeting and the presence of your advocate are not gifts but rights.

The physical setting can provide you with advance information about what's coming. When you sit down to the meeting, note the physical arrangements:

Are you all sitting at a table like a team trying to solve a problem, or is the administrator sitting behind a desk, which is a reminder of his or her authority?

Are you going to have to balance all of your important papers in your lap? If so, this could distract you from the important work at hand. Ask if there is another room available with a table where you can all work with the documents in front of you. If the administrator insists that this is the only room that can be used for the meeting, then ask for an end table or another chair to use for your records. A responsive administrator who is honestly limited to that room will clear his or her desk as the working table. If you are forced to balance things on your lap during the meeting, then do not apologize when it takes you time to find the report you want. You might say, "If we had a better setup, I could find the document more quickly. Unfortunately, I'm afraid you'll just have to bear with me while I look through my file."

Are you meeting in a place free of distractions, or in an office where you are interrupted by various people and calls not of an emergency nature? Sometimes there will be interruptions at the beginning of the meeting. It is up to the administrator to make it clear to staff that he or she is not to be interrupted during this meeting, and most administrators will do that. However, if you find yourself at a meeting with constant disruptions that are seriously undermining the development of the plan, you may want to raise the issue of setting a better time: "Ms. Thomas, in the half hour we've been here, you have taken four calls and left the meeting twice." (Who's counting? You! And you put it in your log or notebook as soon as you suspect that the interruptions are becoming unreasonable.) "Although it was difficult for Mrs. Tate and me to arrange time for the meeting, we are willing to reschedule at a better time for you. You obviously have other commitments today, and we need your full participation at this meeting." If things do not quiet down, insist on rescheduling. IDEA guarantees your child privacy, which doesn't exist if interruptions occur.

In your notebook, list who is at the meeting. You have the school's list of who is attending the meeting; are all of the participants there, especially the individuals you requested? If not, are the excuses valid? "The gym teacher broke his arm in a freak accident in school today" may be a valid excuse; "The speech-language therapist is attending an all-day workshop" is not. You may need a follow-up meeting that includes the gym teacher in the discussion about adaptive physical education. You are justified in feeling that your child's future is more important than any workshop, and that at the very least, because the speech-language therapist knew in advance he would be absent, the meeting should have been scheduled for another time when he could be present for the discussion. You say to the others that it may be necessary for him to be here, but for the time being, you'd like to see his report. If people are not there, they cannot be part of the discussion that is part of developing the IEP. You will then react appropriately to the situation: "No report! Well, without the report we may not be able to finish the program today. Let's see how much we can do." Or "Ah, you have the report. Is this my copy? Give Mrs. Tate and me a few moments to read it."

Leading Off

Before the meeting begins you should ask how much time has been allotted for the meeting. It is a rare IEP that can be done in an hour, and that happens only when there are previous discussions and total agreement. Normally there will be no time for chitchat, or you'll find someone telling you the meeting time is over and another parent is waiting. If this does happen to you, don't panic, because you can always ask for another meeting, and you will be aware of time at the next meeting. But be mindful of just how much time has been set aside to develop your child's IEP.

At the beginning of the meeting, you will be asked to sign an attendance sheet. This is the only paper you will sign at the meeting.

The meeting begins in earnest. The speech report is presented for discussion, and you find that it is written in simple language with definitions of complicated terms. Don't hesitate to compliment the school staff on the clarity of the report: "This is nice. I think I really understand the goals of the speech therapy now." School staff need and deserve praise for a good job, too.

If the report is full of jargon and you can't understand it, you should say so and ask that it be rewritten so that you can understand it because this is an area of great concern to you. You are not being difficult: You want and have a right to know. Besides, the group is making decisions that will seriously affect your child, and you will want to carefully review and understand all recommendations and plans before you sign the IEP. Would you sign a contract without reading and understanding it? If the report is long, you need more time to read it and think about it. Tell the school staff you are taking it home and will get back to them later about your child's speech-language needs. You must never sign an IEP when it's first presented to you at the meeting. You should instead ask for a copy that the team has developed and take it home for a second look.

Being Specific

If you have had time to read the report that was written in language you understand, you may be ready to work through the speech-language goals of your child's IEP. Ask the school staff what they think your child needs and what they have to offer in the way of service. They are the experts; let them go first. They may have developed a speech-language program that is everything you want. However, they may be vague. If so, push for specifics:

> *"Speech-language therapy" should read, "Speech-language therapy twice a week with Mr. Hadley, the speech-language therapist. Each session is 30 minutes. The therapist works with the general education teacher, Ms. Ames, 1 hour twice a week, to assist Ms. Ames to provide a language training program (based on the therapist's evaluation and plan), which will be implemented throughout the school day."*

Everything you want that is agreed upon by the group must be written down in clear and specific terms so that later on, there will be no difference of opinion about the type and quantity of services your child will be receiving. When you have this kind of specificity, you and everyone else understands the kind of service your child will get. You may want to include in the IEP regular meetings for you and the therapist and/or teacher. This can be important if your child is young or has difficulty communicating. Again, be specific—meetings once a month, every 2 months, or perhaps weekly telephone contact. Do you also want objectives to work on at home with your child? Then say so, and get the specifics.

Remember, talk is cheap (verbal agreements are very weak), and when you go back after a few months to check on the implementation of the IEP, you will be able to advocate for only what is written in the program. With verbal agreements, you may find yourself up against honest misunderstandings, vague recollections, or even loss of memory. And without written agreements, you will probably hear about the tight budget and shortage of personnel that does not allow for more service for your child. If it's not written down in the IEP, it's like it never happened.

The business of getting adequate and accurate information presented, discussed, and recorded at the IEP meeting is hard work. You need a guide.

Asking Your 20 Questions

In each program or service area, such as fine motor or vocational skills, you should make sure that you have answers to the following questions:

Assessment

1. Is information regarding your child's present level of performance (what he or she can and can't do) accurately presented, discussed, and agreed upon?

2. Is the information regarding your child's learning style part of the assessment? For example, does your child learn most and best by listening (auditory learner) or by seeing (visual learner)?

Evaluations

3. What evaluations has your child had or does your child need? (These evaluations can be done only with your consent. If the school staff want your child to have a psychiatric evaluation and you don't agree, you can withhold your consent.)

4. Are the evaluations comprehensive and multidisciplinary; that is, do they look at the whole child or just a "piece" of the child? For example, your child is labeled with emotional disturbances and has been seen by a psychologist, but has he or she been seen by a learning disabilities specialist, an occupational therapist, or a neurologist who may uncover some other specific learning problems? (If you are requesting an outside evaluation, the school must provide you with a list of independent evaluators.)

5. Are the evaluations nondiscriminatory? For example, if your child's native Spanish is better than his or her English, is he or she tested in Spanish? Or, if your child has visual disabilities, is he or she given a visual or an auditory test of intelligence? If your child can't make visual discriminations, he or she will score more poorly on the visual test, and the score will be inaccurate.

IEP Goals

6. Are the goals written in the order of priority (e.g., the most important is first, the next most important is second, and so forth), and in the specific descriptive terms that you requested ("one-to-one ratio," not "adequate ratio")?

Implementation of Goals

7.   What service is to be provided?

8.   Who will provide the service? The specialist? The teacher? The aide? Any combination of these people? What are their qualifications, training, or preparation?

9.   How will the service be provided? Which methods or teaching approaches will be used?

10.   Where will the service be provided? What school or building? What setting—class (general education or special education); small group; one-to-one?

11.   How often will the service be provided? One day per week? Three days per week?

12.   How much will be provided? Fifteen-minute sessions? Hour-long sessions?

13.   When will the service start? As soon as the plan is agreed upon and signed? Thirty days later (to allow for hiring special personnel)?

Meeting Procedures

14.   Are the comments and recommendations about the reports being recorded?

15.   Do you have your copy (copies)?

16.   Do you understand what you have been given to read?

17.   Are you and your advocate given enough time and opportunity to discuss and understand the items presented, to ask your own questions, and to present your own recommendations?

18.   If you are not in agreement, are your sound and specific reasons for disagreeing being recorded?

19.   If you are in agreement about the service, has its implementation been written into the plan in the specific language you requested?

20.   Have all of your questions been answered?

Now, let's apply these questions to another area of concern, such as your child's reading program. The following is a hypothetical transcript of a portion of an IEP meeting using the 20 Questions as your guide:

Question 1 (Performance): The teacher discusses her assessment of your child's reading level. Your copy was sent to you before the meeting, so you and your advocate had sufficient time to read the assessment.

The teacher reviews: "Carol is presently reading at a fourth-grade level. However, her comprehension is at a second-grade level."

You know that Carol can read more than she appears to understand because you have done some reading with her at home. You add your general agreement.

Question 2 (Learning style): The teacher continues by showing some samples of things Carol has read and notes that some types of reading materials are better for her:

"Carol seems to do better in comprehending materials that deal in facts, and especially with facts that she can relate to her own experiences. Although her overall comprehension is at a second-grade level, she does a little better with this series." (The teacher shows you and the group one of the readers.)

At this point, the psychologist speaks up: "Carol's reading problems may have something to do with her immaturity and her emotional problems. Her inability to read more abstract material could be a result of her difficulties in dealing with her feelings."

You realize there is a shift here from reading skills to emotional problems, and you intervene: "Before we lose sight of Ms. Payne's assessments, I want to say that my observations of Carol agree with hers. Carol learns and remembers what she can see and do. Emphasizing the concrete can help her read better. She has to understand what she's reading; otherwise, she's only parroting."

Question 3 (Evaluations): The psychologist refers to his earlier evaluations:

"Two years ago when I gave Carol some tests, including an intelligence test, she did poorly. From my other observations in the classroom, I thought Carol was a good deal brighter than the test results would indicate. During the testing, however, she became anxious and distracted, which I attributed to her immaturity. Perhaps we need to test her again to see if she has made progress in her emotional development."

You interrupt: "I understand and appreciate what you are saying, but I don't want to move away from Carol's reading yet."

Note that you resist the psychologist's assumptions and his shift away from reading problems.

Question 4 (Comprehensiveness): You ask, "What other evaluations has Carol had?" and are told that she has undergone several others done by school staff. You note that since Carol has been in school, she has not been seen by a neurologist. Given that her original diagnosis was brain damage, you would like more comprehensive evaluations: specifically, a review by the neurologist, as well as an evaluation by a learning disabilities specialist. You feel that more information is needed than one kind of testing—psychological evaluation—will give. (Throughout the process you may continue to press for multidisciplinary evaluations.)

Question 5 (Fairness): You ask for a description of the past psychological evaluations. As they are described to you, you realize that they are basically verbal tests, and you know that Carol's strengths are visual. You ask, "Aren't there visual tests of intelligence?" and are told, "Yes, but we use the most widely used tests, which happen to be verbal."

"That doesn't seem fair," you respond. "It doesn't give Carol her best shot, does it?" You turn to the school psychologist and ask, "Can you give her some other tests that won't put her at such a disadvantage and test her intelligence rather than test her disability?"

The psychologist is not all that familiar or experienced with other tests; he feels that it would be unfair to Carol to do tests he is not familiar with and suggests that it is best to leave well enough alone and stick with the verbal tests.

You disagree; it is not "well enough" if Carol's true abilities are not being measured. At this point, you may request an evaluation by a neuropsychologist, who can do a wider range of tests. If the school agrees to the independent evaluation you asked for, it is written into the IEP. If they reject further testing, you must say this is an issue we will take to hearing.

Question 6 (Priorities): The teacher wants to discuss her recommendations for reading. "After all," she asks, "isn't reading one of the highest priorities for Carol?"

To you, reading and language are part of the same need for your child, and you say so. If you have to separate them for the IEP, then your priorities will be 1) language/communication, and 2) reading. Both are very important goals. You want to know how the goal for reading will be implemented.

Question 7 (What): The teacher replies that reading instruction will be given, with the goal being to increase Carol's comprehension from a second-grade level to a low fourth-grade level in the coming school year. You ask if that is possible. The teacher tells you that she can't promise that the goal will be attained, but she feels that it is a worthy and realistic goal.

Question 8 (Who): The teacher indicates that she will provide the basic reading instruction. She will work closely with the speech-language therapist to ensure that the materials used will be appropriate to Carol's language and reading needs. In addition, the aide will work with Carol, tutoring on an individual basis.

Question 9 (How): The emphasis, says the teacher, will be on concrete basic reading materials using the series of readers that Carol is now using with success. The aide will specifically work with Carol on preparing experience stories based on Carol's own words and experiences.

Question 10 (Where): The aide in the general education classroom will provide the services in the special education classroom in small-group and in one-to-one instruction.

Question 11 (How often): Small-group reading and one-to-one instruction will occur every day.

Question 12 (How much): The teacher will provide instruction for small-group reading each day for one half-hour. In addition, the aide will provide your child with one-to-one instruction for half an hour each day in the general education classroom. This sounds appropriate to you, but you have one question: "What is a small group?" The teacher responds that, with her knowledge of the programs of the students she will be teaching, it could range from two to four students, but she expects that for most days, three will be the maximum, and that, for 1 or 2 days each week, the group size will be two. You ask that the size of the small group be designated in the IEP as three students.

Note that you required that terms be defined and written down. In this way you can help to prevent that small group from growing to six or eight students and still appearing to be consistent with the IEP. Because of your request for specificity, you have increased the likelihood of the group remaining small.

Question 13 (When): The program is beginning to sound good to you. There is twice as much overall instruction as last year with a substantial increase in individual instruction. "When," you want to know, "will the reading program start?" The teacher explains that she will have a new classroom aide at the beginning of the year and will need a few weeks to train the aide. She anticipates that "within a few weeks," the aide, under her supervision, will begin the additional instruction. The teacher, if the IEP is agreed upon, will begin her daily instruction on the first day of the school year. The discussion should also note the specific time the reading program will be reviewed to measure its success or failure (e.g., 9 weeks? mid-year?).

Question 14 (Recording): The best way to know that all comments and recommendations are being recorded is to ask that they be read back to you. As you listen, check your notes to be sure that the specifics you wanted have been duly noted. If there are omissions or changes, speak up: "That piece about the teacher and the speech-language therapist was left out. I think that's very important. Please include it in the implementation statements about the goal."

Question 15 (Copies): Look at your papers. Do you have copies of all reports? The teacher's recommendations? The psychologist's evaluation? If not, speak up: "I thought Ms. Brousseau's comments on my child were excellent, but I don't seem to have her recommendations. They were not in the reports sent to my home. May I have a copy before we finish this discussion on reading?" Because most schools have copy machines, the school staff can usually produce the material in a few minutes. You will still need 48 hours to review the document, but you are open to hearing discussion.

Question 16 (Clear understanding): When you get the material, read it to see if you understand it. If not, ask for more explanation.

You cannot give your full agreement until you read and understand everything.

Question 17 (Time and opportunity): Make sure you take enough time and make the opportunity to present your own questions, concerns, and recommendations. Even the best-intentioned school staff may leave you out of the discussion if you never speak up. Someone may not notice you shaking your head in disagreement. You must help to make your own time and opportunity. Whether you agree or disagree, say so and explain why.

Question 18 (Disagreement): If you disagree with the reading program being developed, this is the time, when discussion on reading is being wrapped up, for you to say so while the reasons why you disagree are fresh in your mind. The school staff may not like your criticisms now, but they will like them even less when they think the IEP is almost done and you unexpectedly pipe up with, "I don't like the reading plan!" Voice any objections you have when the items are under discussion.

For example, if the teacher, when defining a small group, had told you 10 children instead of 2 to 4, you would want to object because that was the actual class size and not a small group within the class. You would then want recorded not only your objection but also your specific request for instruction in a small group of two to four students. Your specific objection is based on your understanding of your child's need and may in fact make better educational sense than the larger group. It ought to be recorded. (The school should record your disagreement in the discussion. You also record your objections in your own notes.)

Question 19 (Agreement): But you are in agreement! The reading plan looks appropriate and promises some real benefit for your child. Tell the school people, especially the teacher, that you like the recommendations. Ask that the person chairing the committee read back the specifics—the what, who, where, when, and hows of the plan. If any item is vague or has been left out, have that item clarified or recovered and entered into the plan. Work on those additions or corrections until they represent the reading program you are willing to accept. Then, state your agreement and satisfaction, which the school records in the discussion and you record in your log.

Question 20 (Any questions): Surely by now all of your questions about the reading program have been fully answered. Or have they? Review the notes you have been making during the meeting. Remember the discussions with the psychologist about evaluations. That was left up in the air. You may want to seek some closure now or postpone agreement. (If you suspect that the evaluations will be discussed with other components of the IEP, you may prefer to save the discussion of evaluations until later in the meeting. Write it on your list of things to be accomplished before you sign the IEP.)

You begin: "Before we go on to the next service item, I would like to return to the discussion of evaluations. We didn't reach any conclusions that I can remember. I would prefer. . . ." And then you may want to say something like this:

" . . . that no further testing be done at this time. I would like to see the program we have just outlined given a chance to work. Later, we may all feel that further testing will be necessary. When a stronger case can be made, I will be happy to give my consent for further tests."

or

". . .that a neurological evaluation be done along with the psychological testing. I will consent to both evaluations if you can arrange a predominantly visual test of intelligence for Carol."

or

". . .that we settle the matter of evaluations after we have discussed some more of the IEP's components. Because I suspect that Carol has some motor problems, it may be necessary to have more comprehensive evaluations. We may be in a better position to decide later in the meeting which evaluations will be necessary."

In general, as you move from one area of concern to the next (e.g., math, adaptive physical education, social skills), you are asking yourself and the group the same valid 20 questions until the school staff have presented all of their recommendations for the education program. During this time, you and your advocate are taking notes on concerns, agreements, and disagreements, as well as making comments, recommendations, and points.

Adding One or Two More Things

As the meeting seems to be coming to a close, you quickly review your list of concerns and requests for services to see if any have been left out. From your notes, you see that no one has mentioned art, music, or physical education. You want one or all of these items considered in the IEP, and you say so.

Generally the school people feel obligated to present as good a plan (based on their professional skills) as they can within the system's constraints as they see them. If you have been cool, controlled, and prepared, chances are that you have engaged already in some give and take during the discussion of at least some, if not all, issues. In this way, you have established yourself as a reasonable person who is knowledgeable and assertive, as well as concerned and committed.

The wise parent always goes into negotiations with a longer list of services than he or she expects to receive. Your list is made up only of services your child needs (none are frivolous or luxurious), but some services are more important than others. You can star the most important ones—the nonnegotiables—the ones you will insist be met. You are willing to negotiate ones that are less important.

As you review the developing program, you may see that most of your requests have been included, and you note to yourself, "Speech-language program looks good. Reading is a little weak, but the gym program is a disaster, and we haven't even discussed the art program."

Presenting Your Case

Given your understanding of the meeting, you now present your case. Typically you will review what the school system has offered in the developing IEP, compliment the parts of the program you like, and express the reservations you still have about other parts: "Larry's motor problems are a serious concern. He needs a carefully planned physical education program with more individualized instruction from the physical education teacher. But he also needs some art therapy to help him develop fine motor coordination."

You hope for both but you are prepared to accept one. The special education director tells you that the physical education teacher is swamped with work and the art therapist gets to Larry's school once a week and doesn't even get to all of the grades in the school. Here are some examples of how you can respond in this discussion, depending on how you see your child's needs:

"You say that you appreciate the physical education teacher's problems, but wouldn't it be possible for him to assess Larry and develop a plan that could be used by the classroom aide or student teacher for the first 10 minutes of every gym period? This would at least be a start."

Or you express your concern and say that you would like both art and physical education because your child's needs are great, but, for this year, you are willing to accept one if both are not possible.

Or you request that an evaluation by a physical or occupational therapist be done and that the therapist make recommendations for the classroom, art therapy, and gym to meet Larry's needs. (Perhaps you have talked privately to your child's teacher, who agreed with your concerns and who is desperate for help and direction from a specialist.)

Whichever response you give, the message you have communicated is that your child's motor needs are important and you want something done to help him or her. Even your weakest response (you will accept either art or physical education) is said with the understanding that next year you will be back for the service you didn't get this year.

When you review your list of services, you may find yourself thinking, "Hey, I've got the most important services, the speech-language and reading, and that's good. I'd like services to meet all of his needs, but I may have to give a little here." If you are keeping score (and you are), your list of proposed services might look like this example (stars denote priority items):

Speech*—Satisfactory

Reading*—Good but needs more individual attention; make sure time is specified

Math—Satisfactory

Music—Acceptable

Gym—Unsatisfactory (but could be satisfactory if gym teacher and aide work together)

Art—Unsatisfactory (but could be satisfactory if teacher gets help and evaluation from the therapist)

Overall, there are more new and specific recommendations in your child's IEP than there were last year, and you feel his or her needs are being met. You have accomplished what you set out to do. Give yourself a pat on the back or a night on the town: You deserve it.

If, when you review your list, you find that the list of services seems very limited or does not in your opinion meet your child's needs (you may deserve a pat on the back even more for surviving so far), you will speak up and clearly state that if this is the plan, you suspect that after taking it home to share with your spouse, you will probably need to reject it.

If you are asking for things that schools typically resist giving, like Extended School Year (ESY) or an exemption from the discipline code, you have more work to do. If your child needs a year-round program, you ask for an ESY. Note that you do not ask for a "summer program." Even if your child's IEP is carried out at a camp, it is still an ESY. The goals may be similar to the school-year IEP (e.g., language skills) or different (e.g., a plan for therapy to improve motor skills) or more likely a mixture of both. Schools typically are reluctant to provide a year-round program, and they use a regression recoupment argument mostly focused on the rate of recovery for academic skills. For some children, there may be significant loss of academic skills; for others the loss may be in behavioral skills. They frequently dismiss the loss of behavioral skills, which could be due to an absence of occupational or physical therapy or a period of no opportunity to interact with other children in either learning or social situations. They overlook that for a child with a communication disability, language lost is language not acquired over the summer. Getting an ESY will not be easy, but that summer may be a critical time of learning for that student. Early intervention programs, because of the language, motor, and social skills being learned, almost always demand an ESY.

Another challenge the schools do not willingly undertake is to provide an exemption from the school's discipline code. An increasing number of students are being frequently suspended from school, and the majority of these suspended students are students with disabilities. Students with anxiety, panic, emotional, or sensory/neurological disorders, as well as students with other disabilities, are often targeted by school bullies, and usually it is the victim who is blamed for any disruption and suspended.

Schools frequently resist making an exemption from the discipline code, but you can insist that there be something written in the IEP that notes your concern about any discipline taken against your child because of his or her disability. This is discrimination, and it will be tougher for you to deal with if there is no early record of this concern.

———◆———

Miguel had trouble managing the high school corridors, even with his aide. When the bell to change classes rang, he immediately sat on the hall floor. He was immovable. The Vice Principal for Discipline (yes, that was his title) was sent for, and by the time he arrived, the school halls were empty. With a little coaching and some threats from the aggravated Vice Principal for Discipline, Miguel got to his feet. Had not his physical therapist explained that Miguel had perceptual and balance difficulties and his sitting down in the milling halls was a way to make himself safe, the suspension threats would have become real. Instead, the school learned to accommodate him by letting him leave classes early while the occupational therapist worked on Miguel's balance.

———◆———

WRAPPING UP THE IEP

When you have participated in an open and responsive process that leads to an IEP that is appropriate and beneficial for your child, and when that plan has been achieved in an atmosphere of cooperation, collaboration, or friendly negotiation, then you are ready to sign the IEP, right? Not quite. No plan will be harmed by a few days' delay. You are pleased with the plan, but you still want a few days to take it home and sleep on it.

"Just Sign Right Here"

Sometimes you may even be asked to sign an incomplete IEP, with the promise that it will be filled in later (the "we're all friends" approach). You never sign a blank IEP. It's like a blank check: You don't know what will be filled in or not. Usually, your copy of the IEP will be presented with the information filled in at the meeting and all is above board, but you still do not sign on the spot. Always take it home to read it carefully or to show it to your spouse. After a careful reading, you will sign and return it, or if you have any questions, you will call the special education director to have them answered and, with hope, changed and corrected.

Sometimes the school will mail you finished copies at a later date for your review and signature. When you receive the IEP, you and your advocate should sit down with your notes to read and discuss it; be sure the plan is intelligible and says what was said in the rough copy you were given at the meeting before you sign it. Corrections are made before you sign, not after. When you are satisfied with the IEP—you agree with the services and all of your questions have been answered—you return a copy with your signature on the line where it says you agree with the plan. You of course keep an exact copy for your files. If your experiences at the meeting have been positive, you may wish to call the principal or special education director to tell him or her that the signed IEP is on the way, that you felt the meeting was both pleasant and productive, and that you have great hopes for the coming year for your child. In this way, you compliment the school staff on their efforts in the development of the program and, at the same time, drop a hint that the implementation of the program will be of great interest to you.

For the time being, your work is done. Congratulations! Go back to whatever unfinished things you were doing before you learned about parent advocacy while the school staff begin the business of implementing the program. Later you will want to check out the implementation.

"But I Can't Sign This!"

Some of you may find yourselves looking at a plan that is poor, even shabby. Not only does the plan not meet your child's needs but also it may appear to be indifferent to your child's needs. If this happens to you, your response will probably be "How could this happen after all of that hard work and friendly discussion at the meeting? What happened to all of those mutually agreed-upon goals? I did everything you told me, and now this—this is not what we talked about. I feel like I've been taken for a ride."

Maybe you did have a wonderful meeting with all kinds of open and friendly discussion and agreements. But when they handed or mailed you the plan, you saw immediately that it was full of holes or that your top priorities were lost. When you asked about the omissions, you got excuses for answers. For example:

Mr. Klebanoff:	*There's nothing here about the implementation of the speech-language goal—the number of times each week, how long, and all of the specifics we discussed.*
Special Education Director:	*We all know what Vicki needs and we are all in agreement. It isn't necessary to write everything down.*

Mr. Klebanoff:	*Oh, but it is. That information is important and should be written down.*
Special Education Director:	*What if we can't find or even hire another therapist? It's possible with this year's budget that we may have to make do with the staff we've got. There's no point in writing things into the IEP that we may not be able to deliver.*
Mr. Klebanoff:	*The program isn't made on the basis of what you can deliver. It's supposed to be an individualized program based on what's appropriate to Vicki's unique educational needs. I thought it was all set. Why are you backing down now?*
Special Education Director:	*Because it may be impossible to give Vicki therapy in the amounts you want for her.*
Mr. Klebanoff:	*But it's not just me! We agreed on that goal at the meeting.*
Special Education Director:	*I'm sorry you're disappointed, but it's the best we can do. You can accept or reject the IEP. It's up to you.*

Or maybe you had to work even harder at the meeting, where everyone was given a mimeographed copy of an IEP. Because your participation in the development of an IEP is a right that you have under IDEA, the preplanned, photocopied IEP prepared without your participations is not an acceptable product. So you started from scratch, item by item, with your 20 questions to develop a program individualized according to your child's unique needs. It was uphill work, but you thought you were succeeding. However, this thing that they mailed you is practically the same as the mimeographed IEP that they handed out at the start of the meeting. You feel like you've run the marathon without leaving the starting line. When you complained, you were told, "You can reject the IEP if you don't like it. We think it's satisfactory and we can defend it." Most parents won't meet this kind of stone wall, but that's little comfort to those who do.

DEALING WITH YOUR FRUSTRATIONS

Whether you meet your "stone wall" at the beginning of the meeting or face it at the end, it is an extremely frustrating experience for a hard-working and committed parent advocate. You may respond in several ways.

"Where Did I Go Wrong?"

This is often the first response parents make when something bad happens to their child. Parents will search for the flaw in their characters or performance. Of course, it is always possible to look back and find something you could have done differently. For example, "Maybe I should have spoken up more and been more assertive" or "Was I too pushy?"

But if you were prepared and your requests were, in your opinion, reasonable and appropriate, you could give a five-star performance and still not get the important services you asked for. When the system is unresponsive, even rigid, and the process breaks down, don't blame yourself. Your job is tough enough without carrying any useless and undeserved guilt. When the process isn't working, you are actually working harder than the parent who is working with school people interested in the child's needs, and you deserve even more rewards for surviving the process (take two nights on the town!). Success isn't only an easy win; success can be hanging in when the going gets rough and the game is going into extra innings.

"You Can't Beat the System"

"The process is a sham. Why did I even try?" Parents who make this response are blaming the system (and that may be putting the blame squarely where it belongs), but they are also giving up. Maybe the meeting was a sham, but it doesn't have to end there. There are still steps, described in the next chapter, which parents can take. If you give up now, the next time you ask for something for your child, the school people may find it easy to ignore you. You may have participated in the process, but, after all, when the system took a firm stand against you and your child, you gave up, went home, and didn't bother them any more.

"Yes," you may say, "but I showed them. I didn't sign their IEP." That IEP has since been filed away and there is no one but you to question it. Your child is probably being served under that program you found unacceptable or perhaps getting even less service because there is no one like you questioning your child's present IEP. If you did not sign the program, you can reopen the case by writing a letter to the school (copies to the state department of education and others who can help you), stating that you have never accepted the IEP and you are requesting another meeting to develop an appropriate and adequate IEP for your child (see Chapter 8).

"I've Put Too Much in This to Give Up Now"

This is the most productive response parents can make. They may feel anger ("Nobody is going to short-change my kid!"), desperation ("Daniel needs so much! I can't let him down now"), or even cold determination ("I started this business, and I'll see it through to the end").

This response is the starting point for the next phase. All that you have done before is not lost; it is a large part of your preparation for confronting the system. You may add to that preparation, but you are basically relying on the skills and information you have been building.

Actually, most parents will make all of these responses and work through them to gain understanding of the particular process and individuals they have dealt with, reaffirm their commitment to their children's educational future, and remind the school system that every year of their children's education is crucial.

The IEP process is a new, often frightening, and sometimes even depressing experience for parents. As parents go through it for the sake of their children, they begin to recognize their own strengths and skills and become more secure in their ability to advocate, negotiate, and develop the services their children need. Most parents will find a satisfactory and appropriate program at the end of the meeting. When they sign IEPs that benefit their children, they feel good about themselves because they participated in a process that demanded much from them in the way of skills, energy, commitment, and endurance to achieve success. But for those parents who find themselves up against resistance; rigidity; and, on occasion; even hostility, they must temporarily find comfort in their strength and commitment as they continue to work for their goals—the satisfactory conclusion of appropriate IEPs for their children.

The next chapter is devoted to those parents who find themselves facing failure and frustration. They need to learn how to effectively say no to the system. It is time to look at confrontation.

8

Confrontation
When Nice Guys Finish Last

---

questioning the IEP process • how to reject • every state is different • you can't do it alone • hearings and lawyers • prepping your advocate • how money makes a difference • inclusion and resistance

---

Harriet Wendell claims she was too nice. Although she brought to the meeting a list of services she wanted for Darrell, she gave in on practically everything but the speech-language therapy. The school staff finally wrote the speech-language therapy into her son's IEP. Six months later, Darrell does not have a speech-language therapist. What more can she do?

Leonard Lawson met with the school staff just once and contributed very little "because they never intended to serve Sonia anyway." When he received the IEP, he rejected it immediately and requested an appeal. Now that he is engaged in the appeal process, he is worried because he needs to know more about Sonia's school program in order to criticize it.

Although Karen Flynn was prepared and performed well at the IEP meeting, her son Tim did not get the services she thought he deserves. She just received a notice from her state department of education to come to a mediation hearing, and she doesn't want to go because "these professional always support each other."

These parents need to know more about the productive uses of confrontation. Perhaps you have cooperated, collaborated, and negotiated. You've rehearsed for meetings until you were even saying your lines and making self-statements in your sleep. You may have a file of records, laboriously collected, as long as your arm. You have exhausted yourself in your efforts to help develop an appropriate and beneficial plan for your child, yet your child does not have one. Perhaps you feel that you have failed. But is the failure yours or the school system's? Did the school people fail to recognize your child's individual, unique needs? Did they fail to meet your child's unique needs? Did they listen carefully to your concerns for your child and your reasons for requesting specific services? Did they explain to your satisfaction and in words you understood why they chose to select certain services and reject others?

As you review your frustrating experience, you may begin to realize that the school people did not take you seriously. They may have been friendly or intimidating, they may have been up front about their refusal to give your child what you believe he or she needs, or they may have feigned acceptance only to present you with a plan that ignored your requests. However they did it, they said no to your requests and your active involvement in developing the IEP, with the expectation (or at least the hope) that now you would go away and leave them to return to business as usual, that you would be a "nice" guy and not a "troublesome" parent. But nice guys can finish last, and, what is worse, the children of nice guys can end up with poor education programs.

LEARNING TO SAY NO

You may want to go away when the school people reject your recommendations, just as you once were willing to leave your child's education solely in the hands of the professionals. But that was before you read Chapter 3 and learned about the educational myths that have kept parents in their place. Rejecting the IEP is an option that you have the right to choose. Rejecting the IEP may in fact be the biggest contribution you make to your child's educational future. "But it's hard to say no to the experts." Just as you learned to speak up to the experts, you can learn to say no to them. Be wary of the "old school pupil" who may still survive in your relationships with school staff and who may interfere with your ability to say no to people in authority. You can learn to say no in the same way you learned to speak up at meetings as the controlled, rational, and contributing parent.

First, you should get a free copy of the rules and regulations on special education from your state department of education, especially so you will know the timelines for rejecting the plan. You should also get in touch with your state's Parent Information Center (these are listed in the appendix—every state has one) or the organization that represents your child's specific disability. The Parent Information Center may be able to help you with both the regulations and locating the specific disability organization.

Then, properly informed, you plan what you will say; share with others your concerns and reasons for rejecting the IEP in whole or in part, backing up your objections with assessments, observations, and other data; and rehearse in advance of the time when you will say no and say it effectively. Let's look at some examples.

———◆———

Elsa King went to meetings with school people who were friendly and pleasant. She was devastated when she was mailed the IEP for her daughter Elaine. The program was the same as last year's and included none of the services Elsa had requested so carefully at the meetings. Both she and her husband David agreed that the plan was unacceptable and that they had no choice but to reject it. David King wanted to make one last call to the special education director to see if the IEP could be rewritten to reflect the parents' concerns without entering a lengthy process of appeals.

Mr. King:	*My wife and I have carefully reviewed Elaine's IEP that you mailed us, and we feel that we cannot accept it as written.*
Special Education Director:	*I'm sorry to hear that. Just what is wrong?*
Mr. King:	*Well, specifically. . . . (He outlines his objections and backs them up with references to his file of evaluations and reports.) Is there any possibility of rewriting the plan to include these important components?*

Special Education Director:	*I don't know, Mr. King. The committee worked very hard to develop Elaine's IEP.*
Mr. King:	*As the IEP is now written we must reject it.*
Special Education Director:	*Give me a few days to see what I can do.*
Mr. King:	*I appreciate your interest, and I will call on Thursday to see if you can change the IEP. Then we can arrange another meeting to deal with our disagreements. But if that's not possible, Elsa and I will be forced to return this IEP with our rejection.*
Special Education Director:	*Call me on Thursday. I'll see what I can do.*

Note that David King was calm, firm, and specific. His message was clear: The IEP will be rewritten, or it will be rejected. And he gave a deadline (Thursday) for action to be taken. If the special education director comes up with a meeting to revise the IEP to one that the parents can agree with, David and Elsa King will have spared themselves a possibly lengthy appeals procedure by engaging in productive confrontation that is informal and minimal. If, on Thursday, the special education director says that he can do nothing, then the parents will have lost but a few days, and they will object in writing, noting those portions with which they agree and especially those portions or omissions with which they disagree.

◆

Delia Norton, on the other hand, had to deal with school people who were constantly patronizing and who rejected her suggestions by using jargon continually. When she received her son Sal's IEP in the mail, she was not surprised that it was inadequate. After fuming a bit, she called her personal advocate, Evelyn, to bring her up to date on the situation.

Delia:	*Evelyn, I just got Sal's IEP and there's no way I can sign it.*

Evelyn: *Well, we expected that. Can you give me the specifics?*

Delia: *That's the problem: There are no specifics. It's so vague that they can do whatever they want and still meet the IEP as written. For example, they have as an objective "regular gym as the schedule allows." Now I ask you, what kind of objective is that? The rest of it is the same way.*

Evelyn: *Well, Delia, I think you have no choice but to reject the program in writing. The only way to move these people is to show that you mean business. Will you send me a copy of the IEP? Maybe together we can work up a list of reasons for disagreeing with the IEP and stating what we want included in the IEP.*

Delia: *No easy way, is there, Evelyn?*

Evelyn: *We can hope that sending that rejected program back will make them sit up and take notice. It's time someone took them to task.*

In this case, the parent's dealings with the system have been difficult from the first day. Because a telephone call would seem to be of little value, the parent should formally reject in writing the proposed IEP, noting its faults, such as overall ambiguity or lack of specifics, inadequacy of plans for inclusion in particular classrooms and activities, or insufficient amounts of specific therapies needed by the child.

Learning to say no to school systems requires the same skills you learned to use in working to develop the IEP process: knowing your rights, using the telephone, writing letters, keeping records, and gathering allies. It is harder to say no, however, because disagreement and confrontation are generally unpleasant. If you are the kind of person who always strives to get along and keep everyone happy, you may have to practice a lot to prepare yourself for saying no to the school staff. Get out the list of those self-statements you used during the IEP process to shore yourself up when you engage in confrontation.

Earlier you made a commitment to see the process through. Now, as the going gets rough, you must reaffirm that commitment. It may seem paradoxical that the fully committed parent can sometimes avoid a long appeals process to get what he or she wants for his or her child, and yet it is true. School staff know how to recognize the parents who are determined to see that their children's educational rights are served, and they often will provide the requested services or portions when confronted by a committed parent in order to avoid a lengthy, time-consuming, and costly process for the school system. "Are you telling me," you may be thinking, "that I can get what I want just by telling the special education director that I won't accept my child's IEP? That sounds too easy." Surprisingly, it does work that way for some parents, depending on how much disagreement there is; other parents will need to go farther. There are, in fact, a number of ways and times you can confront the school system. Let's look at them now.

RECOGNIZING LEVELS OF CONFRONTATION

Because confrontation involves face-to-face disagreement with people who are responsible for your child's education and well-being, you, like many other parents, may approach confrontation with feelings ranging from discomfort to panic. You may be worried about possible repercussions to your child—loss of present services and the possible development of unfriendly attitudes toward your child—or about looking foolish or failing. Confrontation is hard on parents.

Set your anxieties aside. By your actions (written and verbal), you are in effect focusing a large spotlight on your child. Everything that happens to your child while you are involved in the educational process will be highly visible. Because school staff will be making efforts to look good and to prove that their recommendations for the IEP are better than yours, they are not likely to reduce or stop services or in any way punish you through your child. School staff want to look competent and reasonable, especially when they are faced with rejection of an IEP.

School professionals don't like confrontation either. Like you, they would prefer agreement, but, like you, they may feel that on some services there is no compromise, especially if it involves a substantial amount of money. Because both parties would like to avoid confrontation, confrontation should be treated like strong medicine—used only in the amount needed. And, of course, neither side should engage in name-calling, tears, or other dramatics, which will make confrontation more painful and less productive for all involved.

"Why should I care," you may ask, "if I hurt them? Look what they've done to me and my child!" You care because your performance is best when you are controlled and rational, rather than emotional.

You also care because, however the confrontation is resolved, you will have to go back to working with these school people on your child's education. The maintenance of good relationships will be helpful when that time comes.

Rejecting the IEP: The First Step

When you receive an IEP that you find unacceptable for your child, you must reject it. If, like Elsa and David King, you have reason to hope that you can solve the problem informally, then you should try that approach first. After you have carefully read the plan, discussed it with your advocate, and noted your specific objections for your personal reference, then call your special education director or principal to state your intention to reject the plan, in part or the whole, and your concerns, one of which is finding a way to reach agreement without going through a complicated process involving outsiders. This type of telephone call gives the school people an opportunity to reassess the seriousness of your commitment, to take further steps to resolve the disagreement, and to present a good image. They still have a chance to be "good guys" without having to record and file a rejection of an IEP with the state department of education. For some parents, this can lead to a happy solution. You must, however, set time limits: You expect to hear within a few days whether it is possible to modify the proposed IEP and that a meeting for that purpose can be called within the week. If the school staff promise to reconvene but you can't pin them down to a specific time, you may rightfully begin to suspect that you are being stalled; you should then formally reject the plan.

Formally rejecting the plan means disagreeing with the IEP in writing. Forms may vary somewhat from state to state, but the forms are basically the same. For example, some forms include the line "I do not accept the educational plan." In whatever way the form includes your rejection, you should note in the form the parts of the IEP with which you agree and the parts with which you disagree (e.g., "I agree with the plan for adaptive physical education" and/or "I disagree with the lack of individual speech therapy"). Keep a full copy of the rejected and completed form signed and dated by you. Three things can happen after your formal rejection of the IEP.

One is that you may get a call from the school staff asking you to reconsider your objections to the proposed and now rejected IEP and seeking to work with you to come to some compromise or mutually satisfactory conclusion. If you receive this kind of call, you can afford to be gracious. Yes, you would be very interested in meeting again if that would help to develop the program you believe your child needs and to implement the desired plan as soon as possible. You are willing to do much to see that your child gets the services he or she needs now. By using confrontation to impress the school with the seriousness of your commitment, you have brought the school staff back to the negotiating table to rework the IEP. When they reach out to you, they are demonstrating that they are willing to reconsider your requests and to concede to at least some (if not all) of them. It is important to meet and resolve as many differences as possible. If you get all of your requests (or the most important ones), this will be the end of your experience in confrontation. If you fail to reach agreement, you will still have reduced the number of items disagreed upon and, in this way, will have simplified the continuing process of confrontation.

The second thing that can happen is that you may receive a notice that you are entitled to a reconciliation, voluntary mediation, or hearing to resolve differences between you and the school and to decide on the services to be provided to your child. The process can be somewhat informal (mediation) or very formal (due process hearings). You are entitled to any one or all three. The school system is also entitled to a hearing to resolve differences. It is always best to try to solve your differences in the least aversive way.

The third thing is that nothing can happen. The school people have simply filed away your rejected IEP and are proceeding with business as usual as if the IEP process had never taken place. Of course, few do this because they would be in violation of the law if they have not made clear to you in language that you can understand that you have a right to be heard. Whether you have been informed or not, you can and should follow up on the hearing process, even starting it off. You should initiate the process if needed because each state has its own timelines for the process. You do this by writing to your state department of education, informing them that you have rejected your child's IEP and are requesting an impartial hearing to resolve the differences. Send a copy to your advocate and one to the school system, and keep a clear copy for your records. You can now sit back and wait for notice from your state department of education that the legal (due process) wheels are turning. A higher level and more difficult step of confrontation lies ahead.

Reconciliation

Before you can go to hearing, IDEA requires that a *reconciliation* meeting be held between you and the school system. "Another meeting!" Yes, because it may resolve some if not all of the disagreements between you and the school system, and it is required before you can move to hearing.

The school calls the meeting after discussing with the parents who should be at the meeting to work on resolving the disagreements about the IEP. This may not be the same group you met at the first IEP meeting. It will likely not include the people who would implement those services, goals, and objectives on which you agreed. But it may include some new people who have or will be doing further evaluations. This is not a meeting to bring a lawyer to. You want the group to focus on educational issues for your child.

When you meet, make sure that issues you resolve and agree to implement are set down in writing. Any time you meet, you may resolve some of your differences, with the result that you are dealing with fewer and fewer issues as you approach the hearing. You may even find that a hearing is unnecessary. However, if your disagreements are not resolved at reconciliation, you should consider another part of the due process system available to you—mediation.

Mediation

Before the formal hearing, there is a less formal procedure called *mediation,* which is used to resolve differences between parents and schools. Mediation is voluntary for the school. If the school calls for mediation, parents must participate. If the parents call for mediation, schools don't have to oblige; this was a later change to IDEA. Schools know, however, that mediation is much, much cheaper than hearings, and they will likely agree to mediation, which is cheaper for you because you do not need to bring a lawyer to mediation. Lawyers have no place in mediation. The school saves, too, on not having a lawyer at mediation, so they will most of the time prefer mediation to costly appeals.

Participate in the mediation process to the best of your ability. You may or may not resolve your disagreements, but you may better clarify the issues of disagreement, which will help you in your appeal.

IDEA requires states to offer mediation whether or not either party has filed a due process complaint. It is being used by more and more states to resolve parent–school conflicts over the IEP, and it appears to be successful in a number of cases. In mediation, parents and school people sit down together in the presence of an unbiased third person, the mediator, whose job it is to help parents and school people reach agreement in a structured, yet informal setting. The mediator does not make decisions about the IEP; his or her role is to encourage communication and discussion, maintain some order (no shouting and people talk one at a time), and, if possible, persuade everyone to reach a mutually satisfying agreement.

"How can this third guy, an outsider, help when we have already been over everything and are just getting more frustrated all of the time?"

The mediator can help just because he or she is an outsider. As you and the school staff try to explain to the mediator what your problems and differences are, you will begin to see everyone's behavior improve, and any amount of snipping and sniping at each other will diminish as people on each side make their best case to convince the mediator that they are right. The mediator asks questions and makes suggestions. He or she can help each side understand the other better and, from what may first appear to be two warring factions, create a group of reasonable folks willing to negotiate their differences under the watchful eyes of the impartial mediator. After hearing the presentations and arguments, the mediator may spend some time alone with each side to tell them what their chances are of winning an appeal.

> **Mediator:** *I wanted to share with you privately some of my impressions and experience.*
>
> **Principal:** *You want to tell me that the IEP is inadequate, don't you? We did a lot of work on it.*
>
> **Mediator:** *I don't doubt that. But, looking at those evaluations that Mr. White keeps bringing up, I think he has a strong case for the intensive speech-language program he wants.*
>
> **Principal:** *But I don't have a speech-language therapist in my school.*
>
> **Mediator:** *I understand that it may be difficult for you to provide these services, but those evaluations from the University Medical Center make it clear that Lynnette has a serious language dis-*

> *ability and needs a comprehensive language*
> *program. I have to tell you that, in my opinion,*
> *the parent would win the appeal. I expect the*
> *hearing officer would find the IEP inadequate*
> *and order a new IEP that would include that*
> *service.*

Principal: *Well, maybe the parent won't appeal. I'm sur-*
prised he's hung in this long.

Mediator: *You know I have to share the same information*
with Mr. White. I have to tell him that his
chances of winning an appeal are very good
based on the information I have.

Principal: *I know you do. And that just might keep him*
going. He's already talking about private
schools!

Mediator: *Listen, all I can do is tell you what I know. Your*
chances are slim. Isn't there something you can
do to provide the child with the speech-language
program she seems to need?

When a principal is given information and advice like this, he or
she usually starts to think about a solution that will satisfy the parent.
On returning to the group, the principal may tell the parent, "Maybe
you're right and maybe we should be offering Lynnette more. Would
you be satisfied if we were to hire a speech-language therapist?"

Negotiation, guided by the mediator, follows. The principal offers
something; the parent asks for more. As they bargain, talk of private
schools disappears, and both parents and school people shift from
counterproductive disagreement to working toward a common goal—
in this case, a substantial speech-language program that will benefit
Lynnette in her communication skills and assist her as well in reaching her other educational goals.

Sometimes, parents are told that they are probably asking for too
much. For example:

Mediator: *Zachary is like a lot of kids in his school. You will*
have a hard time making a case that he needs a
private school.

Mrs. Floyd: *But he's not making any progress!*

Mediator: *You made that clear in the discussion. It's obvious that the program needs to be modified to meet his needs, and I think you should work on getting more out of his present school placement.*

Mrs. Floyd: *They've had Zach 3 years now and very little has happened. It's time for someone else to do the job. I'm willing to go to an appeal hearing.*

Mediator: *I know you are, but I'm afraid that if you insist on a private school, you will lose. However, I think you have a strong case for requesting substantially more services from the public school and even an Extended School Year (ESY) program for Zachary.*

Mrs. Floyd: *All I want is for Zach to learn.*

Mediator: *I know that. Why not give the school another chance today to come up with a better plan?*

If the parent agrees with the mediator's advice, the mediation can continue. They can return to the group, where the parent may ask the school people, "How can you provide Zach with the services he needs?"

The school staff may respond with some surprising recommendations because they have also heard from the mediator that the IEP that they proposed is weak and inadequate. They may offer more individual tutoring and a new adaptive physical education program, which are high priorities to the parent. Yet they balk at the idea of an ESY program for Zach. The parent feels that with the improvements in the IEP, she is willing at this time to forego the extended school year program, and both parties are at last in agreement. Or the parent believes that the ESY program is crucial, and in spite of the positive efforts put forth by the school staff, she cannot agree to the plan. She is entitled to disagree. Because mediation is only an attempt to bring the involved parties to agreement, the parent or schools always have the option to refuse the amended program.

The mediator is a kind of matchmaker, a go-between, with no power to decide the content of the IEP. He or she doesn't recommend, doesn't decide. Only the parents and school people can reach a decision, which must be a joint decision. If they do agree, then a formal document of agreement can be written up and signed by both school staff and parents: That agreement is the new and accepted IEP. If they disagree, nothing is written down about the mediation meeting, and nothing discussed in mediation can be used at hearings.

For a growing number of parents, mediation is a workable means of getting good IEPs for their children. You are only required to go through mediation if the schools call for it. If you are concerned about the qualifications of the mediator chosen (he or she is not really an impartial party) or believe that the school staff will use the mediation process to delay the development of a good educational program for your child, then you can move through mediation quickly by continuing to reject the IEP. Most of the time, mediation will help you because it is less adversarial than appeals; your relationship with school staff will be less damaged when mediation is successful. But, for you, mediation is successful only when your child benefits. If necessary, you, the active and committed parent, are ready to take the next step.

Appeals

Within the educational system, appeals are the last resort, and probably the most difficult experiences parents can undergo. The time, emotional, and financial costs are to be avoided if possible. However, if your child's IEP is bad or inadequate, you must take this last step.

Your right to appeal to a higher level of authority in the educational system is guaranteed by IDEA. If you disagree with the school system, you are entitled to an impartial due process hearing. That means that you get to state your case before an impartial and qualified hearing officer—someone who does not work for your school system and who does not have a personal or professional interest that would bias his or her judgment in deciding the case. The impartial hearing officer has the power to decide the issue of the IEP. Unlike the mediator, whose job was to assist both parties in reaching a mutually satisfying agreement, the hearing officer is not concerned with whether the parties agree; he or she makes the decision that the IEP is adequate and appropriate or that it is inadequate and inappropriate to the child's special needs according to the law. Unlike mediation, where discussion may be open and informal, the hearing can be very legalistic, with the hearing officer determining who talks when and what they talk about. (Hearing officers do have different styles; some will be more formal than others. All should be seeking solid information on which to base their judgment or disposition of the appeal.) And unlike mediation, your chances of ending the hearing on a friendly note with the school staff are very slight indeed. Hearings tend to be adversarial; the lines are drawn—it's them or us. This is not to say that you will never be able to talk to the school people again, but, for a while, you may find it hard.

To start the appeals process, you need the assistance of a lawyer who will help you get the regulations on due process. (Each state may differ in its timelines for appeals and/or its requirement that you be represented by a lawyer.) You should carefully pick a lawyer experienced in special education law. No parent should ever try to do appeals alone.

Winning an appeal will require a lot of work from you in documenting and in planning your case. You will need to have a lawyer represent you because schools will bring their own lawyers to represent them at hearings. You may do a lot of work and spend a lot of money, yet lose. You may be wondering, "Why are you painting such a black picture of appeals? If we have come this far on our commitment and efforts, why should we give up now? All along it's been go, go, go! You can do it! Now suddenly, it's 'Take it easy. Don't jump the gun.' Why?"

You're right! This description is discouraging on purpose. Sometimes when parents learn about appeals, they may be tempted to rush through the development of the IEP, reject it, and go for an appeal, thinking they can shorten the time it takes to get what they want for their children. Although you should never put up with any unnecessary delays (e.g., long postponements of meetings, casual cancellations), working with the school staff (even when you find many disagreements) can help you to better formulate your case for rejecting the plan, for seeking mediation, and for requesting a due process hearing. If you rush the procedures, you may have to deal with an unnecessary number of IEP issues, some of which could have been resolved in reconciliation; this could result in a lengthy appeal process while you all go over issues that didn't need to be part of the appeal. You may appear at the hearing only to be accused by the school staff of not working with them to develop the necessary programs for your child while they have made good faith efforts to deal with you. If you go to an appeal that could have been avoided, you will have caused yourself some unnecessary work, expense, and possible grief.

Now that you know all of that, you should also know that parents do win appeals; they win them with lawyers who are experienced and committed to the education and well-being of children with disabilities. They win on the merits of their case: They have done their homework, and they can back up their claims with specifics—evaluations, school reports, and other documentation.

By all means, when the IEP process and mediation have failed, you should move to appeal. If you start the appeals process, the school system just may make a last-ditch effort to satisfy you because appeals are costly to school systems, too. They must hire substitute teachers to free your child's teacher(s) and other school staff to attend the hearing. The special education director's work piles up while he or she is at the hearing. The town counsel (lawyer) may be called away from "more important business to waste a day or more at the state department of education." Or they may have to hire a private lawyer at more expense. School staff do not enjoy appeals. If there is an easier and more acceptable way, they will want to use it to avoid the appeals process.

But appeals are necessary, both to resolve irreconcilable differences and to put teeth into the law. If there were no appeals process, rejected IEPs would merely be more pieces of paper to file, and school people would feel no pressure to satisfy parents' requests for services. The specter of going through an impartial due process hearing can sometimes turn a recalcitrant school system into one that is at least willing to try cooperation.

You, the active and committed parent, are also the judicious parent, avoiding appeals when you can but using them when they will serve your child's best interests. If you find that you need to resort to appeals, then you need to find a lawyer who is knowledgeable and experienced with IDEA.

USING LAWYERS

You should know that although the educational rights are federal, each state has its own way of conducting due process in terms of reconciliation, mediation and hearings, timelines (e.g., scheduling by calendar days or business days), and formats. If you find yourself involved in reconciliations, mediations, and/or hearings, you should not do it alone. For reconciliations and mediation, an experienced lay advocate who may be a parent trained in educational advocacy can help. For hearings, you will need a lawyer experienced in special education law.

This is the time when the public agency conducting the hearing (usually the state department of education) is required by law to provide you with information about free or low-cost legal services available to parents in your area or state. If you do not receive this information, then you should ask for it by phone or, if necessary, by letter. Your Parent Information Center (see Appendix A) can help you with specifics about the hearing process, as well as the school's record on appeals, and may put you in touch with parents who have been through appeals. Talking to other parents can give you good information about which lawyers are knowledgeable and experienced in special education law and who may be learning as they go at your expense, both emotional and financial.

Free legal services? Sounds good! Unfortunately, there are few available, and those that are available are in great demand. Even if you are very poor and entitled to publicly funded legal services, such as protection and advocacy agencies concerned with disabilities, you may find that all you can get is some consultation time. The public agency lawyers may be so overburdened that they find it impossible to represent you at the hearing, but they are generally willing to advise you, if that will help. As for low-cost lawyers, keep in mind that most lawyers charge by the hour, and what is by legal standards a modest fee for representation can overwhelm the average family.

Start with an hour of legal consultation. If you are poor, free legal counsel may be available; if you are of average means, 1 hour of a lawyer's time will not break you, and an experienced lawyer familiar with special education appeals may give some suggestions that could ease your way or may give you some idea of your chances of winning an appeal. Sometimes even a letter of concern from a lawyer can help. It is very important that you find a lawyer who has knowledge or experience in IDEA; otherwise, you may be spending your money and time to bring the lawyer up to your level of expertise about the law.

The lawyer may tell you that, in his or her opinion, you have a strong case or a weak one, that these are the important issues and arguments and that the others are weak, that he or she believes your money will be well spent on legal fees for appeals (get an estimate of the cost to help you decide), or that the issues raised in your child's case are so important to a number of children that your case could set a precedent that would benefit a whole class of children. In this latter case, the lawyer might tell you that an advocacy organization or public interest law firm might be willing to bear the expense if you want them to represent you and your child. If you can get free legal representation, you can move ahead. If not, you must decide whether you can afford to pay for legal representation and how much.

"We've gone to the lawyer and the cost is beyond our means. We'll just have to forget about the appeal."

Not yet! You still have resources to tap—your local parent or advocacy organization, your state's Protection and Advocacy agency (see Appendix A), your long-distance advocate (who may come out for appeals), perhaps a nearby university law student, graduate students in special education, or even professors who may be interested in some front-line action in resolving special education problems. The more contacts you make, the greater the chances of finding help for your appeal. Search out your resources. If in the end all you have is your naive personal advocate, that person can at least be an emotional support to you. If you find that you must go to appeals without a lawyer, explain to the hearing officer why you don't have a lawyer—it doesn't hurt your case any for the hearing officer to know that you wanted counsel but couldn't afford it. But if you find a lawyer willing to take your child's case on a contingency basis, that is, that he or she will be paid only if you win, then go with your lawyer. Lawyers do not take cases on contingency unless in their professional judgment they think they can win.

If you have hired a lawyer, give him or her the best and most accurate information you can; the better the information, the stronger case he or she can present for you. So, prepare your legal advocate as you prepared your personal advocate. (Review The Advocate's Advocate in Chapter 5 and Getting Your Advocate Ready in Chapter 6.) You can hire the best lawyer in the world, but he or she will have a hard time making a case with muddy issues and scanty information. This is true for school systems as well; they can hire high-priced lawyers who will have a hard time defending a poorly designed IEP or obvious violations of parents' and children's rights.

UNDERSTANDING THE MONEY PERSPECTIVE

Because confrontation can be a difficult and discouraging experience, wouldn't it be nice to have some kind of predictor that could tell you whether you will have a short and relatively easy disagreement or a long, tough fight ahead of you? Well, there is a rough predictor that works much of the time and that is based on a simple fact of life:

money. How much are the services you want for your child going to cost the school system?

Some school people will insist that they provide all of the services a child needs and that money is not a factor; other educators see that children need more services and realize that money is an important factor in determining who gets what services, how much, and how often, but they may have little control over how much money is spent. Even the most concerned special education director can have his or her hands tied by the school's fiscal policies. Any increase in costs may result in increased pressure on the school administrator to hold the line on spending. In bad economic times, the pressure on schools to resist additional services can be great. If your requests for your child will require a modest increase in costs, chances are your struggle will be brief and not too unpleasant. If complying with your requests will result in a large expenditure, you may have to prepare for a difficult and drawn-out battle. This simple rule generally works quite well. You must, however, look at costs from the perspective of school administrators. They take into consideration three kinds of costs:

- Short-term costs

- Long-range costs

- Costs of confrontation

Short-Term Costs

These are the immediate actual costs for the new services for your child. Here are some examples:

- Judy needs an extra session with the speech-language therapist, which you estimate will cost the school system about $2,500 for the year.

- Calvin should have regular psychotherapy (a related service); the projected annual cost is about $7,500.

- Charlotte cannot attend school unless certain architectural barriers are removed, access ramps and accessible toilet facilities are provided, and some classes and equipment are relocated: projected costs are approximately $35,000 and up.

- Ross does not benefit from the school program and needs a private school day placement to meet his educational needs and tuition— estimated cost is $45,000 and up, plus the cost of transportation.

- Lorena's disabilities are so extensive and severe that she requires a year-round residential program—estimated cost and tuition is $90,000 and up.

Short-term costs are the school's immediate costs in providing the services and implementing the changes the parents have requested for their children. They can range from a few thousand dollars to $45,000 or more. However, there are often other hidden costs that may be of even greater concern to school administrators in reaching their decision to give the parent what he or she wants, or to stand fast in their refusal. Transportation to out-of-district placements can add up and must be included in actual costs.

Long-Range Costs

What school people often fear is that by agreeing to provide services for your child's educational needs, they will open the floodgates and a horde of angry parents will descend on them to demand expensive services. For a school system with a bad track record for meeting children's needs, this fear may be based on a real possibility—that parents who realize that their children have been denied legitimate services will be angry and demanding. But for those systems that have sincerely attempted to place children in appropriate services, this is much less of a threat.

You may have to guess about what is behind the school's refusal to comply with your request for educational services. But often the school people will help you by making certain kinds of statements.

"We can't set a precedent. If we give it to your child, we'll have to give it to everybody."

"We can't send every student to private school just because a parent asks for it."

"Everybody would send their kids to private schools if the public schools would pay for it."

The key words to listen for are words like "precedent" and "everybody." Some of the statements are patent nonsense. Keep in mind the

I in IEP stands for *individualized*; precedent as a consideration is irrelevant. You would give your right arm if your child could benefit from a special program in his or her own local public school. And what parents would want their children pulled away from a learning program to spend time with an occupational therapist if those children did not have sensory difficulties? Do not allow yourself to be put down or put off by irresponsible statements from resistant school professionals.

Let's look at the earlier examples in the context of long-range costs:

Judy's parents are asking for an increase in services that the school people have already agreed on, and it's a modest increase. There should be little fear of setting a precedent. However, if Judy were in a school system where few or no children were getting speech-language therapy, then giving Judy the service might have the effect of creating a large demand among a number of parents for speech-language programs for their children. The long-range costs could become significant.

Calvin's case is similar. If he is one of a number of students to receive psychotherapy, it is no big deal. But if he is going to be the first, the school people will be considering the costs of providing psychotherapy to 10, 50, or more students (depending on the size of the system).

In Charlotte's case, the school, by maintaining a public program not accessible to individuals with disabilities, is in violation not only of IDEA, but also of the Americans with Disabilities Act (ADA) of 1990 (PL 101-336). Charlotte's parents will point out this fact to the school people. In addition, they will explain that although the cost may seem expensive this time, the building modifications will allow services to be provided to other students with disabilities. In this case, the short-term and long-range costs of the service are the same.

When we look at the requests for private school placement for Ross and Lorena, we can anticipate resistance from most school administrators. The short-term costs are expensive, and the possible threat of other parents requesting private school placement can make the long-range costs appear overwhelming. This is not to suggest that all school systems will refuse to consider private placement, but you should know that this kind of request might tend to create strong resistance.

It is important to look for these long-range costs and try to evaluate them. When you ask for what seems to you a tiny but necessary increase in service and suddenly find yourself up against a stone wall, you should suspect that there is a serious long-range expenditure hanging over the heads of the school people; you should check with other parents in your town (or your agency or professional advocate) about the present status of the service you want. You may find that there is no speech-language therapist for students with disabilities in your town. Depending on the size of your town, there may be one hundred or more students who need this service. Once word gets out about you, there could be a deluge of requests. Your request for service should not be a secret. The more parents know about entitlement to services and get them, the more secure you can feel.

Or you could ask for a private placement for your child with fear and trembling, only to be told by a school administrator that he or she has been thinking about the same thing because the public school is not yet capable or ready to serve a child with needs as severe as those of your child's, although they are working on it. Measure the potential long-range costs by collecting information about the services already available in your town. The state department of education may be a source. They can't tell you who is getting services, but they can and should tell you what kinds of services are being provided by schools in your town and any outside placements your town has made (e.g., public school collaboratives, private day schools, or residential schools).

Costs of Confrontation

Confrontation costs schools extra cash. Appeals require the presence of a number of school people (and you can request or subpoena even more). An administrator and teacher will almost always be there with a lawyer. The lawyer will generally be paid at a rate of $200 or more per hour; every teacher will have to be replaced on the job by a substitute at a rate of about $200 per day; and the administrator can plan on taking the work home for the weekend that he or she could not complete in the office or being behind in the performance of his or her duties.

The hearing can run 1, 2, or more days. By multiplying your best estimate of daily costs, you can come up with a reasonable estimate of the confrontation costs to the school system. Even a 1-day hearing can cost the schools several thousand dollars or more, and an extended hearing can cost tens of thousands of dollars.

A School's-Eye View of Costs

When you have reviewed the costs of the new services that your child needs, looked into the status of special education in your town to help you estimate the possible long-range costs, and made your best guess about the school's costs of confrontation, you will be better able to assess the costs from the school's point of view and to predict roughly the potential resistance of the school administrators to your request for new service(s). Let's try this predictor against the examples.

Regarding Judy, a small increase in a service that is already provided is being requested. The expected short-term cost for the service could be about $2,000. The long-range costs are small or even zero. The costs of confrontation for the school could cost $10,000 (e.g., lawyers, substitute teachers, specialists, some hidden costs to attend the hearing, and more depending on how many days the hearing takes place). If finances are a concern, a school administrator will have a difficult time giving a satisfactory explanation to his or her superiors about how he or she saved the school system $2,000 by spending more than $10,000 doing it! In Judy's case, the easiest and cheapest solution for the school is to give her a little more therapy and be done with it. The parents can anticipate that a telephoned or written rejection will result in negotiations to improve service.

Regarding Calvin, let's assume that if he were to receive the psychotherapy as part of his IEP, he would be the first student in his school system to get this service. The long-range costs could be high: It would mean annual school expenditures of many tens of thousands of dollars. Because confrontation costs in this case are not likely to exceed $10,000, there is a probability that the school system will make a strong effort to resist the parents' request for service. Calvin's parents should prepare themselves with documentation, experts to testify for their side, and advocates, who may include lawyers, for a long, tough fight.

In Charlotte's case, the short-term cost is also the long-range cost. There may be other families waiting for someone like Charlotte's mother to break the architectural barrier; the parents should make an issue of the fact that the school is not only inaccessible to their daughter, but to present and future students with mobility problems as well, and that the public school system is violating not only Charlotte's special needs but also her civil rights. Her parents should get a summary of ADA, which guarantees the civil rights of people with disabilities, and use it when talking to the school people.

The cost of renovating the school facilities will exceed the usual costs of confrontation, but renovation is a one-time cost with long-range benefits. In addition, the issue of inaccessibility can be made so visibly clear that the school may be reluctant to contest the parents' appeal.

If there are no accessible schools in Charlotte's town, a civil rights complaint should be filed by the parents with the U.S. Office of Civil Rights. Parents have the right to expect quick action here.

Occasionally, a school system may offer to place a child in private school to avoid renovation costs. Some parents are willing to accept this placement, especially for their children with severe and multiple disabilities. But Charlotte can benefit from being included in a public school program if they will only widen the doors and let her in. If there is more than one elementary, middle, or junior high school, the school administration may offer to send Charlotte to an accessible school that is in her town but outside her neighborhood. Schools would offer this to avoid the costs of further renovation. This option, however, may be contested as a violation of Charlotte's civil rights to her neighborhood school and that it also violates the educational principle of least restrictive environment, which the school is obligated to provide under IDEA.

Ross's school system prides itself on its low education budget and on the fact that no student has ever "needed" a private placement—that is, the school administrators have refused to consider private placement, no matter what the individual need. Ross's placement could cost $40,000; confrontation costs could be more than $10,000. (The parents are determined to go through the appeals process using several expert witnesses to testify about Ross's needs and the inadequacies of the program the school administration is proposing.) The difference between short-term and confrontation costs is not so great as to push the school system into a long procedure. A long procedure could boost the school's expenses upwards of $20,000. However, Ross's mother believes that there are at least two children with needs similar in severity to Ross's and that the current educational programs of these children consist of inadequate services in an isolated regional school operated by a consortium of adjoining towns' public schools. Ross's mother realizes that the school people are not worried just about spending $40,000 for her son; they are worried about an amount that could exceed $100,000, depending on how many students the town should place in its out-of-district school for students with multiple disabilities. Clearly the long-range costs are the issues here. The school system can be expected to resist.

The residential program that Lorena's father believes will meet his daughter's unique needs costs more than $85,000. This is a heavy cost for Lorena's community to bear. But this community has in the past sent some students to both day and residential private programs when the public school programs were not meeting the students' needs. Although placing students outside the community, the school administrators planned and developed programs for those students and, after a year or two, were able to bring many of them back into the public schools. They do not feel they are ready to serve Lorena but will work on developing an appropriate program over the next year. A community like this is not frightened by the specter of hordes of students requiring expensive outside placements. The school people are more concerned with the short-term costs and costs of confrontation in individual cases. If they believe that they cannot serve Lorena in the public schools, a push from the parents may bring forth the private placement. However, if they feel there hasn't been enough time or opportunity for them to work with Lorena, they may refuse to write the kind of IEP the parents want and begin to prepare for the appeals. Still, here is another case where the cost will drive the school's decision.

"Some rule! Our town will fight to the finish over $5,000 and the other town will shell out $100,000 on request? That's quite a difference!"

You're right. There is a wide difference between towns or school systems. The rule serves as a kind of yardstick that you apply to what you know about your own school system to measure or predict the likelihood of resistance (or compliance) to your special requests for your child's individual educational needs. It is a rough measure, but it can be a useful one when applied to specific cases. And your primary interest is very specific—the IEP to meet your child's needs. Understanding the money perspective from the school's point of view can aid you in making an informed decision about engaging in confrontation, at what level, and for how long.

Schools' Views on Inclusion

IDEA strongly promotes the least restrictive environment (commonly referred to as LRE) and intends that students with disabilities should be included as much as possible in their own communities. This means that your child should not be educated in totally segregated programs. Teresa should not be driven 50 miles or more to a school building that houses only students with disabilities. Mike should not be tucked away in a separate classroom where he never participates in activities with typical students of his age. Token participation, such as being allowed to sit at a special "disabilities-only" table in the school cafeteria, is also not acceptable. The goal of IDEA is that every student receive as much inclusion as possible with appropriate supports to provide a beneficial education.

Supports like a teacher's aide or paraprofessional, assistive technology, and consultation to teachers by specialists do cost money, but they are not major money issues. Some schools may try to take advantage of the push for inclusion to save a few dollars by placing students with disabilities in general education classrooms without supports and related services. When this happens, you must use all of your skills in the IEP process to get those needed supports. You must help the school people understand the difference between the least restrictive environment for your child and "dumping" your child in general education classes. Which classes? How much time (full day or partial)? Which related services? Which curriculum modifications? It is not a free appropriate public education in the least restrictive environment unless your child is actively learning.

However, the major resistance you may encounter from some school systems has nothing to do with money. Schools are bureaucracies and bureaucracies do not like to change. They may have designed nice little separate programs, sometimes set up in isolated facilities with their own staff of specialists—all very tidy, all very "special education," and all administratively convenient. And here you come to rock the boat. What an ungrateful parent! You will hear remarks such as the following:

"Jodie will be lost in that class. Do you want her to sit there and vegetate?" ("No. I want her program modified and supported so she can participate with her typical classmates.")

"The regular students will ignore or even make fun of Jack. Children can be cruel." ("Not if you prepare and expect them to accept Jack.")

"The speech-language therapist is assigned to the special regional school and can't provide services at the local school." ("Doesn't the speech-language therapist drive?")

"You can't allow these children with disabilities to disrupt the 'regular' students." (You wince and are tempted to say, "Some of the 'regular' students I passed in the hall were doing a pretty good job of disrupting themselves!")

When you hear remarks like these, you are encountering resistance to change. You may keep your feelings to yourself, but you are momentarily baffled. Is asking that your child attend the school where the neighborhood children go (his or her friends or potential friends) so outrageous?

If you are the first parent to ask for inclusion or more inclusion (if it is now limited to lunch and maybe recess), then you will seem outrageous to the school staff. You are asking for change, but it is reasonable change that acknowledges your child's full equality. Separate but equal didn't work before and it's not working now.

You should know that some schools have accepted the challenge of inclusion and are successfully providing free and appropriate, fully supported, least restrictive environments to their students with disabilities. Appropriately inclusive programs can be found in some towns and not in others, in the same state or neighboring states. These programs exist as models for other schools that are having difficulty accepting students with disabilities into any part of general education. If your school system has resisted inclusion, they will challenge you, and their resistance may force you into confrontation. Whether you push for full or partial inclusion, it is important to remember that these typical students will be your child's neighbors, and some of them may even become his or her friends and supporters if they have a chance.

MAKING YOUR DECISION

Although disagreeing with the IEP may be a new experience for you, it is something that most parents, faced with an inappropriate education program, can do without much difficulty or even hesitation. Deciding to appeal is a little harder. Rejecting the IEP does not require you to go to appeals, and you may not feel ready to push for a hearing. On getting notice of your disagreement with the IEP, schools should schedule a reconciliation meeting. Meetings should be scheduled at times that do not interfere with parents' jobs. (Check with your state department of education to determine how much time you have to file or respond.) Now that you know something about the process and how to measure potential school resistance to your requests, you have to consider your personal costs. You will have expenses—financial, emotional, and physical—and you will want to be sure that the prize is worth the contest.

You can most easily predict your financial costs. These can include legal fees for consultation or representation at hearings, transportation, babysitters, and/or time away from your job. These are the hard dollars-and-cents facts you can determine from your own situation.

The other costs (e.g., energy, time, feelings) are every bit as real, but are harder to estimate. You might say, "Hey, there isn't anything I wouldn't do to get my child into the right program!" but you might be feeling, "I've worked so hard for so long; I don't think I can do any-more." If you want to go on but are feeling drained, look for ways to get support or relief for yourself. Ask yourself these questions:

- Can I get the emotional support I need from my advocate? From my Parent Information Center? Are there others who can help me?

- Do I need more information about my child's needs, skills, and dis-abilities to make a stronger case for a new IEP? Is there a school in a nearby town that can serve as a model for the program I want?

- Do I need more time? Can the hearing date be postponed if I am anxious about being ready or need to have the date moved up because the waiting is hard for me?

- Do I need more preparation and practice in order to strengthen my new skills (e.g., assertiveness, self-statements) and overcome some of my personal weaknesses (e.g., timidity, short emotional fuse)?

Use these questions to determine what you need to survive the appeals process and to increase your chances of success. You are the best judge of what you can do.

Review your child's needs one more time. Are your requests for services for your child appropriate and beneficial? Should you be asking for even more? Now is the time—before the appeals—to make sure you are asking for all of the things you think belong in your child's education program. Or are you asking too much because you really want revenge on the school staff for all of the things they've done and haven't done? It is natural for parents to be angry with school staff who they believe have neglected their children's education and welfare. However, your best chance of winning the appeal is based on your child's current actual needs. Use your best judgment to make your strongest case. As for your anger, use it to fuel your determination to keep going during the difficult moments at the hearing.

And there will be difficult moments. Confrontation at any level can be unpleasant; appeals especially can be painful. If you are convinced that the IEP you want is essential to your child's educational growth and well-being, then the prize is worth the contest. The way of a parent advocate is never easy; at times it can be tough and painful.

You need to know the worst so you can be prepared to last. If the school people change their minds suddenly and give your child the services you have been asking for, you can live with that kind of pleasant surprise. (Your aura of determination may, in fact, have helped them to change their minds.) But if you are not prepared to deal with confrontation, you can be overwhelmed by it. Knowing about confrontation (and the judicious use of it) is a kind of power to enable you to seek and achieve the IEP that meets your child's needs.

We have put confrontation toward the end of the book for a number of reasons:

- Confrontation is procedurally the last step in developing the IEP.

- Parents should use it as their last resort in dealing with school staff.

- Most parents will not need to use confrontation to get the right IEP.

For those of you who will find it necessary to engage in confrontation and those of you who must finally resort to the appeals process, it is important that you know the worst and prepare for it. Informed and skilled parents can and do win appeals, and their children with disabilities are better served because of their caring parents' valiant efforts.

The steps you will need to take to ensure continued, improved service for your child are outlined in the next chapter. You will learn how to monitor compliance with the IEP, how to deal with noncompliance, and how to sustain your active, ongoing participation in planning for your child's educational future.

9

And the Beat Goes On

The Need for Constant Advocacy

take a break • need for monitoring • when "nit picking" pays off • using your new skills again • always focusing on the IEP • getting help for dealing with noncompliance • the constant advocate in education and beyond

"It was a long haul, but it was worth it."

"I'm glad I did it, but I'm sure glad it's over."

"I've wanted Maya to be included, but will she get the extra help she needs in the general education classroom?"

"How will I know whether my child gets all of the services we agreed on?"

These are the kinds of feelings that parents have when the IEP is finally signed, sealed, and set up to go. You may have put more effort, emotion, and energy into getting an appropriate IEP than you have ever put into anything else. It may have been just plain hard work doing things you have never done before; or, especially if you engaged in confrontation, the whole business may have taken on the dimensions of a bad dream from which you could not awaken. Whatever you experienced, it's over and done. The IEP is written, and now you can sit back and relax or return to whatever ordinary routine you gave up to become your child's advocate. You thought you might never see the end of developing the IEP, but it's over. Take a break.

The need for advocacy remains. The IEP is a legal contract for the school system. For you, it is more—a moral and deeply emotional commitment to your child that you will do all in your power to see that the school fulfills the obligations that are clearly stated in your child's IEP as well as future obligations that the courts and Congress place on schools as the rights of people with disabilities are more fully recognized and protected.

In going through the IEP process, you have developed new skills and resources; you may have had some experiences you will never forget. All of these—skills, resources, allies, and knowledge gained from your experiences—you will use in your constant advocacy.

Yes, developing the IEP is over; but there is still more work to do. Be assured, though, that the hardest, most time-consuming work is done. Take a break; you've earned it. In fact, you want to sit back and give the school a little time to implement the education program before you begin your monitoring of it.

MONITORING

Monitoring is making sure that your child gets what's coming to him or her—the education program you and the school people proposed, discussed, disagreed on, labored over, developed, and finally agreed upon as the necessary, appropriate, and adequate IEP for your child. You certainly did not labor mightily to bring forth a piece of paper; you worked for a program. Your job is to be sure that the piece of paper becomes the real services to which your child is entitled. In order to do that, you must become the watchdog of the IEP implementation. If the IEP says occupational therapy is given for three half-hour sessions each week with the occupational therapist, you want to know that it is given three times every week and not only once a week because the special education director has not hired the additional therapist. If your child, according to the plan, is to be included in general education classes for 60% of the school day and it hasn't happened after the first week of school, you should be aware of that and hold the school system accountable for delivering those services. Read and know the specifics of the IEP so you will know when it is not being followed. In monitoring, you will realize how important the specific language of the IEP is. The IEP is clearly written so it can be read by anyone and followed as a teaching guide. When you were insisting that the number and length of sessions, the location, responsible person, and so forth be written into the IEP in precise language, you may have been made to feel that you were nit-picking and mistrustful. You were not; you were just being careful and thorough. Now your care will pay off.

Why Monitoring Is Necessary

"If the plan is so specific," you may ask, "why do I have to bother the school staff? They can read as well and probably better than I can." You're right. It is not a question of reading ability; it's a question of the "same old pressures," such as budget, lack of personnel, and unqualified staff. (See the discussion in Chapter 4 of the pressures on school people.) School people are often trying to stretch inadequate resources in an effort to keep the budget down. The child of the "good," quiet parent who does not follow through on monitoring is apt to be short-changed. The child of the parent who quotes the IEP (e.g., "It says here that Gloria should have. . . .") is more likely to get most or even all of the services written into the IEP. That parent, in effect, often makes the case for the principal or special education director to bring to the superintendent or school board. He can report that, "Mrs. Lujan is constantly calling about the lack of the special services written in the IEP, and I don't think she's going to go away until we set them up." Usually, the "squeaky" parent gets the "grease" in the form of the services for his or her child required by the IEP.

For a few school systems, the "standard operating procedure" interferes with implementing the IEP: These schools, even when they present few obstacles in writing the IEP, may have little intention of initiating any new services and routinely ignore the requests of parents to deliver promised services. They can and do get away with this because most parents either don't follow up by monitoring because they figure the program is there and the school will do what is required, or because they become apathetic (e.g., "I did everything I was supposed to do, and now they are ignoring the IEP. I knew you couldn't beat the system.").

These systems get away with breaking the law when no one checks up on them and holds them accountable. The more successful they have been at this game in the past, the more effort is required of a parent to get services. Telephone calls requesting information about the start-up of the items in the IEP and letters stating that you are ready to file a complaint against the school system for noncompliance (discussed later in the chapter) can often move a resistant system to act responsibly. The vocal and informed parent monitor can usually get the services by being assertive and relentless.

Sometimes a school will technically put all of the IEP pieces in place and assure the parent that the IEP is being implemented. For example, Jennifer's father felt good until he visited the school and saw that the reading tutorial room was located on the other side of the cafeteria walls and learned that Jennifer was scheduled when the cafeteria was gearing up for lunch, with the result that the teacher and student could only hear half of what they were saying to each other.

Another, and perhaps the most flagrant, example of technical implementation is illustrated in the following example of a student's language program.

———————

Richard's mother did all of the right things in preparing and participating in the IEP process. Her highest priority for her son was speech-language training. The school staff countered her request for more time with the speech-language therapist with the response that there was no money. Through discussion and negotiation, a plan was agreed upon that called for the therapist to continue to see Richard but also to work closely with the classroom teacher and an aide who would implement the therapist's recommendations. The aide, under the supervision of the teacher, would be responsible for language instruction throughout each day. Mrs. Chan realized that this arrangement would provide her son with considerably more language instruction and practice than would an extra weekly session with the speech-language therapist, so she agreed to the compromise.

In September she learned from the school people that the aide had been hired and the plan was underway. In November, during her parent–teacher conference at the school, she learned that the new aide's primary language was Spanish and that she lacked the necessary grasp of English to support Richard, who did not understand Spanish. Although all of the pieces seemed to be in place, Richard's language program was in fact practically nonexistent. It would have been simple for the school to switch aides within the system, locating the Spanish-speaking aide with bilingual or other students who could benefit from her help and finding another aide more capable of implementing Richard's program.

———————

Of course, this is an outrageous example of a school's indifference or incompetence, and it doesn't happen every day. But you should know that it does happen. Parent monitoring would not have prevented the setting up of this arrangement; however, a September visit to the classroom could have put an early end to it. Public and formal disclosure of this arrangement can move a system to apology and action (e.g., "A regrettable error! Of course, we didn't intend. . . ."). For years, of course, the reverse has all too often been true. Students for whom English is not their native language have been taught in classes in which the teachers have little or no skill with the students' language, and in cases where the student has a communication disability and the family has little understanding of English, schools have sometimes ignored the families' need and the federal requirement for a competent interpreter in school and at meetings.

Parent monitoring is essential to proper implementation of IDEA. Schools may appear to be in technical compliance but actually be violating the spirit or intent of the law. For example, a child who is "mainstreamed" into a general education class for a percentage of the school day but who is given little or no work to do and is effectively excluded from most or all classroom activity represents this kind of violation. Mere presence is not enough to satisfy the law. Students must make adequate progress in general education classrooms. They can't just sit there while schools pretend they are providing the least restrictive environment. Schools must adapt the curriculum (age-appropriate materials and individualized methods of instruction) to meet the student's needs and learning style, provide the assistive technology and other related services, and make the classroom truly accessible for the individual student. (This may be as simple as placing the student where he can see or hear what is going on or providing special equipment so the student can respond and participate with his or her classmates.) Visiting teams from the state educational agency may not pick up some of the specific violations because they do not know the individual students. You do know one student very well. For that student—your child—you are potentially the best monitor. Good advocates never assume that the IEP is being well and fully implemented.

How to Monitor

"Okay, I accept," you say. "I will become a snoop and a nag if it will help my child. What do I need to know to monitor?" You basically already know what you need to know. By reading this book and by practicing your new or improved advocacy skills of keeping and using records, evaluating the program, speaking up in person and on the telephone, writing letters, and finding and using allies, you have prepared yourself to be a good monitor. All you need is a timetable for contacts and an awareness of the kinds of contacts you should plan on making.

Telephone Calls

The timing of your first telephone call depends on your school system's past record of providing services to your child and other students. If you have a system that is conscientious about implementing education programs, give the school staff a few days to set things up. Make your first monitoring call to the teacher (or special education director) at the beginning of the second week of school. You are looking for information and assurance that the IEP is being implemented. If there are any delays in the services, such as specialists and partial inclusion into regular classrooms, you want to know why and for how long. If the delays seem to you to be lengthy or unreasonable, express your concern and request that the special education director or principal give immediate attention to your child's program. If all of the services are in place, or one or two remaining are scheduled to start within the week, be sure to express your appreciation to the school staff for doing their job and tell them that you would appreciate hearing from them when those other services are in place.

If, however, you have a system that is notorious for ignoring IEPs, make your first call a few days before school opens. (The administrators are already working; there may also be some teachers and specialists preparing for the new school year.) In this case, your first call serves as a reminder that you are very serious about your child's new program and that you want no delays in its implementation. If the school people tell you, as parents of students with disabilities are sometimes told, that they are too busy getting ready for the opening of school to give any time to your child's individual program, remind them that your child's program is school business and that you expect your child to have the appropriate program the day school starts, just like the other students do. Of course, for any call, you record the date, the name of the person with whom you spoke, and the information you received, especially about the IEP components that are in place, the ones that are still in process, and the dates that the services will be initiated.

Your follow-up call depends on the information you receive from the school staff. You may need to call the next day or the next week, or you may wait a few weeks before further contact. The telephone will be one of the regular monitoring tools you use throughout the school year. You will use it to contact teachers and specialists, as well as administrators. Teachers and specialists can tell you much more about the day-to-day details of the IEP implementation than the administrators can. Of course, you should call at convenient times, which means you do not call when the teacher is with his or her class (you also want your child to have full benefit of the person's expertise and time). You can call the school office to ask about good times to talk to school personnel. Perhaps the person you want to reach prefers to take and return calls during a free period, in the half hour after school is dismissed, or at some other specified time. You should try to respect that preference, if at all possible.

When you call teachers and specialists, have your specific questions and the information you want to share organized and written down in advance. By preparing for your call, you make the best use of your and the school person's time. Any person can be put off by a vague and drawn-out conversation when the next class is about to start or when the only other person left in the school is the janitor, waiting to lock up the building. However, a teacher or specialist would have a difficult time complaining about a parent's call that was 3–5 minutes long and focused on highly specific requests for information. You, the informed and reasonable advocate, should make only reasonable demands that are hard to fault with and to ignore.

Use the telephone to make periodic checks: Has the specialist been hired yet? How much time is Hilary spending in the general education class? The information you receive over the telephone should be a report of events and changes in activities. (You, the parent, are also interested in and entitled to specific information from the school staff; you do not want vague, confusing, or drawn-out explanations.) But there are times when you want more than reports; those are the times when you want to see for yourself.

Visits

When you want firsthand information, you have to visit the program. You have written your visits into the IEP as a component of your child's program. Especially if he or she is very young or has a communication disability (e.g., aphasia, autism, cerebral palsy) it is even more important to observe firsthand.

The information you receive in your reports from teachers and specialists may be accurate and valid, but it is still secondhand information. Your child is also a source of information about his or her program, but that is secondhand information, too. Your check on the accuracy of these reports is your visit to the school.

"That sounds like acting awfully suspicious to me. Why can't I just believe what they tell me?"

The problems with Jennifer's classroom location and Richard's language program reveal why total trust can be dangerous. The parents were contented until they visited the school. Perhaps Jennifer's father arranged his visit because his daughter complained to him that she had a hard time hearing the teacher. In this case, information from the child led the parent to check out the program early in the school year.

Richard's mother was not so lucky because his language disability prevented him from reporting to his mother. If he could have said, "Hey, Ma, my teacher doesn't speak much English," the parent would have investigated in September instead of being shocked in November. For parents whose children have difficulty communicating, the visits are crucial. Because their children are unable to report, the parents are down one source of information. Early school year visits are a must. The schedule of follow-up visits depends on what a parent finds during that first visit and what is written in the IEP.

"But my school discourages (or even prohibits) visits! What can I do?"

The best solution to this problem is to make sure that your schedule of visits is written into the very first IEP and every IEP after that. During the IEP process, you can negotiate the frequency of your visits— biweekly, monthly, or quarterly (not annually or on Parents' Visiting Day or Open House). Base your case on the fact that your child cannot tell you much, if anything, about his or her program, and, as a responsible parent and an equal partner in the IEP process, you feel it is essential that you be scheduled for regular visits. Hold off signing until that provision is written into the IEP. Unlike related services, your visits don't cost the school anything, so they should be agreeable.

Whatever it takes—making telephone calls, writing letters, or including visits in the IEP—you do it because firsthand observation of your child's program is an important part of your job as your child's advocate. You know that plans on paper and people in place do not always add up to an appropriate program for your child. You want to be sure that your child has the program to which he or she is entitled. Visits provide you with those facts.

When you have permission or authorization and a scheduled time to visit your child's program, it is your duty as a responsible parent and an equal partner in the IEP process to prepare yourself by reread-ing your child's IEP (you do know it by heart, right? Read it again any-way) and Chapter 6 on program evaluation. Write down what you want to observe and whom you want to see in your order of impor-tance. The school people may have new items and information they want to discuss with you; they have their lists, too. Of course, you want to listen to their concerns and information, but you want to be sure that your list is taken care of before the visit is completed. When your visit is over, you should also arrange a follow-up time with the teacher to discuss your child and your visit. You arrange a mutually convenient time that does not interfere with teaching.

Perhaps you are worried that the teacher will see you as a poten-tial troublemaker and will resent your monitoring efforts. Remember that a good teacher welcomes an informed and caring parent. Some teachers will distrust and resent you, but maybe they can be won over if you can put them at ease by showing them that you are there only to be sure that all of the components of the IEP are in place and that the setting and support services are appropriate. (See Chapter 6 on reducing your nervousness and the teacher's.) As for the few diehards who firmly believe that parents have no business inside a school, let alone their classrooms, deal with them by being very specific and very informed.

The suggestions and advice offered in The Follow-Up Interview: Using Your Personal Skills in Chapter 6 are relevant to your inter-actions with the teacher as you monitor the implementation of the IEP. If the teacher accepts your help as an ally who will fight for support services written into the IEP but not delivered, you will keep him or her off the hook when you go to the administrator to discuss the school's noncompliance: "I have visited my child's class-room and it seems that certain components of the IEP are not being implemented. Specifically. . . ." You do not say, "The teacher told me that she wants an aide and you haven't been listening to her."

If, however, a teacher feels threatened by your presence as a mon-itor, it will be up to you to minimize the discomfort. The following example incorporates some of the strategies suggested in Chapter 6 (such as opening the conversation with a positive statement about the teacher's efforts), but focuses specifically on the elements of the IEP about which the parent is concerned:

> **Mrs. Lin:** *What a lovely, bright classroom you have here!*
>
> **Teacher:** *Yes, it is nice. You should have seen the room I had last year. It was in the basement and was very dingy.*
>
> **Mrs. Lin:** *I wish I had known that. I would have spoken to the principal. The children cannot be expected to learn in second-rate classrooms. Nor is it fair to you to expect you to teach under poor conditions.*
>
> **Teacher:** *Well, I asked for 2 years before I got a decent classroom.*
>
> **Mrs. Lin:** *That's terrible. I'm glad you have this nice room now. I don't see the teaching aide that is supposed to be here. Is the aide out with another student?*
>
> **Teacher:** *I have requested an aide but I am still waiting.*
>
> **Mrs. Lin:** *With all of these children, surely you are entitled to an aide! Besides, it says in Quentin's IEP that there is supposed to be an aide in your classroom. I'm going to take that up with the principal.*
>
> **Teacher:** *I don't know if that will do any good.*
>
> **Mrs. Lin:** *I hope to use Quentin's IEP and my observations as my argument for the necessary aide.*

Note that this parent did several things to dispel the threat that the teacher might have felt from the visit. The parent commented on the nice room, acknowledged the teacher's efforts (most teachers try to make their classrooms attractive), presented herself as the parent advocate by expressing concern about past poor facilities for students with disabilities, commiserated with the teacher on past (poor classroom) and present (lack of an aide) difficulties, and promised to try to improve the situation by speaking with the principal through the child's IEP rather than the teacher's complaint.

What this parent did is nothing different from what most of us have learned to do in our everyday dealings with people we want to win over to our side—offer compliments, interest, sympathy, and help. When the repair technician finally arrives to fix the furnace, you might be tempted to say, "What took you so long? You should have been here 2 hours ago." But if you want good service, you will probably say, "We have been waiting and we're glad you're here. Today must have been a busy day for you. Should I move these boxes out of the way to make it a little easier for you?" Put your everyday people skills to good use with the school staff.

Base your conversation with the teacher on notes that you have taken during your visit; they will be related to your list of concerns and questions:

Mr. Frankl:	*Could you show me the language program that the speech-language therapist designed for you to use with Tony in the classroom?*
Teacher:	*Sorry, but the speech-language therapist hasn't put it together yet.*
Mr. Frankl:	*I had hoped to talk to him next week. I think I'll start calling tomorrow.*
Teacher:	*I have the program here.*
Mr. Frankl:	*May I have a copy to take home? Perhaps there are some things I can do to help.*
Teacher:	*You'll have to ask someone in the principal's office. They do the copying there.*
Mr. Frankl:	*No problem. I'll ask on my way out.*

When you are satisfied with the information from the teacher, you can decide when you should see the specialists and whether or not there is a need to see the principal or special education director.

Remember, you are always working from the IEP. First you look for the technical compliance. Are all of the people who are to deliver the program in place? Are the hours of therapies and inclusion in place? Then you look for the quality of compliance. Is the classroom setting adequate? Are the program staff qualified and skilled to work with your child?

If after your visit you are satisfied that the IEP is being implemented accurately and appropriately, you can go home, relax, and pat yourself on the back—the program is working. You can continue to take notes on your observations of your child and his or her progress to share with the school staff during your next scheduled classroom visit or parent–teacher conference. (The parent–teacher conference is a chance to exchange information. It is not a substitute for firsthand observation.) If, however, after your visit you see that there is a poor match between the IEP and your child's daily program, you must be ready to shift gears to become, once again, the assertive, advocating parent. When the IEP is not fully implemented, the school staff are in noncompliance: They are not holding up their end of the contractual IEP agreement. School noncompliance means that you must engage in confrontation strategies and actions.

Parents sometimes give up when they find that the IEP they struggled to obtain is being ignored, especially if they have been through a lengthy appeals process. They feel too tired to do more (and they are tired), or they believe that they have basically exhausted the system (they have not) and that nothing they do will make any difference. These parents are like runners in a marathon who have come 25 miles and falter with the finish line just a mile down the road. If you find yourself in this kind of situation, make the last effort to keep going. The end is clearly in sight.

Noncompliance, in fact, is the clearest issue you have to deal with because you are no longer arguing about the who, what, where, when, and why of services. There is no need for more discussion about what should be in the IEP. If you have been through appeals, someone in the state department of education already is familiar with your case and is aware of the school's reluctance to provide services.

You and the school staff have already signed an agreement—a legally binding contract that pinpoints the provisions of the IEP. The school is on record, in black and white, that it will provide the required services. The only question you and the school staff have to consider is, "Are the services in place or not?" If they are not, then the school system is violating the law and its own contractual agreement.

Review Chapter 8 on confrontation for support and direction. Just as you may have told the school staff that you intended to appeal and so moved them to action, you should first tell them you are considering filing a noncompliance complaint. The threat of a complaint may be enough to get those services and programs in place. As always, if nothing happens, you should follow through on what you said you would do; never bluff. As a determined and responsible advocate, you say only what you mean to do and you follow through.

Of course, if the school system has already made good faith efforts to hire a physical therapist, but you live in Northeast Shangri-La and the nearest therapist is a hundred miles away by dogsled, you—the thoughtful parent advocate—may need to suggest other solutions, such as "Because daily physical therapy is impossible, how about having the therapist come once every 4–8 weeks to spend the day (or 2 days) with Kate and her teachers (classroom and gym teachers, and aide) for evaluation and program planning?"

Filing the Complaint

When you have decided to file a complaint against your school system, you will want to use some of the resources you have already used as you worked toward and through the IEP Complaint process. Call your Parent Information Center, advocacy agency, or your personal sophisticated advocate, who can tell you who to contact (name and address) in the state department of education with regard to your complaint. They may give you some suggestions about writing your letter of complaint and ask you to send them a copy and to keep them informed of developments.

A letter of complaint should include the following specific information:

- The name of your town (or school system)

- Your child's name

- The person responsible for implementing the IEP (the designated IEP chairperson)

- The date the IEP was signed

- The amount of time that has elapsed since the IEP was signed

- Other specifics of noncompliance

- Dates of meetings and hearings if you have been through mediation resolution and/or appeals

The letter need not be elaborate; short and simple does the job.

SAMPLE LETTER

October 13, 2010

10 Forest Road
Your Town, State ZIP code

Mr. G. Anthony Sapienza
Director, Bureau of Implementation
Department of Special Education
State Education Department
Your Town, State ZIP code

Dear Mr. Sapienza:
I wish to file a complaint of noncompliance against my child's school system.

My son, Michael, attends school in the Local Regional School District. Last May we completed the plan for my son's individualized education program (IEP) and I signed it on May 22. The special education director, Ms. Davis, told me that the IEP would be in place at the start of the school year.

When I called during the first week of school in September, I was told that they were still in the process of hiring the specialists and making plans to move my child's classroom from the third floor to the first floor. Two weeks later I called Ms. Davis, who said that the school system didn't have the money to hire the personnel specified in the IEP, and there was nothing she could do.

I understand that IDEA guarantees that my son be given the services written into the approved IEP and that you are the person responsible for seeing that school districts comply with the law.

I look to you for help and will be waiting to hear from you.
Sincerely,

Rosa Adamian
cc: Sen. Barry Rosado
          Drew Ferro, Esq.
          Citizens for Educational Compliance, Inc.

Because the state department of education is legally responsible for seeing that school systems carry out their IDEA responsibilities without delay, you can sit back and let the department deal with the school system. Follow-up calls from you to Mr. Ferro, Senator Rosado, and others can accelerate state action.

Moving On

Once the department has done its job and the services are in place, you will begin your monitoring. Realizing that you are dealing with a reluctant school system, you should plan to monitor your child's school program very carefully and perhaps with greater finesse, friendliness, and frequency than you would have done with a more cooperative school system. Not only do you want to be sure that the IEP is properly and thoroughly implemented but you also want specific and solid information on your child's program and progress to present at the annual meeting. This is the information you will use when you work at next year's annual review of your child's education program with the same group of people who hopefully have seen you "develop" into a responsible and rational parent.

If, in your monitoring, you find the school is violating your child's educational or civil rights, then you are not done yet. You have to again consider filing a complaint.

ATTENDING THE ANNUAL MEETING

Although the IEP may be written for 3 years, the law requires the school system to meet at least once each year to review each student's IEP (usually on the anniversary of the first IEP) and to make revisions in the student's program if they are appropriate and necessary. All of the rules and procedures of IDEA discussed earlier in the book are still in effect, including sufficient prior notice in everyday language, the arrangement of mutually convenient meeting times, meetings conducted in language that the parents can understand, parental access to all records and reports, and opportunity for active parental participation at all meetings.

However, there is one important exception in the annual meeting procedures. Federal law allows some states to proceed without parental consent, and in those states, program revisions are not subject to parental consent; in other words, you no longer have to sign the plan in order for it to be implemented.

"You mean, in other words, as a parent, I am without any power to suggest change or negotiate services in my child's IEP?"

Although you do have less power, which is why that first IEP is so important, you are far from powerless. Remember, there is a spirit to the law that is greater than technical compliance. The law intends that all children should be adequately and appropriately educated. The IEP will need to change in time, reflecting the changing needs of your child, increases in inclusion, and plans for the transition to adult life (which IDEA 2004 requires be written into the IEP by the time a student is 16 years old). Especially with these most recently defined new rights and requirements, you have a right to full participation as schools move (or do not move) to add new elements to your child's IEP.

By insisting on your rights to information and participation, you can continue to have a strong voice in planning your child's education. All of the lessons you have learned from this book (e.g., understanding how the system works, recognizing the "good guys" and the "bad guys," keeping records, and finding allies) and the skills you have practiced (e.g., productive assertiveness, using the telephone, writing letters, making positive self-statements, drawing on your own observations of your child and his or her classroom) will continue to serve you. At this point, you will have become the practiced advocate.

Let's look at some examples:

———◆———

Mr. Donato listens to the school staff discussing his daughter Lucia's reading program:

Principal:	*Lucia didn't make much progress in reading this past year. I think we should move her back to her old classroom where she will be more comfortable. She's just not ready for inclusion.*
Mr. Donato:	*You remember that last year I thought Lucia should have her reading program set up and monitored by the reading specialist and that I asked that the specialist see her twice each week. But I agreed to go along with you because you said that the teacher could set up the program and you would bring in the reading specialist if either Lucia or the teacher needed help.*
Principal:	*In my opinion, the teacher was competent. Lucia is just not smart enough to keep up with the other kids. I plan to return her to the old classroom.*
Mr. Donato (bristling at the suggestion of a return to the	*Lucia's problem was that she didn't get enough help to make a difference. She was given "baby" books and pretty much left on her own. With more adequate help, she could be included and*

segregated program): *making progress. Here are my recommenda-tions. . . .*

———◆———

In a situation like this, there are a number of responses a parent can make:

- The parent backs down and Lucia is, of course, moved back to her old segregated classroom behind the gym.

- The parent announces that he plans to put his objections in writing (noting the previous year's discussion) and requests that his letter be placed in his child's school file.

- The parent has discovered, during the past year, that the testing was done by the classroom teacher (or the school psychologist) rather than by a qualified reading specialist and offers his opinion that, because the evaluation may have been inadequate, perhaps the original IEP is invalid.

The first sad response of a frustrated parent will not help the student to have the free appropriate public education due him or her.

In the second example, the insertion into the school record of the parent's disagreement with reference to the statements made by the school people the previous year may be enough to bring the school around to further negotiation.

In the last example, the parent can let the school staff know he is considering filing a complaint based on erroneous, false, or misunderstood information. Lack of accurate information may have violated his and his child's rights during the first crucial process. The school people now face a potential hearing procedure and may prefer to deal with the parent in order to avoid it.

In all of these examples, a parent can, with cause, appeal the school's decision to revise the IEP. Many complaints can be used by a parent to appeal. Obviously, if a parent files an appeal after every annual meeting, the hearing officer might become suspicious of the parent's intentions (unless the school system is consistently disregarding the basic rights granted by IDEA, such as never notifying parents of meetings, and has a reputation for such flagrant disregard).

If you think you have a reasonable cause for filing a complaint against your school system, check with your advocacy or legal resources for help in determining whether your complaint is strong and valid before you move to appeal. As in the original IEP process, you exhaust your basic advocacy skills before you move to confrontation. Confrontation is always your last recourse.

In a large number of annual meetings, even though you may not have sign-off (or veto) power, you will find that you can still be a powerful and effective advocate.

HANGING IN

Each annual review requires your presence and participation if your child is to receive the full benefit of IDEA. To the parents of very young children just starting school, being your child's constant advocate may seem endless, and 18 years of possible education looks like a lifetime. It isn't; ask the parents of a 17- or 20-year-old how fast the years go by. They will tell you that it seems like only yesterday that their children were small and they, the parents, were just starting to seek, fight, or wait for services, and now there are only a few years of education left with which to make a difference in their children's lives. Whatever age your child is, you will use the remaining years to your child's best advantage.

Although you are now the practiced advocate, you still need your personal advocate with you. The more you use your advocacy skills, the more comfortable you will become in your role as advocate. As school people become used to your active participation and learn that their assumptions about emotional and intrusive parents are generally unrealistic, they, too, will relax a bit and become more comfortable in dealing with you. They will recognize that their exaggerated fears of unreasonable and excessively demanding parents getting involved in education have not been fulfilled. With a very few extreme exceptions, parents in fact have been demanding too little of school systems, and if parents can be accused of being unreasonable, their fault lies more in the direction of not asking for more services and not having those services more often.

Many school people still have little experience in working with active parent advocates; you can help them understand that parents, as advocates, can be both reasonable and responsible. The educational issues will become clearer as the status and role issues are diminished. Then one day your active participation in developing IEPs will be over. Your son or daughter will no longer be a school-age child.

However, if your efforts have been successful, you will begin to extend your basic advocacy skills into other areas. The more substantial your child's disability, and, therefore, the more dependent the child is on you, the more likely you are to generalize your advocacy skills to other important areas in your child's life. You will use these skills in dealing with physicians, state and federal agencies, assorted specialists, camp directors, and others before whom you will appear, always, with just a few notes in hand on your questions, observations, references to past records, and suggestions for future services and supports. You will have learned to use your eyes, ears, and common sense, and you won't want to stop. And if you are now a patient, unassertive, "no-trouble-at-all" parent (as the author once was) operating on the old erroneous assumptions about school systems and school people, you can astonish yourself by becoming an upfront, outspoken, persistent, and effective advocate.

To your child, you are the constant advocate; you are always there, faithful and steady, because your child needs you. To the school people, you may become the constant educational gadfly:

"Oh-no, she's here again! This time she's insisting on getting those records (or a meeting or a visit). What can I do?"

"Give them to her and let's be done with it."

Although you are not quite underfoot, your presence is always felt; you do stand fast and are an unremitting, even relentless, advocate. You can appreciate the real problems teachers and principals face, but your focus is always your child.

Your constancy may require great sacrifices on your part, but the ends can justify the sacrifices. There may be moments when you feel close to failure. It's okay to occasionally take a little time out for a modest amount of well-placed and well-deserved self-pity. Then it's back to mustering your skills, getting yourself back on task, and forging ahead.

With the hope that it will ease your way, this book has tried to take you on a simulated but formidable journey through the special education system, pointing out along the way the perils and problems parents have faced and the achievements parents can realize through the rights IDEA grants to them and their children.

Perhaps before you read this book (or spoke to some informed parent advocate), you felt that you and your child were lost in the system, getting nowhere, while outside the rest of the "normal" world was passing you by. Surely there were times when you thought the world had forgotten your existence or simply didn't care. You wanted to find the way through the system for yourself and your child, but, alone and powerless, you feared you would remain trapped forever. IDEA empowers you to deal with school systems. You are not alone and powerless. IDEA is your map, your compass, to keep you headed in the right direction. It reveals the most direct route to the places your child has the right to go. IDEA will get you through the system.

Getting through the system may still be difficult. Even with the map, it may be hard to recognize the right path, or there may be unexpected obstacles blocking it. But all of the time, you will know that you are making progress, getting closer to the goal, and keeping the solemn promises you made to your child to get the education he or she deserves.

Your goal for your child, and your child's right, is an appropriate and beneficial education leading to a brighter future. So follow your map and get through to your destination. And may the road be smooth and even, and may you and your child have a productive and successful journey.

Appendix A

Parent Information Centers

Now that you have read the book, or maybe you couldn't wait to find out where your state Parent Information Center is, you need to know that your Parent Information Center is where you start. It is your first stop for information and support. Pick up the phone and call them for information about the laws (IDEA, ADA, Section 504), IEP preparation and advocacy training for parents who want to help other parents throughout the IEP process, about state and local resources. Most Parent Information Center staff are parents themselves who have been there. They know the challenges and stresses in the IEP process that you are preparing for.

PACER Center, Inc.
8161 Normandale Boulevard
Minneapolis, MN 55437-1044
952-838-9000 Voice / 952-838-
 0190 TTY
pacer@pacer.org
http://www.pacer.org

The more than 100 Parent
Training and Information
Centers (PTIs) are coordinated
by PACER, which is the National
Alliance Center under IDEA.
They can be contacted for
national issues by phone,
1-888-248-0822, by e-mail:
alliance@taalliance.org
and on the web at
http://www.taalliance.org.
PACER also serves as the PTI
in Minnesota. Your own PTI
is listed next.

PARENT INFORMATION CENTERS BY STATE

ALABAMA

Alabama Parent Education Center
10520 U.S. Highway 231
Wetumpka, AL 36092
334-567-2252
http://www.alabamaparent
center.com

ALASKA

Stone Soup Group
307 East Northern Lights
Boulevard, Suite 100
Anchorage, AK 99503

907-561-3701
http://www.stonesoupgroup.org

AMERICAN SAMOA

CPRC in American Samoa
Post Office Box 2191
Pago Pago, AS 96799
684-699-6621
http://www.taalliance.org/ptis/
amsamoa

ARIZONA

Raising Special Kids
5025 East Washington Street,
Suite 204
Phoenix, AZ 85034-2005
602-242-4366 (Voice and TDD)
info@raisingspecialkids.org
http://www.raisingspecialkids.org

ARKANSAS

Arkansas Disability Coalition
1123 South University Avenue,
Suite 225
Little Rock, AR 72204-1605
501-614-7020 (Voice and TDD)
http://www.adcpti.org

**Northwest Arkansas Community
Parent Center**
614 East Emma, Suite 219
Springdale, AR 72764
479-927-4100
http://www.supports.org/cprc

CALIFORNIA

**Chinese Parents Association for
the Disabled**
Post Office Box 2884

San Gabriel, CA 91778-2884
626-307-3837
http://www.cpad.org

DREDF
2212 Sixth Street
Berkeley, CA 94710
510-644-2555 (TDD available)
http://www.dredf.org

Exceptional Parents Unlimited
4440 North First Street
Fresno, CA 93726
559-229-2000
http://www.exceptionalparents.org

Fiesta Educativa
161 South Avenue 24
Los Angeles, CA 90031
323-221-6696
info@fiestaeducativa.org
http://www.fiestaeducativa.org

Foster Youth Resources for Education (FYRE)
2212 Sixth Street
Berkeley, CA 94710
510-644-2555 (TDD available)
http://www.dredf.org

Loving Your Disabled Child
Post Office Box 90633
Los Angeles, CA 90009
323-373-0323
http://www.lydc.org

Matrix Parent Network and Resource Center
94 Galli Drive, Suite C
Novato, CA 94949
415-884-3535
info@matrixparents.org
http://www.matrixparents.org

Parents Educated and Empowered for Partnership
3299 Claremont Way, Suite 3
Napa, CA 94558
707-253-7444
parents@parentscan.org
http://www.parentscan.org

Parents Helping Parents
Sobrato Center for Nonprofits–San Jose
1400 Parkmoor Avenue, Suite 100
San Jose, CA 95126
408-727-5775 Voice /
408-727-7655 TDD
info@php.com
http://www.php.com

Parents of Watts
10828 Lou Dillon Avenue
Los Angeles, CA 90059
323-566-7556
pow90059@yahoo.com

Rowell Family Empowerment of Northern CA
962 Maraglia Street
Redding, CA 96002
530-226-5129
http://www.rfenc.org

Support for Families of Children with Disabilities
2601 Mission Street 606
San Francisco, CA 94110-3111
415-282-7494
http://www.supportforfamilies.org

TASK, San Diego
3180 University Avenue, Suite 430

San Diego, CA 92104
619-794-2947
http://www.taskca.org

Team of Advocates for Special Kids (TASK)
100 West Cerritos Avenue
Anaheim, CA 92805
714-533-8275
http://www.taskca.org

Vietnamese Parents of Disabled Children, Inc.
7526 Syracuse Avenue
Stanton, CA 90680
949-724-2359
http://www.VPDCA.org

COLORADO

Denver Metro Community Parent Resource Center
14501 East Alameda Ave, Suite 205
Aurora, CO 80012
303-365-2772
info@denvermetrocprc.org
http://www.denvermetrocprc.org

PEAK Parent Center, Inc.
611 North Weber, Suite 200
Colorado Springs, CO 80903
719-531-9400 Voice /
719-531-9403 TDD
info@peakparent.org
http://www.peakparent.org

CONNECTICUT

AFCAMP, Hartford-New Haven CPRC
60 Weston Street, Suite B
Hartford, CT 06120

860-297-4358
afcamp@sbcglobal.net

CPAC
338 Main Street
Niantic, CT 06357
860-739-3089 (Voice and TDD)
cpac@cpacinc.org
http://www.cpacinc.org

DELAWARE

Parent Information Center of Delaware (PIC/DE)
5570 Kirkwood Highway
Wilmington, DE 19808-5002
302-999-7394
http://www.picofdel.org

DISTRICT OF COLUMBIA

Advocates for Justice and Education
2041 Martin Luther King Avenue Southeast, Suite 400
Washington, DC 20020
202-678-8060
http://www.AJE-DC.org

Advocates for Justice and Education CPRC
4201 Georgia Ave, NW
Washington, DC 20011
202-265-1432
http://www.AJE-DC.org

FLORIDA

Central Florida Parent Center
Assistance with Achieving Results in Education
1021 Delaware Avenue
Palm Harbor, FL 34683
727-789-2400

cfpc@cflparents.org
http://www.cflparents.org

Parent Education Network Project
2196 Main Street, Suite K
Dunedin, FL 34698
727-523-1130
pen@fndfl.org
http://www.fndfl.org/pen/index.
htm

Parent to Parent of Miami, Inc.
7990 Southwest 117th Avenue,
Suite 200
Miami, FL 33183
305-271-9797
info@ptopmiami.org
http://www.ptopmiami.org

Parents of the Panhandle Information Network
541 E Tennessee Street, Suite 103
Tallahassee, FL 32308
850-847-0010
popin@fndfl.org
http://www.fndfl.org/popin.htm

GEORGIA

Parent to Parent of Georgia, Inc.
3805 Presidential Parkway,
Suite 207
Atlanta, GA 30340
770-451-5484
info@p2pga.org
http://http://www.parenttoparentofga.org

HAWAII

Hawaii Parent Training and Information Center
245 North Kukui Street Suite 205

Honolulu, HI 96817
808-536-9684 (Voice) /
808-536-2280 (Voice and TTY)
http://www.ldahawaii.org

IDAHO

Idaho Parents Unlimited, Inc.
1878 West Overland
Boise, ID 83705
208-342-5884 (Voice and TDD)
parents@ipulidaho.org
http://www.ipulidaho.org

ILLINOIS

Family Matters
1901 South 4th Street, Suite 209
Effingham, IL 62401
217-347-5428
info@fmptic.org or
deinhorn@fmptic.org
http://www.fmptic.org

Family Resource Center on Disabilities
20 East Jackson Boulevard,
Room 300
Chicago, IL 60604
312-939-3513 (Voice)
frcdptiil@ameritech.net
http://www.frcd.org

INDIANA

IN*SOURCE
1703 South Ironwood Drive
South Bend, IN 46613
574-234-7101;
219-239-7275 TTD
insource@insource.org
http://www.insource.org

IOWA

Access for Special Kids (ASK)
5665 Greendale Road, Suite D
Johnston, IA 50131
515-243-1713
http://www.askresource.org

KANSAS

Families Together, Inc.
3033 West Second, Suite 106
Wichita, KS 67203
316-945-7747
http://www.familiestogetherinc.
org

KENTUCKY

FIND of Louisville
1151 South 4th Street, Suite 101
Louisville, KY 40203
502-587-6500
http://www.findoflouisville.org

**KY Special Parent Involvement
Network (KY-SPIN)**
10301 B Deering Road
Louisville, KY 40272
502-937-6894
spininc@kyspin.com
http://www.kyspin.com

LOUISIANA

**Louisiana Parent Training and
Information Center**
201 Evans Road, Building 1
Suite 100
Harahan, LA 70123
504-888-9111
http://www.laptic.org

**Pyramid Community Parent
Resource Center**
3132 Napoleon Avenue
New Orleans, LA 70125
504-899-1505
PyramidCPRC@aol.com

MAINE

Maine Parent Federation
Post Office Box 2067
Augusta, ME 04338-2067
207-623-2144
parentconnect@mpf.org
http://www.mpf.org

MARYLAND

The Parents' Place of Maryland
801 Cromwell Park Drive,
Suite 103
Glen Burnie, MD 21061
410-768-9100
info@ppmd.org
http://www.ppmd.org

MASSACHUSETTS

Federation for Children with Special Needs
1135 Tremont Street, Suite 420
Boston, MA 02120-2140
617-236-7210 (Voice and TTY)
fcsninfo@fcsn.org
http://www.fcsn.org

Urban PRIDE
15 North Beacon Street, Suite
NR-2B
Allston, MA 02134
617-206-4570
http://www.urbanpride.org

MICHIGAN

Michigan Alliance for Families–Region 1
51 West Hancock
Detroit, MI 48201
313-833-3883
http://www.michiganallia
nceforfamilies.org

Michigan Alliance for Families–Region 2
1380 East Napier Avenue, Suite 4
Benton Harbor, MI 49022
269-934-9471
http://www.michiganalliance
forfamilies.org

MINNESOTA

discapacitados abriendose caminos
621 Marie Avenue
South St. Paul, MN 55075
651-293-1748
discapacitados@qwestoffice.net
http://www.dacfamilycenter.org

PACER Center, Inc.
8161 Normandale Boulevard
Minneapolis, MN 55437-1044
952-838-9000 Voice /
  952-838-0190 TTY
pacer@pacer.org
http://www.pacer.org

MISSISSIPPI

Empower Community Resource Center
136 South Poplar Street
Post Office Box 1733
Greenville, MS 38702-1733

662-332-4852
empower@suddenlinkmail.com

MS PTI
5 Old River Place, Suite 101
Jackson, MS 39202
601-969-0601
mspti@mscoalition.com
http://www.mspti.org

MISSOURI

Missouri Parents Act (MPACT)
8301 State Line Road Suite 204
Kansas City, MO 64114
816-531-7070 / 816-931-2992
  TDD
http://www.ptimpact.org

MONTANA

Parents Let's Unite for Kids
516 North 32nd Street
Billings, MT 59101
406-255-0540
plukinfo@pluk.org
http://www.pluk.org

NEBRASKA

PTI Nebraska
3135 North 93rd Street
Omaha, NE 68134
402-346-0525
info@pti-nebraska.org
http://www.pti-nebraska.org

NEVADA

Nevada Parents Encouraging Parents (PEP)
2355 Red Rock Street, #106
Las Vegas, NV 89146

702-388-8899
pepinfo@nvpep.org
http://www.nvpep.org

NEW HAMPSHIRE

Parent Information Center
Post Office Box 2405
Concord, NH 03302-2405
603-224-7005 (Voice and TDD)
http://www.parentinfor
mationcenter.org

NEW JERSEY

Association for Special Children & Families
Post Office Box 494
Hewitt, NJ 07421
973-728-8744
ascfamily@hotmail.com
http://www.ascfamily.org

Statewide Parent Advocacy Network (SPAN)
35 Halsey Street, 4th Floor
Newark, NJ 07102
973-642-8100
http://www.spannj.org

NEW MEXICO

Education for Parents of Indian Children with Special Needs
Post Office Box 1043
Bernalillo, NM 87004
505-404-2070
http://www.epicsproject.org

Parents Reaching Out
1920 "B" Columbia Drive SE
Albuquerque, NM 87106

505-247-0192
http://www.parentsreachin-
gout.org

NEW YORK

Advocates for Children of NY
151 West 30th Street
5th Floor
New York, NY 10001
212-822-9513
http://www.advocatesforchil-
dren.org

The Advocacy Center
590 South Avenue
Averill Court
Rochester, NY 14620
585-546-1700
http://www.advocacycenter
.com

Parent Network of WNY
1000 Main Street
Buffalo, NY 14202
716-332-4170
info@parentnetworkwny.org
http://www.parentnetworkwny
.org

Resources for Children with Special Needs, Inc.
116 East 16th Street,
5th Floor
New York, NY 10003
212-677-4650
http://www.resourcesnyc.org

Sinergia/Metropolitan Parent Center
2082 Lexington Avenue
4th Floor
New York, NY 10032

212-643-2840
http://www.sinergiany.org

United We Stand
91 Harrison Avenue
Brooklyn, NY 11206
718-302-4313
uwsofny@aol.com
http://www.uwsofny.org

NORTH CAROLINA

**Exceptional Children's
Assistance Center
(ECAC), Inc.**
907 Barra Row, Suite 102 and
  103
Davidson, NC 28036
704-892-1321
http://www.ecac-
parentcenter.org

F.I.R.S.T.
Post Office Box 802
Asheville, NC 28802
828-277-1315, 828-216-7742
(Spanish)
first@firstwnc.org
http://www.firstwnc.org

Hope Parent ResourceCenter
300 Enola Road
Morganton, NC 28655
828-438-6540
(English/Spanish)
828-433-2825 (Hmong)
http://www.fsnhope.org

NORTH DAKOTA

ND Pathfinder PTI
Arrowhead Shopping Center
1600 2nd Avenue Southwest

Suite 30
Minot, ND 58701-3459
701-837-7500 Voice /
701-837-7501 TDD
ptidirector@srt.com
http://www.pathfinder-nd.org

OHIO

OCECD
165 West Center Street,
Suite 302
Marion, OH 43302-3741
740-382-5452
(Voice and TDD)
ocecd@gte.net
http://www.ocecd.org

OKLAHOMA

Oklahoma Parents Center, Inc.
Post Office Box 512
700 North Hinckley
Holdenville, OK 74848
405-379-6015
info@oklahomaparentscenter.org
http://www.oklahomaparents-
center.org

OREGON

Oregon FIRST
830 NE 47th Avenue
Portland, OR 97213
503-215-2268
info@orfirst.org
http://www.orfirst.org

Oregon PTI
2288 Liberty Street NE
Salem, OR 97301

503-581-8156
(Voice and TDD)
info@orpti.org
http://www.orpti.org

PENNSYLVANIA

Hispanos Unidos para Niños
Excepcionales
2200 North Second Street
Philadelphia, PA 19133
215-425-6203
huneinc@aol.com
http://www.huneinc.org

Mentor Parent Program, Inc.
Post Office Box 47
Pittsfield, PA 16340
814-563-3470
mentorparentprogram@veri-
zon.net
http://www.mentorparent.org

Parent Education & Advocacy
Leadership Center
1119 Penn Avenue, Suite 400
Pittsburgh, PA 15222-4205
412-281-4404 Voice / 412-281-
4409 TTY
http://www.pealcenter.org

Parent Education Network
2107 Industrial Highway
York, PA 17402-2223
717-600-0100 (Voice and TTY)
pen@parentednet.org
http://www.parentednet.org

PUERTO RICO

APNI
Post Office Box 21280
San Juan, PR 00928-1280
787-763-4665

centroinfo@apnipr.org
http://www.apnipr.org

RHODE ISLAND

RI Parent Info Network, Inc.
(RIPIN)
1210 Pontiac Avenue
Cranston, RI 2920
401-270-0101
http://www.ripin.org

SOUTH CAROLINA

Parent Training & Resource
Center
1575 Savannah Highway
Suite 6
Charleston, SC 29407
843-266-1318
http://www.frcdsn.org

PRO-PARENTS of SC
652 Bush River Road
Suite 203
Columbia, SC 29210
803-772-5688
proparents@proparents.org
http://www.proparents.org

SOUTH DAKOTA

South Dakota Parent Connection
3701 West 49th Street, Suite 102
Sioux Falls, SD 57106
605-361-3171 (Voice and TDD)
http://www.sdparent.org

TENNESSEE

Chattanooga Area Resource and
Education Project
3700 Bonny Oaks Drive
Chattanooga, TN 37406

423-645-0504
http://www.lifelinefamilies.org

Support & Training for Exceptional Parents, Inc.
712 Professional Plaza
Greeneville, TN 37745
423-639-0125 Voice /
423-639-8802 TDD
information@tnstep.org
http://www.tnstep.org

TEXAS

Partners Resource Network–PATH Project
1090 Longfellow Drive
Beaumont, TX 77706
409-898-4684 (Voice and TDD)
partnersresource@sbcglobal.net
http://www.PartnersTX.org

Partners Resource Network–PEN Project
1001 Main Street, Suite 804
Lubbock, TX 79401
806-762-1434
wtxpen@sbcglobal.net
http://www.PartnersTX.org

Partners Resource Network–TEAM Project
5005 West 34th Street, Suite 207A
Houston, TX 77092
713-524-2147
prnteam@sbcglobal.net
http://www.PartnersTX.org

Special Kids, Inc. (SKI)
Post Office Box 266958
Houston, TX 77207-6958
713-734-5355

specialkidsinc@yahoo.com
http://www.specialkidsinc.org

UTAH

Utah Parent Center
2290 East 4500 South, Suite 110
Salt Lake City, UT 84117-4428
801-272-1051
upcinfo@utahparentcenter.org
http://www.utahparentcenter.org

VERMONT

Vermont Family Network
600 Blair Park Road, Suite 240
Williston, VT 05495
802-876-5315 (Voice and TDD)
http://www.vermontfamilynet-work.org

VIRGIN ISLANDS

V.I. FIND
9500 Wheatley Shopping Center
II, Unit 8
St. Thomas, US VI 00802
340-774-1662
vifind@islands.vi
http://www.taalliance
.org/ptis/vifind/

VIRGINIA

Parent Educational Advocacy Training Center
100 North Washington Street
Suite 234
Falls Church, VA 22046
703-923-0010
partners@peatc.org
http://www.peatc.org

WASHINGTON

Parent to Parent Power
1118 South 142nd Street,
Suite B
Tacoma, WA 98444
253-531-2022
http://www.p2ppower.org

Washington PAVE
6316 South 12th Street, Suite B
Tacoma, WA 98465-1900
253-565-2266 (Voice and TDD)
http://www.washingtonpave.org

WEST VIRGINIA

*West Virginia Parent
Training and Information*
1701 Hamill Avenue
Clarksburg, WV 26301
304-624-1436 (Voice and TTY)
wvpti@aol.com
http://www.wvpti.org

WISCONSIN

Alianza Latina Aplicando Soluciones
1615 South 22nd Street
Suite 109
Milwaukee, WI 53204
414-643-0022
alianza.latina07@yahoo.com
alianzalatinawi.org

Wisconsin FACETS
2714 North Dr. Martin Luther
King Drive
Milwaukee, WI 53212
414-374-4645 Voice /
414-374-4635 TTD
wifacets@wifacets.org
http://www.wifacets.org

WYOMING

Parent Information Center
500 West Lott Street, Suite A
Buffalo, WY 82834
307-684-2277 (Voice and TDD)
http://www.wpic.org

NATIONAL PARENT INFORMATION CENTERS

Specialized Training of Military Parents (STOMP)

6316 South 12th Street, Suite B
Tacoma, WA 98465-1900
253-565-2266 (Voice and TTY)
stomp@washingtonpave.com
http://www.stompproject.org

VISIONS

2196 Main Street, Suite K
Dunedin, FL 34698
727-523-1130
http://www.fndvisions.org

National Parent Technical Assistance Center (NPTAC)
PACER Center
8161 Normandale Boulevard
Minneapolis, MN 55437
952-838-9000
http://www.taalliance.org

REGIONAL PARENT TECHNICAL ASSISTANCE CENTERS (RPTACS)

Region 1
SPAN
35 Halsey Street, 4th Floor
Newark, NJ 07102

973-642-8100
http://www.spannj.org

Region 2

ECAC
907 Barra Row, Suite 102 and 103
Davidson, NC 28036
704-892-1321
http://www.ecac-parentcenter.org/

Region 3

Partners Resource Network
1090 Longfellow Drive, Suite B
Beaumont, TX 77706
409-898-4684
http://www.partnerstx.org

Region 4

WI FACETS
2714 North Dr. Martin Luther King Drive

Milwaukee, WI 53212
414-374-4645
http://www.wifacets.org

Region 5

PEAK Parent Center
611 North Weber, Suite 200
Colorado Springs, CO 80903
719-531-9400
http://www.peakparent.org

Region 6

Matrix
94 Galli Drive, Suite C
Novato, CA 94949
415-884-3535
http://www.matrixparents.org

Appendix B

Other Resources

Here is a list of other resources you can access on your computer. They are organizations, agencies, associations, and groups who can provide information and support to families and professionals working with people with disabilities. These resources are divided into four categories: general information, advocacy, inclusive education, and legal information. The Internet address and a brief description are provided for each web site. This list is meant to give you a starting place for gathering information; it is by no means exhaustive—there are hundreds, if not thousands, of disability-related organizations, and there are multiple organizations related to each specific disability. If you want to find information about your child's specific disability, you can find some information by searching the Internet for your child's disability. You can ask your child's doctor, teacher, or other service provider for information about a local group. The library is another place to find information through books, articles, and other media.

The Internet is an incredible tool for finding information, but there is little regulation over posted information, so it is important that you read critically and check the information with your personal and other resources. A final note of caution: Be sure to read web site content descriptions carefully and consult with your family, friends, colleagues, or professionals whom you trust if you are unsure of something. Some web sites may be more interested in trying to sell you something, or in pushing a particular practice or product.

INFORMATION ON DISABILITIES

Disability Is Natural
http://www.disabilityisnatural.com
Presents positive messages about disabilities and offers in-depth information about person-first language

LD OnLine
http://www.ldonline.org
Guide to learning disabilities and disorders for parents, teachers, and children

National Center for Education in Maternal and Child Health (NCEMCH)
http://www.ncemch.org
Articles and materials on maternal and child health

National Institute of Child Health and Human Development (NICHD)
http://www.nichd.nih.gov/
Research related to health in children and adults

National Institute on Deafness and Other Communication Disorders (NIDCD)
http://www.nidcd.nih.gov/
Research on hearing impairments and communication difficulties

National Institutes of Health (NIH)
http://www.nih.gov/
Medical research

National Library of Medicine
http://www.nlm.nih.gov/
Searchable health information

National Rehabilitation Information Center
http://www.naric.com/
Extensive resources on disability- and rehabilitation-oriented research and services

ZERO TO THREE: National Center for Infants, Toddlers, and Families
http://www.zerotothree.org
Resources about early childhood development

FAMILY SUPPORT AND ADVOCACY

About.com: Parenting Special Needs
http://specialchildren.about.com

Collection of resources and information for parenting children
with special needs

The ARC
http://www.thearc.org
Services and support for people of all ages with intellectual and
developmental disabilities and their families

Beach Center on Disability
http://www.beachcenter.org/
Information and resources for families

Center on Human Policy
http://thechp.syr.edu/
Advocacy and policy information and resources focused on expanding the
rights of people with disabilities

Exceptional Parent Magazine
http://www.eparent.com
Periodical addressing wide range of topics for parents of children with
disabilities

Family Center on Technology and Disability
http://www.fctd.info/
A range of training resources on assistive technology

Family Village
http://www.familyvillage.wisc.edu/
A community of disability-related resources

Inclusion Daily Express
http://www.inclusiondaily.com
News service focusing on disability rights

National Association for the Education of Young Children (NAEYC)
http://www.naeyc.org/
Information on early childhood education and resources for parents of
young children

National Dissemination Center for Children with Disabilities
http://www.nichcy.org
Large compilation of information about disabilities, IDEA and other laws,
and inclusive education practices

National Early Childhood Technical Assistance Center (NECTAC)
http://www.nectac.org/

Contact information and resources related to early childhood services

National Respite Locator Service
http://chtop.org/ARCH/National-Respite-Locator.html
Directory of temporary care support providers

Our-Kids
http://www.our-kids.org
Community for supporting children with disabilities

Regional Resource Center Program
http://www.rrfcnetwork.org
Listing of federally supported regional resource centers on disabilities

Sibling Support Project
http://www.siblingsupport.org/
Workshops, networking, and information to support siblings of children with disabilities

Special Education Resources on the Internet (SERI)
http://seriweb.com
Large directory of links related to disabilities and special education

Support for Families of Children with Disabilities
http://www.supportforfamilies.org
Information and assistance for families of children with special needs

TASH: Disability Advocacy Worldwide
http://www.tash.org
Grassroots advocacy to promote inclusion

Technical Assistance Alliance for Parent Centers
http://www.taalliance.org
Listings of parent centers and wide range of resources

INCLUSIVE EDUCATION RESOURCES

AbleData
http://www.abledata.com
Objective information about assistive technology products

The Access Center
http://www.k8accesscenter.org
Technical assistance for schools to provide better access for students with disabilities

Association on Higher Education and Disability (AHEAD)
http://www.ahead.org/
Resources for transition to postsecondary education

Center for Accessible Technology
http://www.cforat.org
Resources and services to make computers more accessible for people with disabilities

Center for Applied Special Technology (CAST)
http://www.cast.org/
Wide range of information on assistive technology, Universal Design for Learning, and other inclusive educational practices

Center on Positive Behavioral Interventions and Support
http://www.pbis.org
Strategies for effective schoolwide and individualized behavior support

Circle of Inclusion
http://www.circleofinclusion.org/
Information about inclusion in early childhood education

Closing the Gap
http://www.closingthegap.com
Reviews assistive technology and offers guidance on its use

Council for Exceptional Children (CEC)
http://www.cec.sped.org
Largest professional organization working with children with disabilities on issues related to education and advocacy

The Educator's Reference Desk
http://www.eduref.org/
Broad·directory of information and special skills for educators

Education Resources Information Center
http://www.eric.ed.gov/
Directory of education publications and articles

HEATH Resource Center
http://www.heath.gwu.edu
Clearinghouse on postsecondary education for individuals with disabilities

IDEA Partnership
http://www.ideapartnership.org
Collaboration of several agencies to provide tools and resources for working with special education

Inclusion Press International
http://www.inclusion.com
Resources and training for person-centered planning

Inclusive Schools Network
http://www.inclusiveschools.org
Networking for families and schools collaborating to build inclusive education practices

Institute for Community Inclusion
http://www.communityinclusion.org
Information on a wide range of topics related to inclusion

Institute on Community Integration
http://ici.umn.edu/
Research and resource center focusing on community inclusion

Institute on Disability/UCEDD, University of New Hampshire
http://www.iod.unh.edu
Training, technical assistance, and resources for families and schools

National Alternate Assessment Center
http://www.naacpartners.org
Extensive resources and research related to alternate assessments for students with significant disabilities

National Association of State Directors of Special Education
http://nasdse.org
Leadership support for more effective policy and practice

National Center for Educational Outcomes (NCEO)
http://education.umn.edu/nceo/
Research related to participation of students with disabilities in large-scale assessments, standards-setting efforts, and graduation requirements

The National Center on Response to Intervention
http://www.rti4success.org
Technical assistance and information on RTI for school districts, teachers, and parents

OSEP (Office of Special Education Programs) Ideas that Work
http://www.osepideasthatwork.org/
Tool kits and resources for translating special education research into practice

Postsecondary Education Programs Network
http://www.pepnet.org/
Tools to enhance educational opportunities for students who are deaf or have hearing impairments

SpecialEdCareers.org
http://www.specialedcareers.org
Clearinghouse on careers and professions related to early intervention and
education for children with disabilities

Urban Special Education Leadership Collaborative
http://www.urbancollaborative.org
Professional development and technical assistance for urban special educators

LEGAL AND GOVERNMENT INFORMATION

ADA Home Page
http://www.ada.gov
Information and technical assistance on the Americans with Disabilities Act

Bazelon Center for Mental Health Law
http://www.bazelon.org/welcome.html
Advocacy and legal information for people with mental health issues and
developmental disabilities

Center for the Study and Advancement of Disability Policy (CSADP)
http://www.disabilitypolicycenter.org/
Policy information and analysis

Consortium for Appropriate Dispute Resolution in Special Education (CADRE)
http://www.directionservice.org/cadre
Information on mediation and other collaborative strategies for resolving
special education disputes

Disability.gov
http://www.disability.gov
Federal clearinghouse for disability information and resources

Early Childhood Learning and Knowledge Center
http://eclkc.ohs.acf.hhs.gov/hslc
Head Start and other early childhood program information

FedWORLD Information Service (NTIS)
http://www.fedworld.gov
Tool for searching federal agencies and information

FindLaw, Your Online Legal Resource
http://findlaw.com
Legal information and resources for finding lawyers

National Council on Disability (NCD)

http://www.ncd.gov/
Agency to advance disability policy

National Disability Rights Network

http://www.napas.org
The Protection and Advocacy (P&A)/Client Assistance Programs (CAP) network provides training and technical assistance, legal support, and legislative advocacy. The P&A agencies are federally funded and are established in every state.

Nolo.com Self-Help Law Center

http://www.nolo.com/ChunkKID/KID.index.html
Legal information and resources including a lawyer directory

Office of Civil Rights (OCR)

http://www.ed.gov/OCR/
Information on filing complaints based on discrimination

Social Security Administration

http://www.ssa.gov
Information on benefits and work incentives

Supreme Court Decisions

http://supct.law.cornell.edu/supct/index.html
Directory of cases before the U.S. Supreme Court

Thomas Legislative Information

http://thomas.loc.gov
Directory for all laws and bills before Congress

U.S. Department of Education

http://www.ed.gov
Direct information on implementation of federal education laws

U.S. Department of Health and Human Services (DHHS)

http://www.hhs.gov
Support for maintaining health and obtaining assistance with daily life

U.S. DHHS, Administration for Children and Families

http://www.acf.hhs.gov/
Information about federal assistance for families

U.S. DHHS, Centers for Medicare & Medicaid Services

http://www.cms.hhs.gov/
Information on federal support for health care

U.S. Department of Transportation (ADA compliance)

http://www.dot.gov/accessibility/
Information on equal access to transportation

Wrightslaw
http://www.wrightslaw.com
Articles, publications, and extensive information on special education law
and advocacy

Index

Page references followed by *f* indicate figures.